SEW
step by step

SEW
step by step

Alison Smith

DK

LONDON, NEW YORK, MUNICH,
MELBOURNE, DELHI

DK INDIA
Editor Alicia Ingty
Assistant Editor Ekta Sharma
Senior Art Editor Neha Ahuja
Assistant Art Editors Divya PR, Era Chawla,
Mansi Nagdev, Mini Dhawan
Editorial Manager Glenda Fernandes
Senior Art Editor (Lead) Navidita Thapa
Production Manager Pankaj Sharma
DTP Manager Sunil Sharma
Senior DTP Designers Dheeraj Arora, Jagtar Singh
DTP Designer Tarun Sharma
Assistant DTP Designer Sourabh Challariya

DK UK
Project Editor Danielle Di Michiel
Project Art Editor Jane Ewart
Editorial Assistant Roxanne Benson-Mackey
Managing Editor Dawn Henderson
Managing Art Editor Marianne Markham
Senior Jacket Creative Nicola Powling
Production Editor Ben Marcus
Senior Production Controller Alice Sykes
Creative Technical Support Sonia Charbonnier

First published in Great Britain in 2011
by Dorling Kindersley Limited,
80 Strand, London WC2R 0RL

Penguin Group (UK)
2 4 6 8 10 9 7 5 3 1
001 – 179845 – Feb/2011
Copyright © 2011 Dorling Kindersley Limited
All rights reserved.

A CIP catalogue record for this book
is available from the British Library.
ISBN 978-1-4053-6112-2

Colour reproduction by Media Development & Printing Ltd
Printed and bound in Singapore by Tien Wah Press

Discover more at **www.dk.com**

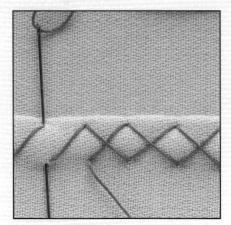

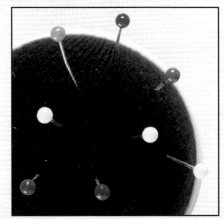

CONTENTS

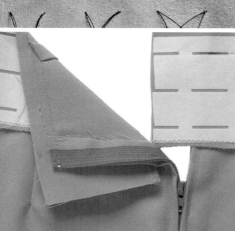

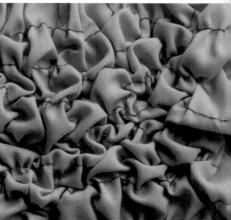

INTRODUCTION

If you are new to sewing and eager to master the key techniques, *Sew Step by Step* is the book for you. These clearly laid out pages cover all the basics (plus a bit more) to help you make and restyle simple soft furnishings, clothes, and accessories.

Starting with equipment and haberdashery and moving on through fabrics to the many techniques, *Sew Step by Step* demonstrates all the basic stitches, shows you how to master seams, hems, and edges, teaches you easy ways to add shape to clothing, with gathers, darts, and waistlines, and how to finish your work with pockets and fasteners.

I hope this book will encourage you to enjoy this satisfying hobby, and inspire you to create beautiful things – for yourself or for your family and friends.

Happy Sewing!

Alison Smith

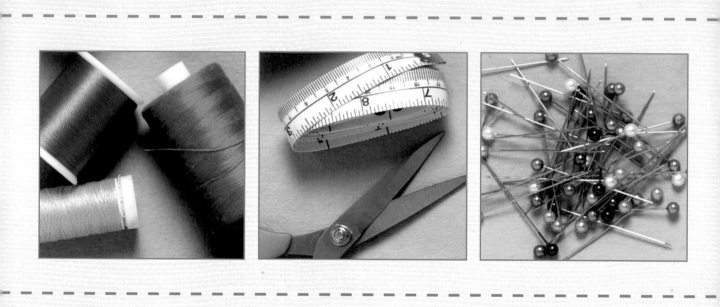

SEWING EQUIPMENT

Basic sewing kit

A well-equipped sewing kit will include all of the items shown below and many more, depending on the type of sewing that you do regularly. It is important that a suitable container is used to keep your tools together, so that they will be readily to hand, and to keep them tidy.

Thimble..................
This is useful to protect the end of your finger when hand sewing. Thimbles are available in various shapes and sizes. **See page 16.**

Tape measure..................
Essential, not only to take body measurements, but also to help measure fabric, seams, etc. Choose one that gives both metric and imperial. A tape made of plastic is best as it will not stretch. **See page 14.**

Zips..................
It is always a good idea to keep a couple of zips in your sewing kit. Black, cream, and navy are the most useful colours. **See pages 133–139.**

Threads..................
A selection of threads for hand sewing and machine/overlocker sewing in a variety of colours. Some threads are made of polyester, while others are cotton or rayon. See pages 20–21.

Haberdashery..................
All the odds and ends a sewer needs, including everything from buttons and snaps to trimmings and elastic. A selection of buttons and snaps in your basic kit is useful for a quick repair. **See pages 18–19.**

Pins..................
Needed by every sewer to hold the fabric together prior to sewing it permanently. There are different types of pins for different types of work. **See page 23.**

Safety pins..................
In a variety of sizes and useful for emergency repairs as well as threading elastics. **See page 23.**

Embroidery scissors
Small pair of scissors with very sharp points, to clip threads close to the fabric. See page 13.

Cutting shears
Required for cutting fabric. When buying, select a pair that feels comfortable in your hand and that is not too heavy. See pages 12–13.

Needles
A good selection of different types of needles for sewing by hand. This will enable you to tackle any hand-sewing project. See page 22.

Seam ripper
Also called a stitch ripper, to remove any stitches that have been sewn in the wrong place. Various sizes of seam rippers are available. Keep the cover on when not in use to protect the sharp point. See page 12.

Pin cushion
To keep your needles and pins safe and clean. Choose one that has a fabric cover and is firm. See page 23.

Sewing gauge
A handy gadget for small measurements. The slide can be set to measure hem depths, buttonhole diameters, and much more. See page 14.

Buttonhole chisel
An exceedingly sharp mini-chisel that gives a clean cut through machine buttonholes. Place a cutting mat underneath when using this tool, or you might damage the blade. See page 12.

BUILD UP YOUR SEWING KIT

CUTTING TOOLS 12–13
Bent-handled shears
Paper scissors
Pinking shears
Snips
Trimming scissors

MEASURING TOOLS 14
Other tape measures

MARKING AIDS 15
Chalk pencil
Chalk propelling pencil
Tailor's chalk
Tracing wheel and carbon paper
Water/air-soluble pen

USEFUL EXTRAS 16
14-In-1 measure
Beeswax
Collar point turner
Emergency sewing kit
Glue pen
Liquid sealant
Loop turner
Tweezers

NEEDLE THREADERS 22

PRESSING AIDS 17
Iron
Ironing board
Pressing cloth
Pressing mitten
Tailor's ham

Cutting tools

There are many types of cutting tools, but one rule applies to all: buy good-quality products that can be re-sharpened. When choosing cutting shears, make sure that they fit the span of your hand – this means that you can comfortably open the whole of the blade with one action, which is very important to allow clean and accurate cutting lines. Shears and scissors of various types are not the only cutting tools that are required, as everyone will at some time need a seam ripper to remove misplaced stitches or to unpick seams for mending.

← Cutting shears
The most popular type of shear, used for cutting large pieces of fabric. The length of the blade can vary from 20–30cm (8–12in) in length.

↑ Seam ripper
A sharp, pointed hook to slide under a stitch, with a small cutting blade at the base to cut the thread. Various sizes of seam ripper are available, to cut through light to heavyweight fabric seams.

← Snips
A very useful, small, spring-loaded tool that easily cuts the ends of thread. Not suitable for fabrics.

↑ Buttonhole chisel
A smaller version of a carpenter's chisel, to cut cleanly and accurately through buttonholes. As this is so sharp it must be used with a self-healing cutting mat.

← Bent-handled shears
This type of shear has a blade that can sit flat against the table when cutting out, due to the angle between the blade and handle. Popular for cutting long, straight edges.

← Trimming Scissors
These scissors have a 10cm (4in) blade and are used to trim away surplus fabric and neaten ends of machining.

← Embroidery scissors
A small and very sharp scissor used to get into corners and clip threads close to the fabric.

↑ Paper scissors
Use these to cut around pattern pieces – cutting paper will dull blades of fabric scissors and shears.

← Pinking shears
Similar in size to cutting shears but with a blade that cuts with a zigzag pattern. Used for neatening seams and decorative edges.

Cutting tools   **13**

Measuring tools and marking aids

A huge range of tools enables a sewer to measure accurately. Choosing the correct tool for the task in hand is important, so that your measurements are precise. The next step is to mark your work using the appropriate marking technique or tool.

Measuring tools

There are many tools available to help you measure everything from the width of a seam or hem, to body dimensions, to the area of a window. One of the most basic yet invaluable measuring tools is the tape measure. Be sure to keep yours in good condition – once it stretches or gets snipped on the edges, it will no longer be accurate and should be replaced.

← Metal tape for windows
A metal tape that can be secured when extended is used to measure windows and soft furnishings.

Tape measure →
Available in various colours and widths. Try to choose one that is the same width as standard seam allowance (1.5cm/⅝in), because it will prove exceedingly useful.

Retractable tape →
Very useful to have in your handbag when shopping as you never know when you may need to measure something!

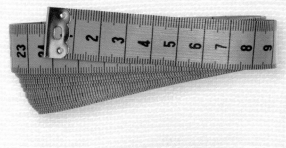

← Extra-long tape
This is usually twice the length of a normal tape measure, at 300cm (10ft) long. Use it when making soft furnishings. It's also useful to help measure the length of bridal trains.

← Sewing gauge
A handy small tool about 15cm (6in) long, marked in centimetres and inches, with a sliding tab. Use as an accurate measure for small measurements such as hems.

Marking aids

Marking certain parts of your work is essential, to make sure that things like pockets and darts are placed correctly and seamlines are straight as drawn on the pattern. With some marking tools, such as pens and a tracing wheel and carbon paper, it is always a good idea to test on a scrap of fabric first to make sure that the mark made will not be permanent.

← Tailor's chalk

Also known as French chalk, this solid piece of chalk in either a square or triangular shape is available in a large variety of colours. The chalk easily brushes off fabric.

← Chalk propelling pencil

Chalk leads of different colours can be inserted into this propelling pencil, making it a very versatile marking tool. The leads can be sharpened.

← Chalk pencil

Available in blue, pink, and white. As it can be sharpened like a normal pencil, it will draw accurate lines on fabric.

Tracing wheel →
and carbon paper

These two items are used together to transfer markings from a paper pattern or a design on to fabric. Not suitable for all types of fabric though, as marks may not be able to be removed easily.

← Water/air-soluble pen

This resembles a felt marker pen. Marks made can be removed from the fabric with either a spray of water or by leaving to air-dry. Be careful – if you press over the marks, they may become permanent.

Useful extras

There are many more accessories that can be purchased to help with your sewing, and knowing which products to choose and for which job can be daunting. The tools shown here can be useful aids, although it depends on the type of sewing that you do – dressmaking, craft work, making soft furnishings, or running repairs – as to whether you would need all of them in your sewing kit.

← Beeswax
When hand sewing, this will prevent the thread from tangling, and will strengthen it. First draw the thread through the wax, then press the wax into the thread by running your fingers along it.

Collar point turner ↑
This is excellent for pushing out those hard-to-reach corners in collars and cuffs.

14-in-1 measure →
A strange-looking tool that has 14 different measurements on it. Use to turn hems or edges accurately. Available in both metric and imperial.

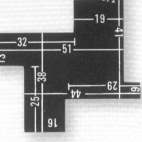

Tape maker ↑
Available in 12, 18, and 25mm (½, ¾, and 1in) widths, this tool evenly folds the edges of a fabric strip, which can then be pressed to make binding.

Thimble →
An essential item for many sewers, to protect the middle finger from the end of the needle. Choose a thimble that fits your finger comfortably as there are many varieties to choose from.

Tweezers ↑
These can be used for removing stubborn tacking stitches that have become caught in the machine stitching. An essential aid to threading the overlocker.

Liquid sealant →
Used to seal the cut edge of ribbons and trims to prevent fraying. Also useful to seal the ends of overlock stitching.

Glue pen →
Similar to a glue pen for paper, this will hold fabric or trims temporarily in place until they can be secured with stitches. It will not damage the fabric or make the sewing needle sticky.

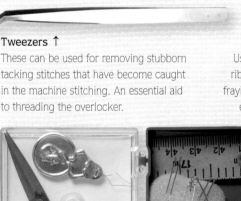
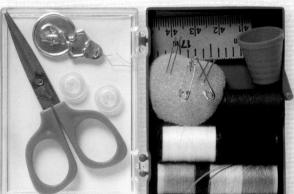

← Emergency sewing kit
All the absolute essentials to fix loose buttons or dropped hems while away from your sewing machine. Take it with you when travelling.

Loop turner →
A thin metal rod with a latch at the end. Use to turn narrow fabric tubes or to thread ribbons through a slotted lace.

Pressing aids

Successful sewing relies on successful pressing. Without the correct pressing equipment, sewing can look too "home-made", whereas if correctly pressed any sewn item will have a neat, professional finish.

Pressing mitten →
Slips on to your hand to enable more control over where you are pressing.

Iron ↑
A good-quality steam iron is a wonderful asset. Choose a reasonably heavy iron that has steam and a shot of steam facility.

Pressing cloth →
Choose a cloth made from silk organza or muslin as you can see through it. The cloth will stop the iron marking fabric and prevent burning delicate fabrics.

Ironing board ↑
Essential to iron on. Make sure the board is height-adjustable.

Tailor's ham ↑
A ham-shaped pressing cushion that is used to press darts and the shape into curves of collars and shoulders, and in making tailored garments.

Haberdashery items

The term haberdashery covers all of the bits and pieces that a sewer tends to need, for example fasteners such as buttons, snaps, hooks and eyes, and Velcro™. But haberdashery also includes elastics, ribbons, trimmings of all types, and boning.

Buttons

Buttons can be made from almost anything – shell, bone, coconut, nylon, plastic, brass, silver. They can be any shape, from geometric to abstract to animal shapes. A button may have a shank or have holes on the surface to enable it to be attached to fabric.

Other fasteners

Hooks and eyes (below left), snaps (below centre), and Velcro™ (below right) all come in a wide variety of forms, differing in size, shape, and colour. Some hooks and eyes are designed to be seen, while snaps and Velcro™ are intended to be hidden fasteners.

Trimmings, decorations, fringes, and braids

Decorative finishing touches – fringes, strips of sequins, ric-rac braids, feathers, pearls, bows, flowers, and beads – can dress up a garment, embellish a bag, or personalize soft furnishings. Some are designed to be inserted into seams while others are surface-mounted.

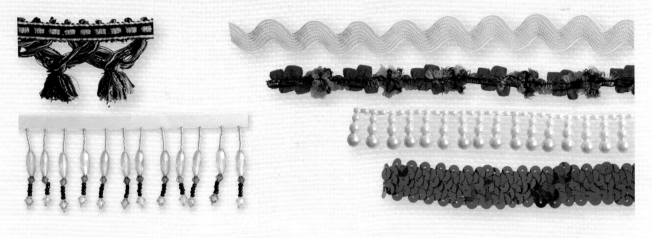

Ribbons

From the narrowest strips to wide swathes, ribbons are made from a variety of yarns, such as nylon, polyester, and cotton. They can be printed or plain and may feature metallic threads or wired edges.

Elastic

Elastic is available in many forms, from very narrow, round cord to wide strips (below left). It may have buttonhole slots in it (below right) or even have a decorative edge.

Boning

You can buy various types of boning in varying widths. Polyester boning (bottom left), used in boned bodices, can be sewn through, while nylon boning (bottom right), also used on boned bodices, has to be inserted into a casing. Specialist metal boning (below left and right), which may be either straight or spiral, is for corsets and bridal wear.

Threads

There are so many threads available and knowing which ones to choose can be confusing. There are specialist threads designed for special tasks, such as machine embroidery or quilting. Threads also vary in fibre content, from pure cotton to rayon to polyester. Some threads are very fine while others are thick and coarse. Failure to choose the correct thread can spoil your project and lead to problems with the stitch quality of the sewing machine.

Cotton thread ↓

A 100% cotton thread. Smooth and firm, this is designed to be used with cotton fabrics and is much favoured by quilters.

Metallic thread ↓

A rayon and metal thread for decorative machining and machine embroidery. This thread usually requires a specialist sewing-machine needle.

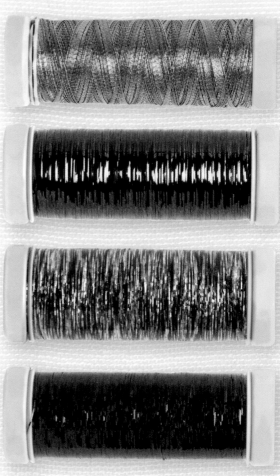

Elastic thread ↓

A thin, round elastic thread normally used on the bobbin of the sewing machine for stretch effects such as shirring.

Embroidery thread ↓

Often made from a rayon yarn for shine. This is a finer thread designed for machine embroidery. Available on much larger reels for economy.

Polyester all-purpose thread ↓

A good-quality polyester thread that has a very slight "give", making it suitable to sew all types of fabrics and garments, as well as soft furnishings. The most popular type of thread.

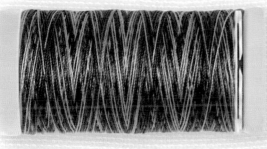

Top-stitching thread ↓

A thicker polyester thread used for decorative top-stitching and buttonholes. Also for hand sewing buttons on thicker fabrics and some soft furnishings.

Needles and pins

Using the correct pin or needle for your work is so important, as the wrong choice can damage fabric or leave small holes. Needles are made from steel and pins from steel or occasionally brass. Look after them by keeping pins in a pin cushion and needles in a needle case – if kept together in a small container they could become scratched and blunt.

Needles and threaders

Needles are available for all types of fabrics and projects. A good selection of needles should be to hand at all times, whether it be for emergency mending of tears, or sewing on buttons, or adding trimmings to special-occasion wear. With a special needle threader, inserting the thread through the eye of the needle is simplicity itself.

← Sharps
A general-purpose hand-sewing needle, with a small, round eye. Available in sizes 1 to 12. For most hand sewing use a size 6 to 9.

Darner's →
A long, thick needle that is designed to be used with wool or thick yarns and to sew through multiple layers.

← Betweens or quilting
Similar to a milliner's needle but very short, with a small, round eye. Perfect for fine hand stitches and favoured by quilters.

Chenille →
This looks like a tapestry needle but it has a sharp point. Use with thick or wool yarns for darning or heavy embroidery.

← Beading
Long and exceedingly fine, to sew beads and sequins to fabric. As it is prone to bending, keep it wrapped in tissue when not in use.

Self-threading needle →
A needle that has a double eye. The thread is placed in the upper eye through the gap, then pulled into the eye below for sewing.

← Tapestry
A medium-length, thick needle with a blunt end and a long eye. For use with wool yarn in tapestry. Also for darning in overlock threads.

Milliner's or straw →
A very long, thin needle with a small, round eye. Good for hand sewing and tacking as it doesn't damage fabric. A size 8 or 9 is most popular.

← Bodkin
A strange-looking needle with a blunt end and a large, fat eye. Use to thread elastic or cord. There are larger eyes for thicker yarns.

Crewel →
Also known as an embroidery needle, a long needle with a long, oval eye that is designed to take multiple strands of embroidery thread.

← Wire needle threader
A handy gadget, especially useful for needles with small eyes. Also helpful in threading sewing-machine needles.

← Automatic needle threader
This threader is operated with a small lever. The needle, eye down, is inserted and the thread is wrapped around.

Pins

There is a wide variety of pins available, in differing lengths and thicknesses, and ranging from plain household pins to those with coloured balls or flower shapes on their ends.

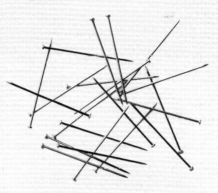

Household ↑
General-purpose pins of a medium length and thickness. Can be used for all types of sewing.

Pearl-headed ↑
Longer than household pins, with a coloured pearl head. They are easy to pick up and use.

Extra fine ↑
Extra long and extra fine, this pin is favoured by many professional dressmakers, because it is easy to use and doesn't damage finer fabrics.

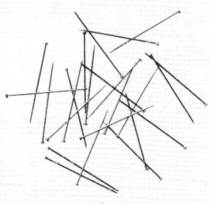

Dressmaker's ↑
Similar to a household pin in shape and thickness, but slightly longer. These are the pins for beginners to choose.

Glass-headed ↑
Similar to pearl-headed pins but shorter. They have the advantage that they can be pressed over without melting.

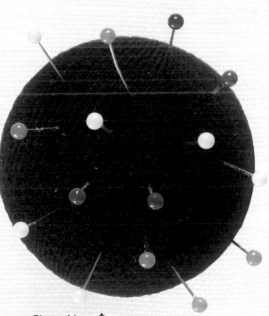

Pin cushions ↑
To keep pins clean and sharp. Choose a fabric cover: a foam cushion may blunt pins.

Safety pins →
Available in a huge variety of sizes and made either of brass or stainless steel. Used for holding two or more layers together.

Sewing machine

A sewing machine will quickly speed up any job, whether it be a quick repair or a huge home-sewing project. Most sewing machines today are aided by computer technology, which enhances stitch quality and ease of use. Always spend time trying out a sewing machine before you buy, to really get a feel for it.

Threading guides ....
Markings to help guide you
in threading the machine.

Tension dial ....
To control the stitch tension on the
upper thread, i.e. how fast the thread
feeds through the sewing machine.

Automatic needle threader
A pull-down gadget to aid threading
the machine needle. ....

Buttonhole sensor
A pull-down sensor that automatically
judges the size of the buttonhole
required to fit the button chosen. ....

Needle ....
The machine needle. Replace it regularly
to ensure good stitch quality. See page 26.

Presser foot ....
To hold the fabric in place while
stitching. Various feet can be used here
to aid different sewing processes.
See pages 26–27.

Removable free arm
This section of the machine will pull
away to give a narrow work bed that
can be used when inserting sleeves. It
also contains a useful storage section. ....

Dog feeds
These metal teeth grip ....
the fabric and feed it
through the machine.

Shank :
To hold the
various feet
in place.

Needle plate
A transparent removable cover
reveals the bobbin. This plate
is gridded to help stitch seams
of various widths.

Speed control
A slide, to control the
speed of your machine.

Spool holder
To hold your sewing
thread in place.

Bobbin winder
Winds the thread from the spool on to
the bobbin, keeping it under tension.
See page 26.

Balance wheel
This can be turned towards you to move
the needle up or down manually.

LCD screen
An illuminated screen that indicates
which stitch you are using.

Touch buttons
Use these to change the type of stitch you
are using and to increase and decrease size
and width of stitch.

Buttons
To provide various
functions, such as
reverse, locking
stitch, and needle-in.

Touch buttons
These quickly select the most popular
stitches such as zigzag and buttonhole.

Stitch library
All the different stitches this
machine can stitch. You just
have to key in the number.

Sewing-machine accessories

Many accessories can be purchased for your sewing machine to make certain sewing processes so much easier. There are different machine needles not only for different fabrics but also for different types of threads. There is also a huge number of sewing-machine feet, and new feet are constantly coming on to the market. Those shown here are some of the most popular.

PLASTIC BOBBIN

The bobbin is for the lower thread. Some machines take plastic bobbins, others metal. Always check which sort of bobbin your machine uses as the incorrect choice can cause stitch problems.

METAL BOBBIN

Also known as a universal bobbin, this is used on many types of sewing machine. Be sure to check that your machine needs a metal bobbin before you buy.

MACHINE NEEDLES

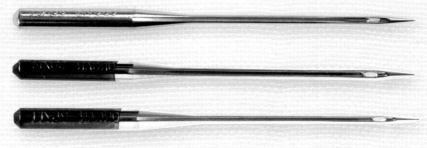

There are different types of sewing machine needle to cope with different fabrics. Machine needles are sized from 60 to 100, a 60 being a very fine needle. There are special needles for machine embroidery and also for metallic threads.

EMBROIDERY FOOT

A clear plastic foot with a groove underneath that allows linear machine embroidery stitches to pass under.

BUTTONHOLE FOOT

This extends and the button is placed in the back of the foot. The machine will stitch a buttonhole to fit due to the buttonhole sensor.

ROLLED HEM FOOT

This foot rolls the fabric while stitching with a straight stitch or a zigzag stitch.

OVEREDGE FOOT

A foot that runs along the raw edge of the fabric and holds it stable while an overedge stitch is worked.

BLIND HEM FOOT

Use this foot in conjunction with the blind hem stitch to create a neat hemming stitch.

WALKING FOOT

This strange-looking foot "walks" across the fabric, so that the upper layer of fabric does not push forward. Great for matching checks and stripes and also for difficult fabrics.

ZIP FOOT

This foot fits to either the right or left-hand side of the needle to enable you to stitch close to a zip.

CONCEALED ZIP FOOT

A foot that is used to insert a concealed zip – the foot holds open the coils of the zip, enabling you to stitch behind them.

FABRICS

Wool fabrics

A natural fibre, wool comes primarily from sheep – Australian merino sheep's wool is considered to be the best. However, we also get wool fibres from goats (mohair and cashmere), rabbits (angora), camels (camel hair), and llamas (alpaca). A wool fibre is either short and fluffy, when it is known as a woollen yarn, or it is long, strong, and smooth, when it is called worsted. The term virgin (or new) wool denotes wool fibres that are being used for the first time. Wool may be reprocessed or reused and is then often mixed with other fibres.

PROPERTIES OF WOOL

- comfortable to wear in all climates as it is available in many weights and weaves
- warm in the winter and cool in the summer, because it will breathe with your body
- absorbs moisture better than other natural fibres – will absorb up to 30 per cent of its weight before it feels wet
- flame-resistant

- relatively crease-resistant
- ideal to tailor as it can be easily shaped with steam
- often blended with other fibres to reduce the cost of fabric
- felts if exposed to excessive heat, moisture, and pressure
- will be bleached by sunlight with prolonged exposure
- can be damaged by moths

CASHMERE

Wool from the Kashmir goat, and the most luxurious of all the wools. A soft yet hard-wearing fabric available in different weights.
Cutting out: as cashmere often has a slight pile, use a nap layout
Seams: plain, neatened with overlocker stitch or pinking shears (a zigzag stitch would curl the edge of the seam)

Thread: a silk thread is ideal, or a polyester all-purpose thread
Needle: machine size 12/14, depending on the thickness of the fabric; sharps for hand sewing
Pressing: steam iron on a steam setting, with a pressing cloth and seam roll
Use for: jackets, coats, men's wear; knitted cashmere yarn for sweaters, cardigans, underwear

CHALLIS

A fine wool fabric, made from a worsted yarn that has an uneven surface texture. Challis is often printed as well as plain.
Cutting out: a nap layout is not required unless the fabric is printed
Seams: plain, neatened with overlocker or zigzag stitch; a run and fell seam can also be used

Thread: polyester all-purpose thread
Needle: machine size 11/12; sharps for hand sewing
Pressing: steam iron on a steam setting, with a pressing cloth; fabric will stretch while warm so handle with care
Use for: dresses, jackets, garments with pleating or draping detail

CREPE

A soft fabric made from a twisted yarn, which is what produces the uneven surface. It is important to preshrink this fabric prior to use by giving it a good steaming, because it will have stretched on the bolt and it is prone to shrinkage.
Cutting out: a nap layout is not required

Seams: plain, neatened with overlocker (a zigzag stitch may curl the edge of the seam)
Thread: polyester all-purpose thread
Needle: machine size 12; sharps or milliner's for hand sewing
Pressing: steam iron on a wool setting; a pressing cloth is not always required
Use for: all types of clothing

FLANNEL

A wool with a lightly brushed surface, featuring either a plain or twill weave. Used in the past for underwear.

Cutting out: use a nap layout

Seams: plain, neatened with overlocker or zigzag stitch or Hong Kong finish

Thread: polyester all-purpose thread

Needle: machine size 14; sharps for hand sewing

Pressing: steam iron on a wool setting with a pressing cloth; use a seam roll as the fabric is prone to marking

Use for: coats, jackets, skirts, men's wear

GABARDINE

A hard-wearing suiting fabric with a distinctive weave. Gabardine often has a sheen and is prone to shine. It can be difficult to handle as it is springy and frays badly.

Cutting out: a nap layout is advisable as the fabric has a sheen

Seams: plain, neatened with overlocker or zigzag stitch

Thread: polyester all-purpose thread or 100% cotton thread

Needle: machine size 14; sharps for hand sewing

Pressing: steam iron on a wool setting; use just the toe of the iron and a silk organza pressing cloth as the fabric will mark and may shine

Use for: men's wear, jackets, trousers

MOHAIR

From the wool of the Angora goat. A long, straight, and very strong fibre that produces a hairy cloth or yarn for knitting.

Cutting out: use a nap layout, with the fibres brushing down the pattern pieces in the same direction, from neck to hem

Seams: plain, neatened with overlocker or pinking shears

Thread: polyester all-purpose thread

Needle: machine size 14; sharps for hand sewing

Pressing: steam iron on a wool setting; "stroke" the iron over the wool, moving in the direction of the nap

Use for: jackets, coats, men's wear, soft furnishings; knitted mohair yarns for sweaters

TARTAN

An authentic tartan belongs to a Scottish clan, and each has its own unique design that can only be used by that clan. The fabric is made using a twill weave from worsted yarns.

Cutting out: check the design for even/uneven check as it may need a nap layout or even a single layer layout

Seams: plain, matching the pattern and neatened with overlocker or zigzag stitch

Thread: polyester all-purpose thread

Needle: machine size 14; sharps for hand sewing

Pressing: steam iron on a wool setting; may require a pressing cloth, so test first

Use for: traditionally kilts, but these days also skirts, trousers, jackets, soft furnishings

TWEED, MODERN

A mix of chunky and nobbly wool yarns. Modern tweed is often found in contemporary colour palettes as well as plain, and with interesting fibres in the weft such as metallics and paper. It is much favoured by fashion designers.
Cutting out: use a nap layout
Seams: plain, neatened with overlocker or zigzag stitch; the fabric is prone to fraying

Thread: polyester all-purpose thread
Needle: machine size 14; sharps for hand sewing
Pressing: steam iron on a wool setting; a pressing cloth may not be required
Use for: jackets, coats; also skirts, dresses, soft furnishings

TWEED, TRADITIONAL

A rough fabric with a distinctive warp and weft, usually in different colours, and often forming a small check pattern. Traditional tweed is associated with the English countryside.
Cutting out: a nap layout is not required unless the fabric features a check
Seams: plain, neatened with overlocker or zigzag stitch; can also be neatened with pinking shears

Thread: polyester all-purpose thread or 100% cotton thread
Needle: machine size 14; sharps for hand sewing
Pressing: steam iron on a steam setting; a pressing cloth may not be required
Use for: jackets, coats, skirts, men's wear, soft furnishing

VENETIAN

A wool with a satin weave, making a luxurious, expensive fabric.
Cutting out: use a nap layout
Seams: plain, neatened with overlocker or zigzag stitch
Thread: polyester all-purpose thread or 100% cotton thread
Needle: machine size 14; sharps for hand sewing

Pressing: steam iron on a steam setting with a silk organza cloth to avoid shine; use a seam roll under the seams to prevent them from showing through
Use for: jackets, coats, men's wear

WOOL WORSTED

A light and strong cloth, made from good-quality thin, firm filament fibres. Always steam prior to cutting out as the fabric may shrink slightly after having been stretched around a bolt.
Cutting out: use a nap layout
Seams: plain, neatened with overlocker or zigzag stitch or Hong Kong finish

Thread: polyester all-purpose thread
Needle: machine size 12/14, depending on fabric; milliner's or sharps for hand sewing
Pressing: steam iron on a wool setting, with a pressing cloth; use a seam roll to prevent the seam from showing through
Use for: skirts, jackets, coats, trousers

Cotton fabrics

One of the most versatile and popular of all fabrics, cotton is a natural fibre that comes from the seed pods, or bolls, of the cotton plant. It is thought that cotton fibres have been in use since ancient times. Today, the world's biggest producers of cotton include the United States, India, and countries in the Middle East. Cotton fibres can be filament or staple, with the longest and finest used for top-quality bed linen. Cotton clothing is widely worn in warmer climates as the fabric will keep you cool.

PROPERTIES OF COTTON

- absorbs moisture well and carries heat away from the body
- stronger wet than dry
- does not build up static electricity
- dyes well

- prone to shrinkage unless it has been treated
- will deteriorate from mildew and prolonged exposure to sunlight
- creases easily
- soils easily, but launders well

BRODERIE ANGLAISE
A fine, plain-weave cotton that has been embroidered in such a way as to make small holes. Usually white or a pastel colour.
Cutting out: may need layout to place embroidery at hem edge
Seams: plain, neatened with overlocker or zigzag stitch; a French seam can also be used

Thread: polyester all-purpose thread
Needle: machine size 12/14; sharps for hand sewing
Pressing: steam iron on a cotton setting; a pressing cloth is not required
Use for: baby clothes, summer skirts, blouses

CALICO
A plain weave fabric that is usually unbleached and quite stiff. Available in many different weights, from very fine to extremely heavy.
Cutting out: a nap layout is not required
Seams: plain, neatened with overlocker or zigzag stitch

Thread: polyester all-purpose thread
Needle: machine size 11/14, depending on thickness of thread; sharps for hand sewing
Pressing: steam iron on a steam setting; a pressing cloth is not required
Use for: toiles (test garments), soft furnishings

CHAMBRAY
A light cotton that has a coloured warp thread and white weft thread. Chambray can also be found as a check or a striped fabric.
Cutting out: a nap layout should not be required
Seams: plain, neatened with overlocker or zigzag stitch

Thread: polyester all-purpose thread
Needle: machine size 11; sharps for hand sewing
Pressing: steam iron on a cotton setting; a pressing cloth is not required
Use for: blouses, men's shirts, children's wear

CHINTZ
A floral print or plain cotton fabric with a glazed finish that gives it a sheen. It has a close weave and is often treated to resist dirt.
Cutting out: use a nap layout
Seams: plain, neatened with overlocker or zigzag stitch; a run and fell seam can also be used

Thread: polyester all-purpose thread or 100% cotton thread
Needle: machine size 14; milliner's for hand sewing
Pressing: steam iron on a cotton setting; a pressing cloth may be required due to sheen on fabric
Use for: soft furnishings

CORDUROY

A soft pile fabric with distinctive stripes (known as wales or ribs) woven into it. The name depends on the size of the ribs: baby or pin cord has extremely fine ribs; needle cord has slightly thicker ribs; corduroy has 10–12 ribs per 2.5cm (1in); and elephant or jumbo cord has thick, heavy ribs.
Cutting out: use a nap layout with the pile on the corduroy brushing up the pattern pieces from hem to neck, to give depth of colour

Seams: plain, stitched using a walking foot and neatened with overlocker or zigzag stitch
Thread: polyester all-purpose thread
Needle: machine size 12/16; sharps or milliner's for hand sewing
Pressing: steam iron on a cotton setting; use a seam roll under the seams with a pressing cloth
Use for: trousers, skirts, men's wear

CRINKLE COTTON

Looks like an exaggerated version of seersucker (see page 36), with creases added by a heat process. Crinkle cotton may require careful laundering as it often has to be twisted into shape when wet to put the creases back in.
Cutting out: a nap layout is not required unless the fabric is printed
Seams: plain, neatened with overlocker or zigzag stitch

Thread: polyester all-purpose thread
Needle: machine size 12; milliner's for hand sewing
Pressing: steam iron on a cotton setting; take care not to press out the crinkles
Use for: blouses, dresses, children's wear

DAMASK

A cotton that has been woven on a jacquard loom to produce a fabric usually with a floral pattern in a self colour. May have a sheen to the surface.
Cutting out: use a nap layout
Seams: plain, neatened with overlocker or zigzag stitch
Thread: polyester all-purpose thread or 100% cotton thread

Needle: machine size 14; sharps for hand sewing
Pressing: steam iron on a cotton setting; a pressing cloth may be required if the fabric has a sheen
Use for: home furnishings; coloured jacquards for jackets, skirts

DENIM

Named after Nîmes in France. A hard-wearing twill-weave fabric with a coloured warp and white weft, usually made into jeans. Available in various weights and often mixed with an elastic thread for stretch. Denim is usually blue, but is also available in a variety of other colours.
Cutting out: a nap layout is not required

Seams: run and fell or top-stitched plain
Thread: polyester all-purpose thread with top-stitching thread for detail top-stitching
Needle: machine size 14/16; sharps for hand sewing
Pressing: steam iron on a cotton setting; a pressing cloth should not be required
Use for: jeans, jackets, children's wear

DRILL

A hard-wearing twill or plain-weave fabric with the same colour warp and weft. Drill frays badly on the cut edges.
Cutting out: a nap layout is not required
Seams: run and fell; or plain, neatened with overlocker or zigzag stitch

Thread: polyester all-purpose thread with top-stitching thread for detail top-stitching
Needle: machine size 14; sharps for hand sewing
Pressing: steam iron on a cotton setting; a pressing cloth is not required
Use for: men's wear, casual jackets, trousers

GINGHAM

A fresh, two-colour cotton fabric that features a check of various sizes. A plain weave made by having groups of white and coloured warp and weft threads.
Cutting out: usually an even check, so nap layout is not required but recommended; pattern will need matching
Seams: plain, neatened with overlocker or zigzag stitch

Thread: polyester all-purpose thread
Needle: machine size 11/12; sharps for hand sewing
Pressing: steam iron on a cotton setting; a pressing cloth should not be required
Use for: children's wear, dresses, shirts, home furnishings

JERSEY

A fine cotton yarn that has been knitted to give stretch, making the fabric very comfortable to wear. Jersey will also drape well.
Cutting out: a nap layout is recommended
Seams: 4-thread overlock stitch; or plain seam stitched with a small zigzag stitch and then seam allowances stitched together with a zigzag

Thread: polyester all-purpose thread
Needle: machine size 12/14; a ballpoint needle may be required for overlocker and a milliner's for hand sewing
Pressing: steam iron on a wool setting as jersey may shrink on a cotton setting
Use for: underwear, drapey dresses, leisurewear, bedding

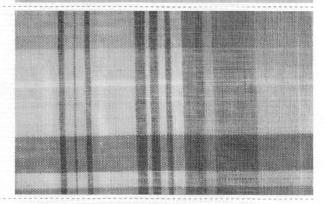

MADRAS

A check fabric made from a fine cotton yarn, usually from India. Often found in bright colours featuring an uneven check. An inexpensive cotton fabric.
Cutting out: use a nap layout and match the checks
Seams: plain, neatened with overlocker or zigzag stitch

Thread: polyester all-purpose thread
Needle: machine size 12/14; sharps for hand sewing
Pressing: steam iron on a cotton setting; a pressing cloth is not required
Use for: shirts, skirts, home furnishings

MUSLIN

A fine, plain, open-weave cotton. Can be found in colours but usually sold a natural/unbleached or white. Makes great pressing cloths and interlinings. It is a good idea to wash prior to use.
Cutting out: a nap layout is not required
Seams: 4-thread overlock stitch; or plain seam, neatened with overlocker or zigzag stitch; a French seam could also be used
Thread: polyester all-purpose thread
Needle: machine size 11; milliner's for hand sewing
Pressing: steam iron on a cotton setting; a cloth is not required
Use for: curtaining and other household uses

SEERSUCKER

A woven cotton that has a bubbly appearance woven into it, due to stripes of puckers. Do not over-press, or the surface effect will be damaged.
Cutting out: use a nap layout, due to puckered surface effect
Seams: plain, neatened with overlocker or zigzag stitch
Thread: polyester all-purpose thread
Needle: machine size 11/12; milliner's for hand sewing
Pressing: steam iron on a cotton setting (be careful not to press out the wrinkles)
Use for: summer clothing, skirts, shirts, children's wear

SHIRTING

A closely woven, fine cotton, with coloured warp and weft yarns making stripes or checks.
Cutting out: use a nap layout if fabric has uneven stripes
Seams: plain, neatened with overlocker or zigzag stitch; a run and fell seam can also be used
Thread: polyester all-purpose thread
Needle: machine size 12; milliner's for hand sewing
Pressing: steam iron on a cotton setting; a pressing cloth is not required
Use for: ladies' and men's shirts

TOWELLING

A cotton fabric with loops on the surface; top-quality towelling has loops on both sides. It is highly absorbent. Wash before use to preshrink and make it fluffy.
Cutting out: use a nap layout
Seams: 4-thread overlock stitch; or plain seam, neatened with overlocker or zigzag stitch
Thread: polyester all-purpose thread
Needle: machine size 14; sharps for hand sewing
Pressing: steam iron on a cotton setting; a pressing cloth is not required
Use for: bathrobes, beachwear

VELVET

A pile-weave fabric, made by using an additional yarn that is then cut to produce the pile. Difficult to handle and can be easily damaged if seams have to be unpicked.
Cutting out: use a nap layout with the pile brushing up from hem to neck, to give depth of colour
Seams: plain, stitched using a walking foot (stitch all seams from hem to neck) and neatened with overlocker or zigzag stitch
Thread: polyester all-purpose thread
Needle: machine size 14; milliner's for hand sewing
Pressing: only if you have to; use a velvet board, a bit of steam, toe of iron, and silk organza cloth
Use for: jackets, coats

Silk fabrics

Often referred to as the queen of all fabrics, silk is made from the fibres of the silkworm's cocoon. This strong and luxurious fabric dates back thousands of years to its first development in China, and the secret of silk production was well protected by the Chinese until 300AD. Silk fabrics can be very fine or thick and chunky. They need careful handling as some silk fabrics can be easily damaged.

PROPERTIES OF SILK

- keeps you warm in winter and cool in summer
- absorbs moisture and dries quickly
- dyes well, producing deep, rich colours
- static electricity can build up and fabric may cling
- will fade in prolonged strong sunlight
- prone to shrinkage
- best dry-cleaned
- weaker when wet than dry
- may water-mark

CHIFFON
A very strong and very fine, transparent silk with a plain weave. Will gather and ruffle well. Difficult to handle.
Cutting out: place tissue paper under the fabric and pin the fabric to the tissue, cutting through all layers if necessary; use extra fine pins

Seams: French
Thread: polyester all-purpose thread
Needle: machine size 9/11; fine milliner's for hand sewing
Pressing: dry iron on a wool setting
Use for: special occasion wear, over-blouses

CREPE DE CHINE
Medium weight, with an uneven surface due to the twisted silk yarn used. Drapes well and often used on bias-cut garments.
Cutting out: if to be bias-cut, use a single layer layout; otherwise use a nap layout

Seams: a seam for a difficult fabric or French
Thread: polyester all-purpose thread
Needle: machine size 11, milliner's or betweens for hand sewing
Pressing: dry iron on a wool setting
Use for: blouses, dresses, special-occasion wear

DUCHESSE SATIN
A heavy, expensive satin fabric used almost exclusively for special-occasion wear.
Cutting out: use a nap layout
Seams: plain, with pinked edges
Thread: polyester all-purpose thread

Needle: machine size 12/14; milliner's for hand sewing
Pressing: steam iron on a wool setting with a pressing cloth; use a seam roll under the seams to prevent shadowing
Use for: special-occasion wear

DUPION
Similar to hand-woven dupion (see page 38) but woven using a much smoother yarn to reduce the amount of nubbly bits in the weft.
Cutting out: use a nap layout to prevent shadowing
Seams: plain, neatened with overlocker or zigzag stitch

Thread: polyester all-purpose thread
Needle: machine size 12; milliner's for hand sewing
Pressing: steam iron on a wool setting, with a pressing cloth as fabric may water-mark
Use for: dresses, skirts, jackets, special-occasion wear, soft furnishings

---

DUPION, HAND-WOVEN

The most popular of all the silks. A distinctive weft yarn with many nubbly bits. Available in hundreds of colours. Easy to handle, but it does fray badly.
Cutting out: use a nap layout as the fabric shadows
Seams: plain, neatened with overlocker or zigzag stitch

Thread: polyester all-purpose thread
Needle: machine size 12; milliner's for hand sewing
Pressing: steam iron on a wool setting, with a pressing cloth to avoid water-marking
Use for: dresses, special-occasion wear, jackets, soft furnishings

GEORGETTE

A soft, filmy silk fabric that has a slight transparency. Does not crease easily.
Cutting out: place tissue paper under the fabric and pin fabric to tissue, cutting through all layers if necessary; use extra-fine pins
Seams: French

Thread: polyester all-purpose thread
Needle: machine size 11; milliner's for hand sewing
Pressing: dry iron on a wool setting (fabric can be damaged by steam)
Use for: special-occasion wear, loose-fitting overshirts

HABUTAI

Originally from Japan, a smooth, fine silk that can have a plain or a twill weave. Fabric is often used for silk painting.
Cutting out: a nap layout is not required
Seams: French

Thread: polyester all-purpose thread
Needle: machine size 9/11; very fine milliner's or betweens for hand sewing
Pressing: steam iron on a wool setting
Use for: lining, shirts, blouses

MATKA

A silk suiting fabric with an uneven-looking yarn. Matka can be mistaken for linen.
Cutting out: use a nap layout as silk may shadow
Seams: plain, neatened with overlocker or zigzag stitch or Hong Kong finish
Thread: polyester all-purpose thread

Needle: machine size 12/14; milliner's for hand sewing
Pressing: steam iron on a wool setting with a pressing cloth; a seam roll is recommended to prevent the seams from showing through
Use for: dresses, jackets, trousers

ORGANZA

A sheer fabric with a crisp appearance that will crease easily.

Cutting out: a nap layout is not required

Seams: French or a seam for a difficult fabric

Thread: polyester all-purpose thread

Needle: machine size 11; milliner's or betweens for hand sewing

Pressing: steam iron on a wool setting; a pressing cloth should not be required

Use for: sheer blouses, shrugs, interlining, interfacing

SATIN

A silk with a satin weave that can be very light to quite heavy in weight.

Cutting out: use a nap layout in a single layer as fabric is slippy

Seams: French; on thicker satins, a seam for a difficult fabric

Thread: polyester all-purpose thread (not silk thread as it becomes weak with wear)

Needle: machine size 11/12; milliner's or betweens for hand sewing

Pressing: steam iron on a wool setting, with a pressing cloth as fabric may water-mark

Use for: blouses, dresses, special-occasion wear

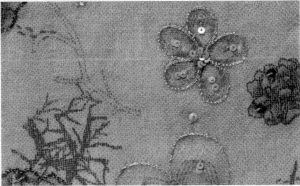

SILK AND WOOL MIX

A fabric made by mixing wool and silk fibres or wool and silk yarns. The fabric made may be fine in quality or thick, like a coating.

Cutting out: use a nap layout

Seams: plain, neatened with overlocker or zigzag stitch

Thread: polyester all-purpose thread

Needle: machine size 11/14, depending on fabric; sharps for hand sewing

Pressing: steam iron on a wool setting; seams will require some steam to make them lie flat

Use for: suits, skirts, trousers, coats

TAFFETA

A smooth, plain-weave fabric with a crisp appearance. It makes a rustling sound when worn. Can require special handling and does not wear well.

Cutting out: use a nap layout, with extra-fine pins in seams as they will mark the fabric

Seams: plain; fabric may pucker, so sew from the hem upwards, keeping the fabric taut under the machine; neaten with overlocker or pinking shears

Thread: polyester all-purpose thread

Needle: machine size 11; milliner's or betweens for hand sewing

Pressing: cool iron, with a seam roll under the seams

Use for: special-occasion wear

Linen fabrics

Linen is a natural fibre that is derived from the stem of the flax plant. It is available in a variety of qualities and weights, from very fine linen to heavy suiting weights. Coarser than cotton, it is sometimes woven with cotton as well as being mixed with silk.

PROPERTIES OF LINEN

- cool and comfortable to wear
- absorbs moisture well
- shrinks when washed
- does not ease well
- has a tendency to crease
- prone to fraying
- resists moths but is damaged by mildew

COTTON AND LINEN MIX

Two fibres may have been mixed together in the yarn or may have mixed warp and weft yarns. It has lots of texture in the weave. Silk and linen mix is treated in the same way.
Cutting out: a nap layout should not be required
Seams: plain, neatened with overlocker or zigzag stitch
Thread: polyester all-purpose thread
Needle: machine size 14; sharps for hand sewing
Pressing: a steam iron on a steam setting, with a silk organza pressing cloth
Use for: summer-weight jackets, tailored dresses

DRESS-WEIGHT LINEN

A medium-weight linen with a plain weave. The yarn is often uneven, which causes slubs in the weave.
Cutting out: a nap layout is not required
Seams: plain, neatened with overlocker or zigzag stitch or a Hong Kong finish
Thread: polyester all-purpose thread with a top-stitching thread for top-stitching
Needle: machine size 14; sharps for hand sewing
Pressing: steam iron on a cotton setting (steam is required to remove creases)
Use for: dresses, trousers, skirts

PRINTED LINENS

Many linens today feature prints or even embroidery. The fabric may be light to medium weight, with a smooth yarn that has few slubs.
Cutting out: use a nap layout
Seams: plain, neatened with overlocker or zigzag stitch
Thread: polyester all-purpose thread
Needle: machine size 14; sharps for hand sewing
Pressing: steam iron on a cotton setting (steam is required to remove creases)
Use for: dresses, skirts

SUITING LINEN

A heavier yarn is used to produce a linen suitable for suits for men and women. Can be a firm, tight weave or a looser weave.
Cutting out: a nap layout is not required
Seams: plain, neatened with overlocker or a zigzag stitch and sharps hand-sewing needle
Thread: polyester all-purpose thread with a top-stitching thread for top-stitching
Needle: machine size 14; sharps for hand sewing
Pressing: steam iron on a cotton setting (steam is required to remove creases)
Use for: men's and women's suits, trousers, coats

Leather and suede

Leather and suede are natural fabrics derived from either a pig or a cow and are sold as skins. Depending on the curing process that has been used, the skin will be either a suede or a leather. The fabrics require special handling.

LEATHER AND SUEDE
As the pattern pieces cannot be pinned on to leather and suede, you will need to draw around them using tailor's chalk. After cutting out, the chalk will rub off and will not damage the skin.

Cutting out: a complete pattern is required, left and right-hand halves; use a nap layout for suede, as it will brush one way
Seams: lapped or plain, using a walking foot or an ultra-glide foot; neatening is not required
Thread: polyester all-purpose thread

Needle: machine size 14 (a special leather needle may actually damage the skin); hand sewing is not recommended
Pressing: steam iron, with a silk organza pressing cloth
Use for: skirts, trousers, jackets, soft furnishings

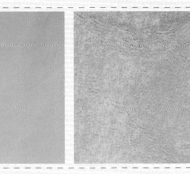

Man-made fabrics

The term "man-made" applies to any fabric that is not 100 per cent natural. Many of these fabrics have been developed over the last hundred years, which means they are new compared to natural fibres. Some man-made fabrics are made from natural elements mixed with chemicals while others are made entirely from non-natural substances.

ACETATE
Introduced in 1924, acetate is made from cellulose and chemicals. The fabric has a slight shine and is widely used for linings. Acetate can also be woven into fabrics such as acetate taffeta, acetate satin, and acetate jersey.

Properties of acetate:
• dyes well
• can be heat-set into pleats
• washes well
Cutting out: use a nap layout due to sheen on fabric
Seams: plain, neatened with overlocker or zigzag stitch, or 4-thread overlock stitch

Thread: polyester all-purpose thread
Needle: machine size 11; sharps for hand sewing
Pressing: steam iron on a cool setting (fabric can melt)
Use for: special-occasion wear, linings

ACRYLIC
Introduced in 1950, acrylic fibres are made from ethylene and acrylonitrile. The fabric resembles wool and makes a good substitute for machine-washable wool. Often seen as a knitted fabric, the fibres can be mixed with wool.

Properties of acrylic:
• little absorbency
• tends to retain odours
• not very strong
Cutting out: a nap layout may be required
Seams: 4-thread overlock stitch on knitted fabrics; plain seam on woven fabrics

Thread: polyester all-purpose thread
Needle: machine size 12/14, but a ballpoint needle may be required on knitted fabrics; sharps for hand sewing
Pressing: steam iron on a wool setting
Use for: knitted yarns for sweaters; wovens for skirts, blouses

NYLON
Developed by DuPont in 1938, the fabric takes its name from a collaboration between New York and London. Nylon is made from polymer chips that are melted and extruded into fibres. The fabric can be knitted or woven.

Properties of nylon:
• very hard-wearing
• does not absorb moisture
• washes easily, although white nylon can discolour easily
• very strong
Cutting out: a nap layout is not required unless the fabric is printed
Seams: plain, neatened with overlocker or zigzag stitch

Thread: polyester all-purpose thread
Needle: machine size 14, but a ballpoint needle may be required for knitted nylons; sharps for hand sewing
Pressing: steam iron on a silk setting (fabric can melt)
Use for: sportswear, underwear

POLYESTER

One of the most popular of the man-made fibres, polyester was introduced in 1951 as a washable man's suit! Polyester fibres are made from petroleum by-products and can take on any form, from a very fine sheer fabric to a thick, heavy suiting.

Properties of polyester:
- non-absorbent
- does not crease
- can build up static
- may "pill"

Cutting out: a nap layout is only required if the fabric is printed

Seams: French, plain, or 4-thread overlock, depending on the weight of the fabric

Thread: polyester all-purpose thread

Needle: machine size 11/14; sharps for hand sewing

Pressing: steam iron on a wool setting

Use for: workwear, school uniforms

RAYON

Also known as viscose and often referred to as artificial silk, this fibre was developed in 1889. It is made from wood pulp or cotton linters mixed with chemicals. Rayon can be knitted or woven and made into a wide range of fabrics. It is often blended with other fibres.

Properties of rayon:
- is absorbent
- is not static
- dyes well
- frays badly

Cutting out: a nap layout is only required if the fabric is printed

Seams: plain, neatened with overlocker or zigzag stitch

Thread: polyester all-purpose thread

Needle: machine size 12/14; sharps for hand sewing

Pressing: steam iron on a silk setting

Use for: dresses, blouses, jackets

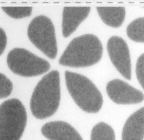

SPANDEX

Introduced in 1958, this is a lightweight, soft fibre than can be stretched 500% without breaking. A small amount of spandex is often mixed with other fibres to produce wovens with a slight stretch.

Properties of spandex:
- resistant to body oils, detergents, sun, sea, and sand
- can be difficult to sew
- can be damaged by heat
- not suitable for hand sewing

Cutting out: use a nap layout

Seams: 4-thread overlock stitch or a seam stitched with a small zigzag

Thread: polyester all-purpose thread

Needle: machine ballpoint size 14 or a machine stretch needle

Pressing: steam iron on a wool setting (spandex can be damaged by a hot iron)

Use for: swimwear, foundation wear, sportswear

SYNTHETIC FURS

Created using a looped yarn that is then cut on a knitted or a woven base, synthetic fur can be made from nylon or acrylic fibres. The furs vary tremendously in quality and some are very difficult to tell from the real thing.

Properties of synthetic furs:
- easy to sew
- require careful sewing
- can be heat-damaged by pressing
- not as warm as real fur

Cutting out: use a nap layout, with the fur pile brushed from the neck to the hem; cut just the backing carefully and not through the fur pile

Seams: plain, with a longer stitch and a walking foot; no neatening is required

Thread: polyester all-purpose thread

Needle: machine size 14; sharps for hand sewing

Pressing: if required, use a cool iron (synthetic fur can melt under a hot iron)

Use for: outerwear

SYNTHETIC LEATHER AND SUEDE

Made from polymers, these are non-woven fabrics. Some synthetic leathers and suedes can closely resemble the real thing.

Properties of synthetic leather and suede:
- do not fray
- do not ease well
- can be difficult to sew by hand, so this is not recommended

Cutting out: use a nap layout

Seams: plain, stitched using a walking foot and neatened with pinking shears; can also use top-stitched seams and lapped seams

Thread: polyester all-purpose thread

Needle: machine size 11/14

Pressing: steam iron on a wool setting, with a pressing cloth

Use for: jackets, skirts, trousers, soft furnishings

Fabric construction

Most fabric is made by either knitting or weaving. A knitted fabric is constructed by interlocking looped yarns. For a woven fabric, horizontal and vertical yarns go under and over each other. The warp yarn, which is the strongest, runs vertically and the weft crosses it at right angles. There are also non-woven fabrics created by a felting process where tiny fibres are mixed and squeezed together, then rolled out.

PLAIN WEAVE
As the name suggests, this is the simplest of all the weaves. The weft yarn passes under one warp yarn, then over another one.

SATIN WEAVE
This has a long strand known as a float on the warp yarn. The weft goes under four warp yarns, then over one. This weave gives a sheen on the fabric.

HERRINGBONE WEAVE
The distinctive herringbone zigzag weave is made by the weft yarn going under and over warp yarns in a staggered pattern.

TWILL WEAVE
The diagonal twill weave is made by the weft yarn going under two warp yarns, then over another two, with the pattern moved one yarn across each time.

WARP KNIT
This is made on a knitting machine, where one yarn is set to each needle (latch). The knit is formed in a vertical and diagonal direction.

WEFT KNIT
Made in the same way as knitting by hand on needles, this uses one yarn that runs horizontally.

Interfacings

An interfacing is a piece of fabric that is attached to the main fabric to give it support or structure. An interfacing fabric may be woven, knitted, or non-woven. It may also be fusible or non-fusible. A fusible interfacing (also called iron-on) can be bonded to the fabric by applying heat, whereas a non-fusible interfacing needs to be sewn to the fabric with a tacking stitch. Always cut interfacings on the same grain as the fabric, regardless of its construction.

Fusible interfacings

Be sure to buy fusibles designed for the home sewer, because the adhesive on the back of fusible interfacings for commercial use cannot be released with a normal steam iron. Do all pattern marking after the interfacing has been applied to the fabric.

HOW TO APPLY A FUSIBLE INTERFACING

1 Place fabric on pressing surface, wrong side up, making sure it is straight and not wrinkled.

2 Place the chosen interfacing sticky side down on the fabric (the sticky side feels gritty).

3 Cover with a dry pressing cloth and spray the cloth with a fine mist of water.

4 Place a steam iron, on a steam setting, on top of the pressing cloth.

5 Leave the iron in place for at least 10 seconds before moving it to the next area of fabric.

6 Check to see if the interfacing is fused to the fabric by rolling the fabric – if the interfacing is still loose in places, repeat the pressing process.

7 When the fabric has cooled down, the fusing process will be complete. Then pin the pattern back on to the fabric and transfer the pattern markings as required.

WOVEN
A woven fusible is always a good choice for a woven fabric as the two weaves will work together. Always cut on the same grain as the fabric. This type of interfacing is suitable for crafts and for more structured garments.

LIGHTWEIGHT WOVEN
A very light, woven fusible that is almost sheer, this can be difficult to cut out as it tends to stick to the scissors. It is suitable for all light to medium-weight fabrics.

KNITTED
A knitted fusible is ideally suited to a knit fabric as the two will be able to stretch together. Some knitted fusibles only stretch one way, while others will stretch in all directions. A knitted fusible is also a good choice on fabrics that have a percentage of stretch.

NON-WOVEN
Non-woven fusibles are available in a variety of weights – choose one that feels lighter than your fabric. You can add a second layer if one interfacing proves to be too light. This is suitable for supporting collars and cuffs, and facings on garments.

Non-fusible interfacings

These sew-in interfacings require tacking to the wrong side of facings or the main garment fabric around the seam allowances. They are useful for sheer or fine fabrics where the adhesive from a fusible interfacing might show through.

HOW TO APPLY A NON-FUSIBLE INTERFACING

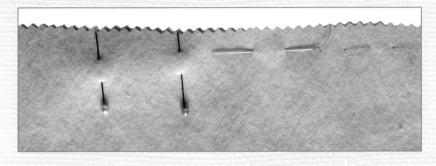

1 Place the interfacing on to the wrong side of the fabric, aligning the cut edges.

2 Pin in place.

3 Using a basic tacking stitch, tack the interfacing to the fabric or facing at 1cm (⅜in) within the seam allowance.

ALPACA
A tailorings canvas made from wool and alpaca, this interfacing is excellent to use in difficult fabrics such as velvet, because the alpaca can be steamed into shape.

COLLAR CANVAS
A firm, white cotton canvas, this will stiffen shirt collars and also boned bodices. It is available as firm and soft collar canvas although there is little difference between the two. Collar canvas is also useful in crafts, such as handbags.

MUSLIN
A cotton muslin interfacing is a good choice on summer dresses as well as for special-occasion wear. Muslin can also be used to line fine cotton dresses.

ORGANZA
A pure silk organza makes an excellent interfacing for sheer fabric to give support and structure. It can also be used for structure in much larger areas such as bridal skirts.

NON-WOVEN SEW-IN INTERFACING
A non-woven material is ideal for crafts and small areas of garments, such as cuffs and collars. Use it in garments when a woven or fusible alternative is not available.

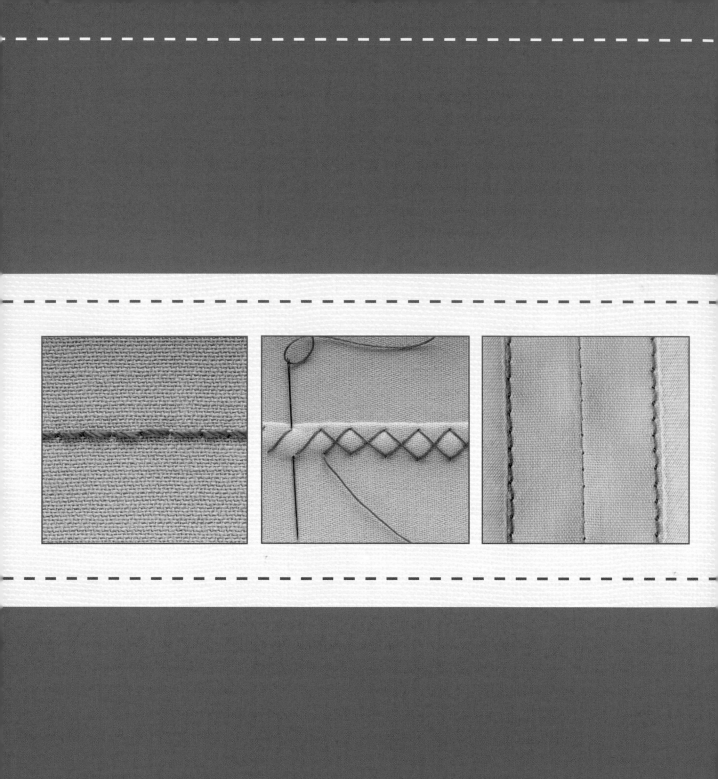

STITCH
ESSENTIALS

Stitches for hand sewing

It is necessary to use hand stitching to prepare the fabric prior to permanent stitching – these temporary tacking stitches will eventually be removed. Permanent hand stitching is used to finish a garment and to attach fasteners, as well as to help out with a quick repair.

Threading the needle

When sewing by hand, cut your piece of thread to be no longer than the distance from your fingertips to your elbow. If the thread is much longer than this, it will knot as you sew.

HOW TO THREAD A NEEDLE

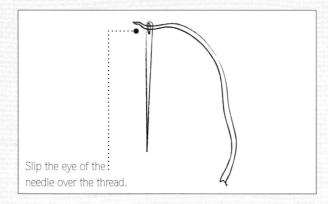

Slip the eye of the needle over the thread.

1 Hold your needle in your right hand and the end of the thread in your left. Keeping the thread still, place the eye of the needle over the thread.

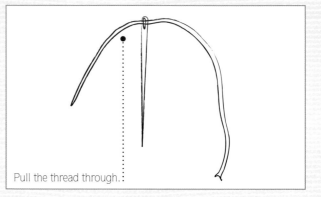

Pull the thread through.

2 If the needle will not slip over the thread, dampen your fingers and run the moisture across the eye of the needle. Pull the thread through.

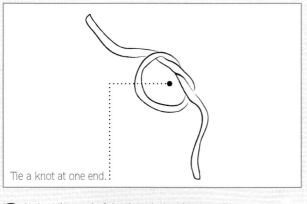

Tie a knot at one end.

3 At the other end of the thread, tie a knot as shown or secure the thread as shown opposite.

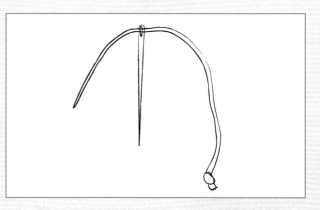

4 You are now ready to start your sewing.

Securing the thread

The ends of the thread must be secured firmly, especially if the hand stitching is to be permanent. A knot (see opposite page) is frequently used and is the preferred choice for temporary stitches. For permanent stitching a double stitch is a better option.

DOUBLE STITCH

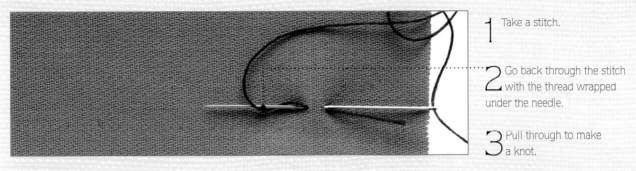

1 Take a stitch.

2 Go back through the stitch with the thread wrapped under the needle.

3 Pull through to make a knot.

BACK STITCH

..................Make two small stitches in the same place.

LOCKING STITCH

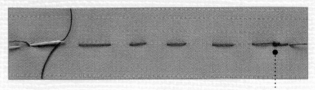

Start the stitching with a knot and finish..........
by working a knot at the end.

Tacking stitches

Each of the many types of tacking stitches has its own individual use. Basic tacks hold two or more pieces of fabric together. Long and short tacks are an alternative version of the basic tacking stitch, often used when the tacking will stay in the work for some time. Diagonal tacks hold folds or overlaid fabrics together, while slip tacks are used to hold a fold in fabric to another piece of fabric.

BASIC TACKS

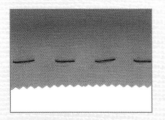

Starting with a knot and, using single thread, make straight stitches, evenly spaced.

LONG AND SHORT TACKS

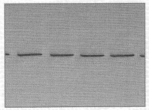

Make long stitches with a short space between each one.

DIAGONAL TACKS

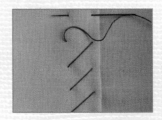

Work vertically, taking horizontal stitches.

SLIP TACKS

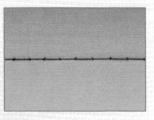

Take a stitch into the fold and then a stitch into the base fabric.

Hand stitches

There are a number of hand stitches that can be used during construction of a garment or other item. Some are for decorative purposes while others are more functional.

BACK STITCH

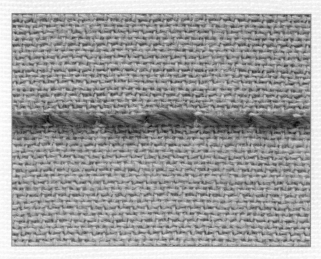

A **strong stitch** that could be used to construct a piece of work. Work from right to left. Bring the needle up, leaving a space, and then take the thread back to the end of the last stitch.

RUNNING STITCH

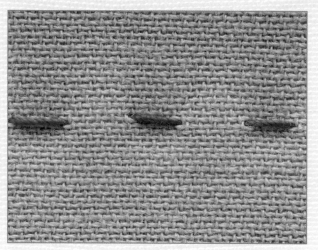

Very similar to tacking (see page 49), but used more for decorative purposes. Work from right to left. Run the needle in and out of the fabric to create even stitches and spaces.

WHIP STITCH

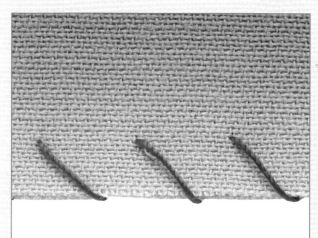

A **diagonal stitch** sewn with a single thread along a raw edge to prevent fraying. Work from right to left. Take a stitch through the edge of the fabric. The depth of the stitch depends on the thickness of the fabric – for a thin fabric take a shallow stitch.

BUTTONHOLE STITCH

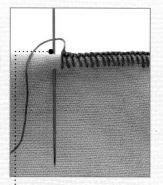 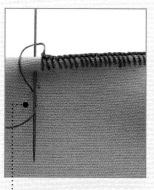

1 **Used to make** hand-worked buttonholes and also to secure fastenings. It is always stitched on an edge with no spaces between the stitches. Work from right to left. Push the needle from the top edge into the fabric.

2 **Wrap the thread** behind the needle as the needle goes in and again as the needle leaves the fabric. Pull through and a knot will appear at the edge. This is an essential stitch for all sewers and is not difficult to master.

HERRINGBONE STITCH

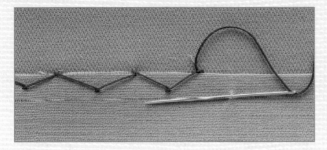

A very useful stitch as it is secure yet has some movement in it. It is used to secure hems and interlinings. Work from left to right. Take a small horizontal stitch into one layer and then the other, so the thread crosses itself.

FLAT FELL STITCH

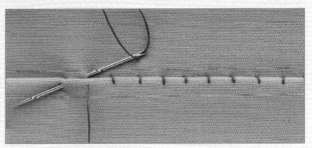

A strong, secure stitch to hold two layers permanently together. This stitch is often used to secure bias bindings and linings. Work from right to left. Make a short, straight stitch at the edge of the fabric.

SLIP HEM STITCH

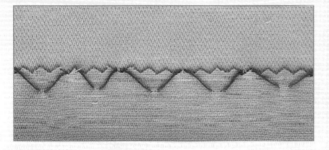

Also called a catch stitch, this is used primarily for securing hems. It looks similar to herringbone (above). Work from right to left. Take a short horizontal stitch into one layer and then the other.

BLIND HEM STITCH

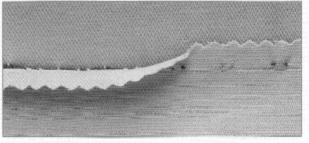

As the name suggests this is for hemming a garment. As the stitch is under the edge of the fabric it should be discreet. Work from right to left and use a slip hem stitch (left).

BLANKET STITCH

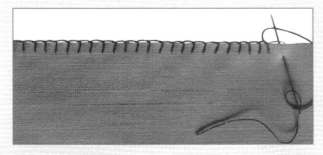

Similar to buttonhole stitch but without the knot. Blanket stitch is useful to neaten edges and for decorative purposes. Always leave a space between the stitches. Push the needle into the fabric and, as it appears at the edge, wrap the thread under the needle.

CROSS STITCH

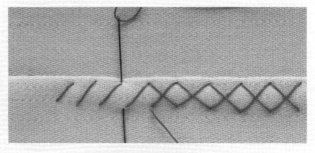

A temporary securing stitch used to hold pleats in place after construction. It can also be used to secure linings. Work a row of even diagonal stitches in one direction and then a row back over them to make crosses.

Machine stitches and seams

Fabric is joined together using seams – whether it be for an item of clothing, craft work, or soft furnishings. The most common seam is a plain seam, which is suitable for a wide variety of fabrics and items. However, there are many other seams to be used as appropriate, depending on the fabric and item being constructed. Some seams are decorative and can add detail to structured garments.

Securing the thread

Machine stitches need to be secured at the end of a seam to prevent them from coming undone. This can be done by hand, tying the ends of the thread, or using the machine with a reverse stitch or a locking stitch, which stitches three or four stitches in the same place.

TIE THE ENDS

1 Pull on the top thread and it will pull up a loop – this is the bobbin thread.

2 Pull the loop through to the top.

3 Tie the two threads together.

REVERSE STITCH

LOCKING STITCH

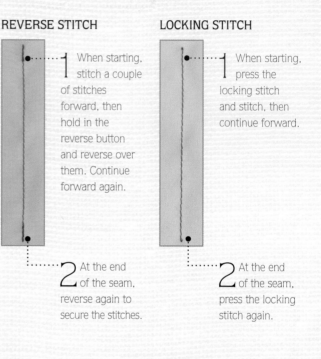

REVERSE STITCH

1 When starting, stitch a couple of stitches forward, then hold in the reverse button and reverse over them. Continue forward again.

2 At the end of the seam, reverse again to secure the stitches.

LOCKING STITCH

1 When starting, press the locking stitch and stitch, then continue forward.

2 At the end of the seam, press the locking stitch again.

Stitches made with a machine

The sewing machine will stitch plain seams and decorative seams as well as buttonholes of various styles. The length and width of all buttonholes can be altered to suit the garment or craft item.

STRAIGHT STITCH

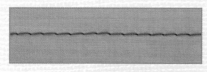

Used for most applications. The length of the stitch can be altered from 0.5 to 5.0 on most sewing machines.

ZIGZAG STITCH

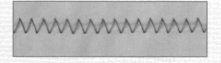

To neaten seam edges and for securing and decorative purposes. Both the width and the length of this stitch can be altered.

3-STEP ZIGZAG STITCH

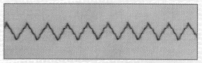

Made up of small, straight stitches. This stitch is decorative as well as functional, and is often found in lingerie. The stitch length and width can be altered.

BLIND HEM STITCH

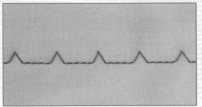

Made in conjunction with the blind hem foot. A combination of straight stitches and a zigzag stitch (see opposite page). Used to secure hems.

OVEREDGE STITCH

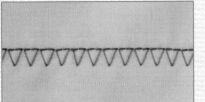

Made in conjunction with the overedge foot. The stitch is used for neatening the edge of fabric. The width and length of the stitch can be altered.

STRETCH STITCH

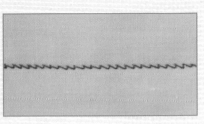

Also known as a lightening stitch. This stitch is recommended for stretch knits but is better used to help control difficult fabrics.

BASIC BUTTONHOLE STITCH

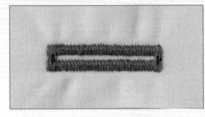

Square on both ends. Used on all styles of garment.

ROUND-END BUTTONHOLE STITCH

One square end and one round end. Used on jackets.

KEYHOLE BUTTONHOLE STITCH

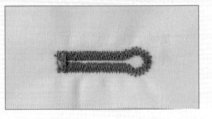

One square end and one end shaped like a loop. Used on jackets.

DECORATIVE STITCHES

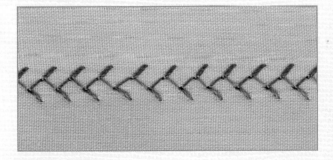

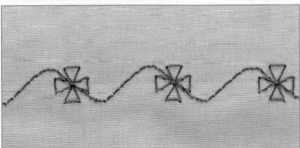

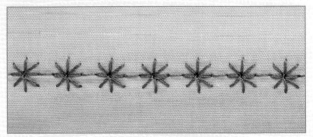

Sewing machines are capable of producing decorative linear stitches. These can be used to enhance the surface of work or a seam as they add interest to edges. Or, when worked as many rows together, they can be used to create a piece of embroidered fabric.

How to make a plain seam

A plain seam is 1.5cm (⅝in) wide. It is important that the seam is stitched accurately at this measurement, otherwise the item being made will come out the wrong size and shape. There are guides on the plate of the sewing machine that can be used to help align the fabric.

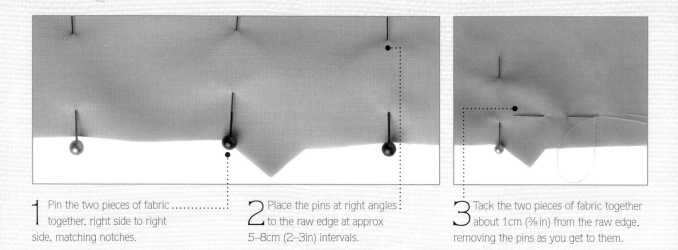

1 Pin the two pieces of fabric together, right side to right side, matching notches.

2 Place the pins at right angles to the raw edge at approx 5–8cm (2–3in) intervals.

3 Tack the two pieces of fabric together about 1cm (⅜in) from the raw edge, removing the pins as you get to them.

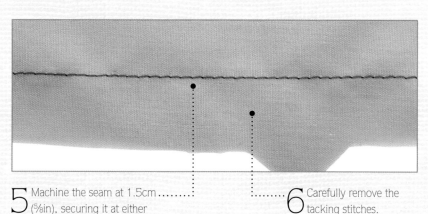

4 Using the seam guide on the machine plate to help you, place the fabric under the machine foot. Turn the balance wheel to place the needle into the fabric, then lower the presser foot on the sewing machine.

5 Machine the seam at 1.5cm (⅝in), securing it at either end by your chosen technique.

6 Carefully remove the tacking stitches.

7 Press the seam flat as it was stitched, then press the seam open.

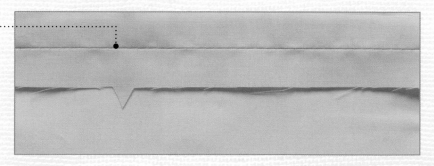

Seam neatening

It is important that the raw edges of the seam are neatened or finished – this will make the seam hard-wearing and prevent fraying. The method of neatening will depend on the style of item that is being made and the fabric you are using.

PINKED

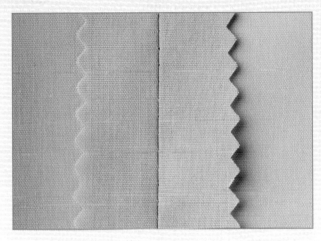

This method of neatening is ideal to use on fabrics that do not fray badly. Using pinking shears, trim as little as possible off the raw edge.

ZIGZAGGED

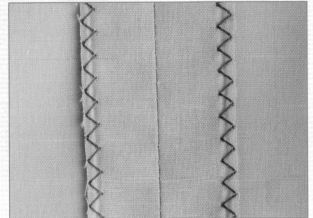

All sewing machines will make a zigzag stitch. It is an ideal stitch to use to stop the edges fraying and is suitable for all types of fabric. Stitch in from the raw edge, then trim back to the zigzag stitch. On most fabrics, use a stitch width of 2.0 and a stitch length of 1.5.

OVEREDGE STITCHED

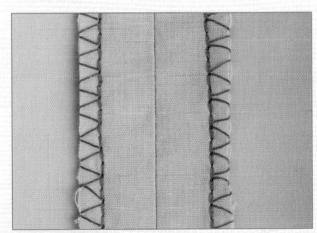

This is found on most sewing machines. Select the overedge stitch on your machine. Using the overedge machine foot and the pre-set stitch length and width, machine along the raw edge of the seam.

CLEAN FINISH

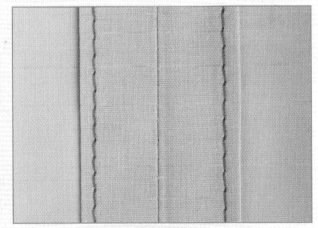

This is a very hard-wearing finish and is ideal for cottons and fine fabrics. Using a straight stitch, turn under the raw edge of the seam allowance by 3mm (⅛in) and straight stitch along the fold.

Hong Kong finish

This is a great finish to use on wools and linens, to neaten the seams on unlined jackets. It is made by wrapping the raw edge with bias-cut strips.

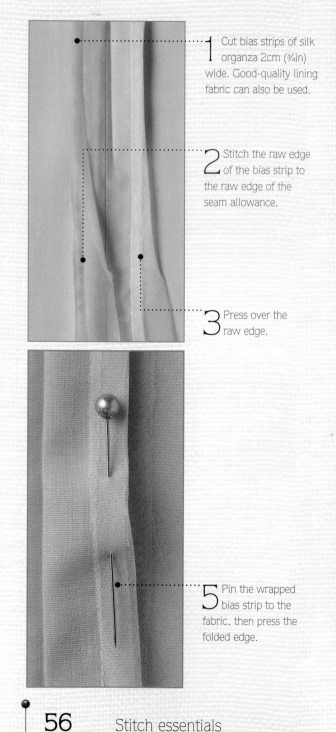

1 Cut bias strips of silk organza 2cm (¾in) wide. Good-quality lining fabric can also be used.

2 Stitch the raw edge of the bias strip to the raw edge of the seam allowance.

3 Press over the raw edge.

5 Pin the wrapped bias strip to the fabric, then press the folded edge.

4 Wrap to the wrong side of the raw edge, with the raw edge of the bias strip against the stitching of the seam.

6 Machine the wrapped bias strip to the seam, from the upper side of the seam, stitching alongside the edge of the bias.

Stitching corners and curves

Not all sewing is straight lines. The work will have curves and corners that require negotiation, to produce sharp clean angles and curves on the right side. The technique for stitching a corner shown below applies to corners of all angles. On a thick fabric, the technique is slightly different, with a stitch taken across the corner, and on a fabric that frays badly the corner is reinforced with a second row of stitches.

STITCHING A CORNER

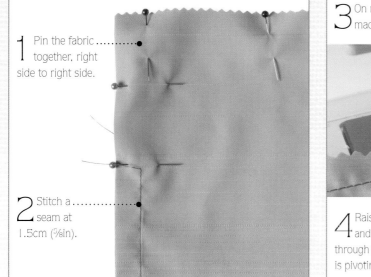

1 Pin the fabric together, right side to right side.

2 Stitch a seam at 1.5cm (⅝in).

3 On reaching the corner, insert the machine needle into the fabric.

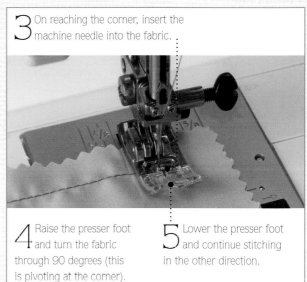

4 Raise the presser foot and turn the fabric through 90 degrees (this is pivoting at the corner).

5 Lower the presser foot and continue stitching in the other direction.

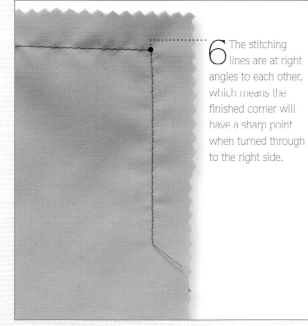

6 The stitching lines are at right angles to each other, which means the finished corner will have a sharp point when turned through to the right side.

STITCHING A CORNER ON HEAVY FABRIC

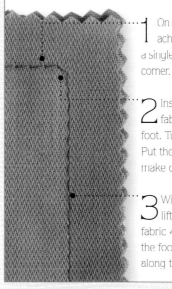

1 On thick fabric it is difficult to achieve a sharp point, so instead a single stitch is taken across the corner. Stitch to the corner.

2 Insert the needle into the fabric, then lift the presser foot. Turn the fabric 45 degrees. Put the foot down again and make one stitch.

3 With the needle in the fabric, lift the foot and turn the fabric 45 degrees again. Lower the foot and continue stitching along the other side.

STITCHING A REINFORCED CORNER

1 On the wrong side of the fabric, stitch along one side of the corner to make a 1.5cm (⅝in) seam.

2 Take the machining through to the edge of the fabric.

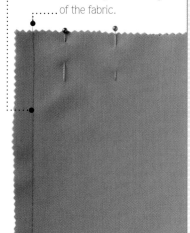

3 Stitch the other side of the corner at a 1.5cm (⅝in) seam allowance, again machining through the edge of the fabric.

4 The two stitching lines will overlap at the corner.

5 Stitch exactly over the first two stitching lines, this time pivoting at the corner (see Stitching a corner, steps 3–5, page 57).

6 Remove the surplus stitches in the seam allowance by unpicking.

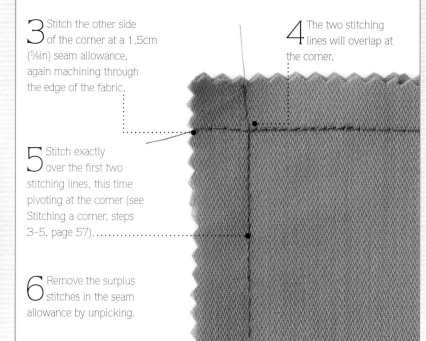

STITCHING AN INNER CORNER

1 Machine accurately at 1.5cm (⅝in) from the edge, pivoting at the corner (see Stitching a corner, steps 3–5, page 57).

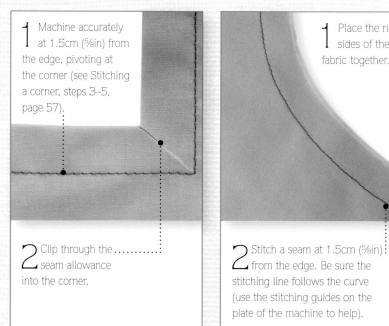

2 Clip through the seam allowance into the corner.

STITCHING AN INNER CURVE

1 Place the right sides of the fabric together.

2 Stitch a seam at 1.5cm (⅝in) from the edge. Be sure the stitching line follows the curve (use the stitching guides on the plate of the machine to help).

STITCHING AN OUTER CURVE

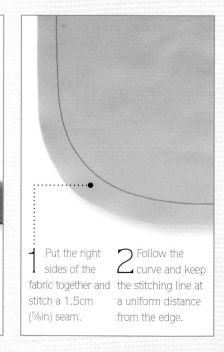

1 Put the right sides of the fabric together and stitch a 1.5cm (⅝in) seam.

2 Follow the curve and keep the stitching line at a uniform distance from the edge.

Reducing seam bulk

It is important that the seams used for construction do not cause bulk on the right side. To make sure this does not happen, the seam allowances need to be reduced in size by a technique known as layering a seam. They may also require V shapes to be removed, which is known as notching, or the seam allowance may be clipped.

Layering a seam

On the majority of fabrics, if the seam is on the edge of the work, the fabric in the seam needs reducing. The seam allowance closest to the outside of the garment or item stays full width, while the seam allowance closest to the body or inside is reduced.

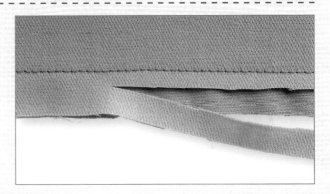

Cut along one side of the seam to reduce the fabric in the seam allowance by half to one-third of its original width.

Reducing seam bulk on an inner curve

For an inner curve to lie flat, the seam will need to be layered and notched, then understitched to hold it in place (see page 60).

1 Stitch the seam on the inner curve.

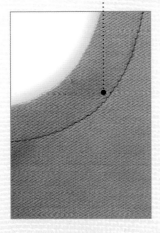

2 Layer the seam (see above), then cut out V notches to reduce the bulk.

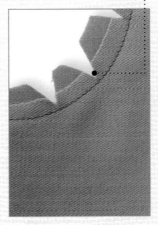

3 Turn to the right side and press.

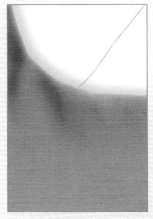

4 Understitch the seam allowances on to the wrong side.

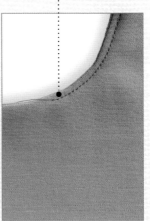

Reducing seam bulk on an outer curve

An outer curve also needs layering and notching or clipping to allow the fabric to turn to the right side, after which it is understitched.

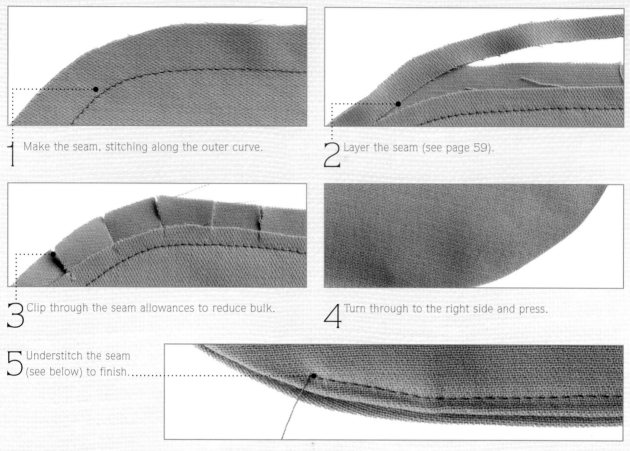

1 Make the seam, stitching along the outer curve.

2 Layer the seam (see page 59).

3 Clip through the seam allowances to reduce bulk.

4 Turn through to the right side and press.

5 Understitch the seam (see below) to finish.

Stitch finishes

Top-stitching and understitching are two methods to finish edges. Top-stitching is meant to be seen on the right side of the work, whereas understitching is not visible from the right side.

TOP-STITCHING

A top-stitch is a decorative, sharp finish to an edge. Use a longer stitch length, of 3.0 or 3.5, and machine on the right side of the work, using the edge of the machine foot as a guide.

UNDERSTITCHING

Used to secure a seam that is on the edge of a piece of fabric. It helps to stop the seam from rolling to the right side. First make the seam, then layer, turn, and press on to the right side. Open the seam again and push the seam allowance over the layered seam allowance. Machine the seam allowance down.

French seam

A French seam is a seam that is stitched twice, first on the right side of the work and then on the wrong side, enclosing the first seam. The French seam has traditionally been used on delicate garments such as lingerie and on sheer and silk fabrics.

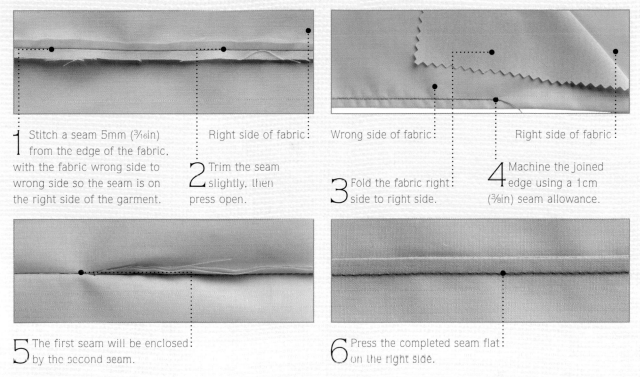

1 Stitch a seam 5mm (³⁄₁₆in) from the edge of the fabric, with the fabric wrong side to wrong side so the seam is on the right side of the garment.

Right side of fabric

2 Trim the seam slightly, then press open.

Wrong side of fabric

Right side of fabric

3 Fold the fabric right side to right side.

4 Machine the joined edge using a 1cm (³⁄₈in) seam allowance.

5 The first seam will be enclosed by the second seam.

6 Press the completed seam flat on the right side.

Run and fell seam

Some garments require a strong seam that will withstand frequent washing and wear and tear. A run and fell seam, also known as a flat fell seam, is very strong. It is made on the right side of a garment and is used on the inside leg seam of jeans, and on men's tailored shirts.

1 Stitch a 1.5cm (⁵⁄₈in) seam on the right side of the fabric. Press open.

Right side of fabric

2 Trim the side of the seam allowance that is towards the back of the garment down to one-third of its width.

3 Wrap the other side of the seam allowance around the trimmed side and pin in position.

4 Machine along the folded pinned edge through all layers. Press.

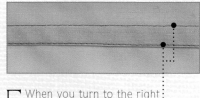

5 When you turn to the right side, there will be two rows of parallel stitching.

Top-stitched seam

A top-stitched seam is very useful as it is both decorative and practical. This seam is often used on crafts and soft furnishings as well as garments.

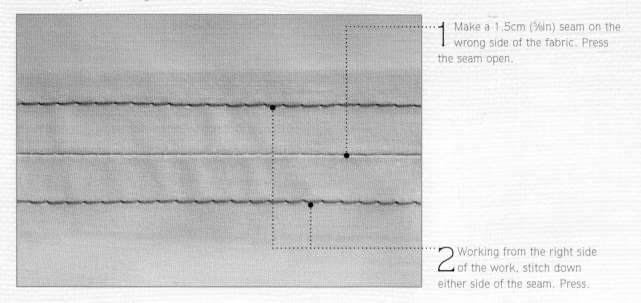

1 Make a 1.5cm (⅝in) seam on the wrong side of the fabric. Press the seam open.

2 Working from the right side of the work, stitch down either side of the seam. Press.

Lapped seam

Also called an overlaid seam, a lapped seam is constructed on the right side of the garment. It is a very flat seam when it is finished.

1 Press under 1.5cm (⅝in) on one side of the seamline to the wrong side.

3 Machine close to the fold.

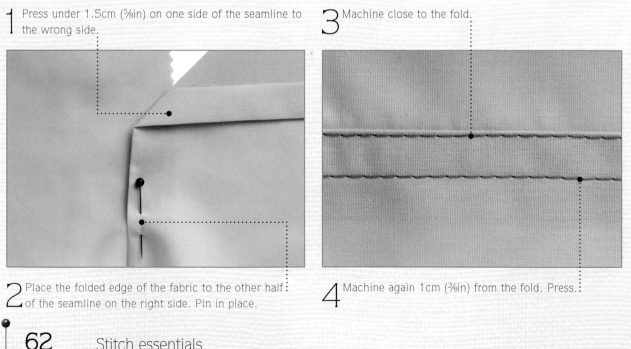

2 Place the folded edge of the fabric to the other half of the seamline on the right side. Pin in place.

4 Machine again 1cm (⅜in) from the fold. Press.

Seams on difficult fabrics

Some fabrics require specialist care for seam construction because they are very bulky, as you find with a fur fabric, or so soft and delicate that they appear too soft to sew. On a sheer fabric, the seam used is an alternative to a French seam; it is very narrow when finished and presses very flat. Making a seam on suede is done by means of a lapped seam. As some suede-effect fabric has a fake fur on the other side, the seam is reversible.

A SEAM ON SHEER FABRIC

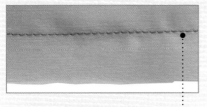 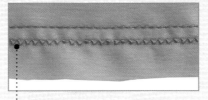 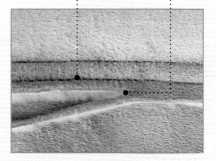

1 On the wrong side of the work, make a 1.5cm (⅝in) seam.

2 Machine again 5mm (³⁄₁₆in) from the first stitching, using either a very narrow zigzag stitch or a stretch stitch. Press.

3 Trim the raw edge of the fabric close to the second row of stitching.

A SEAM ON SUEDE OR SUEDE-EFFECT FABRIC

1 On all seams, trace tack the stitching line 1.5cm (⅝in) from the edge.

2 Trace tack again 1.5cm (⅝in) away from the first row of stitching.

3 Overlap one side of the seam over the other, matching the 1.5cm (⅝in) tack lines. The raw edge should touch the second row of tacks.

5 Stitch again 1cm (⅜in) from the first stitching line.

6 Trim the raw edge by about 3mm (⅛in).

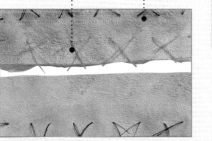

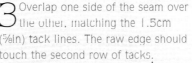

4 Using a walking foot and a longer than normal stitch length of 3.5, machine the two layers together along the tacks marking the 1.5cm (⅝in) seam allowance.

A SEAM ON FUR FABRIC

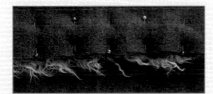  

1 Pin the fabric together right side to right side, placing the pins in alternate directions to stop the fur moving.

2 Using a walking foot and a longer than normal stitch length, machine the seam.

3 Finger press the seam open.

4 Trim the surplus fur fabric off the seam allowances.

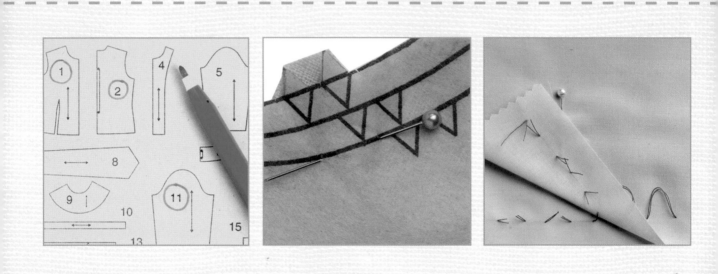

PATTERNS

Reading patterns

A pattern has three main components: the envelope, the pattern, and the instructions. The envelope gives an illustration of the item together with fabric suggestions and requirements. The pattern sheets inside the envelope are normally printed on tissue and contain a wealth of information, while the instructions tell you how to construct the item.

Reading a pattern envelope

The envelope front illustrates the finished garment or item. The different versions are known as views. On the reverse of the envelope there is usually an illustration of the back view and the standard body measurement chart that has been used for this pattern, plus a chart that will help you purchase the correct amount of fabric for each view.

Number of pattern pieces

Code number for ordering

Description of garment or item, giving details of style and different views included in pattern

List of pattern sizes in metric and imperial measurements for bust, waist, and hips in each size

Suggested fabrics suitable for garment or item as well as unsuitable fabrics

Notions required for each view

5678
15 PIECES

MISSES' UNLINED JACKET, SKIRT, SHORTS, AND PANTS. Unlined, semi-fitted, V-neck jacket has short sleeves, front buttons, optional waistline darts, and optional breast pocket. Straight skirt, above mid-knee, and trousers or shorts with straight legs, have waistband, front pleats, side seam pockets, and back zip.

FABRICS: Jacket, skirt, shorts, and trousers: wool crepe, soft cottons, sheeting, linen, silk, silk types, and lightweight woollens. Skirt, shorts, and trousers also challis, jacquards, and crepe. Unsuitable for fabrics printed with obvious diagonals. Allow extra fabric in order to match plaids, stripes, or one-way design fabrics.

Use nap yardages/layouts for shaded, pile, or one-way design fabrics. *with nap. ** without nap
NOTIONS: Thread. Jacket: three 1.2 cm (⅞ in) buttons; 6mm (¼ in) shoulder pads. Skirt, trousers: pkg of 3.2 cm (1 ¼ in) waistband interfacing; 18 cm (7 in) zip; and one hook and eye closure.

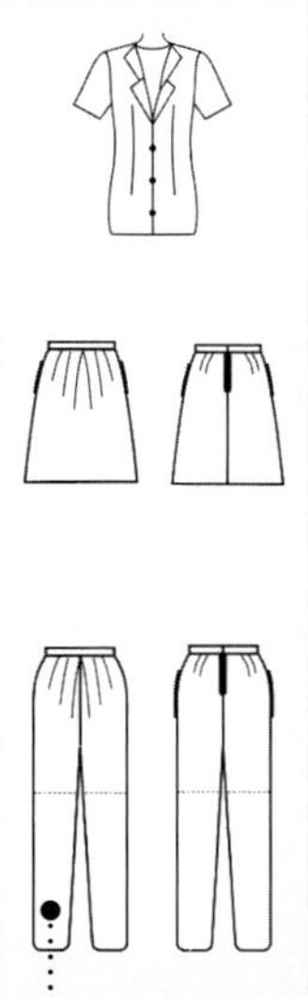

METRIC

Body measurements	(6	8	10)	(12	14	16)	(18	20	22)
Bust	78	80	83	87	92	97	102	107	112 cm
Waist	58	61	63.5	66	71	76	81	86	94 cm
Hip	81	84	86	91	96.5	102	107	112	117 cm

Fabric needed		(6	8	10)	(12	14	16)	(18	20	22)
Jacket	115 cm*/**	1.70	1.70	1.70	1.80	1.80	2.10	2.20	2.20	2.20 m
	150 cm*/**	1.30	1.30	1.30	1.40	1.70	1.70	1.70	1.80	1.80 m
Interfacing		1 m of 55–90 cm lightweight fusible or non-fusible								
Skirt A	115 cm*/**	1.6	1.6	1.6	1.6	1.9	1.9	1.9	1.9	2 m
	150 cm*/**	1.2	1.2	1.3	1.3	1.3	1.3	1.4	1.4	1.5 m
Shorts B	115 cm*/**	1.6	1.6	1.6	1.6	1.9	1.9	1.9	1.9	2 m
	150 cm*/**	1.2	1.2	1.3	1.3	1.3	1.3	1.4	1.4	1.5 m
Pants B	115 cm*/**	2.4	2.4	2.4	2.4	2.4	2.4	2.4	2.7	2.7 m
	150 cm*	2	2	2	2	2.1	2.1	2.2	2.3	2.3 m
	150 cm**	1.6	1.6	1.8	2	2	2.1	2.2	2.3	2.3 m

Garment measurements	(6	8	10)	(12	14	16)	(18	20	22)
Jacket bust	92	94.5	97	101	106	111	116	121	126 cm
Jacket waist	81	83	86	89.5	94.5	100	105	110	116 cm
Jacket back length	73	73.5	74	75	75.5	76	77	77.5	78 cm
Skirt A lower edge	99	101	104	106	112	117	122	127	132 cm
Skirt A length	61	61	61	63	63	63	65	65	65 cm
Shorts B leg width	71	73.5	76	81	86.5	94	99	104	109 cm
Shorts B side length	49.5	50	51	51.5	52	52.5	53.5	54	54.5 cm
Pants B leg width	53.5	53.5	56	56	58.5	58.5	61	61	63.5 cm
Pants B side length	103	103	103	103	103	103	103	103	103 cm

IMPERIAL

Body measurements	(6	8	10)	(12	14	16)	(18	20	22)
Bust	30½	31½	32½	34	36	38	40	42	44 in
Waist	23	24	25	26½	28	30	32	34	37 in
Hip	32½	33½	34½	36	38	40	42	44	46 in

Fabric needed		(6	8	10)	(12	14	16)	(18	20	22)
Jacket	45 in*/**	1⅞	1⅞	1⅞	1⅞	2	2⅜	2⅜	2⅜	2⅜ yd
	60 in*/**	1⅜	1⅜	1⅜	1½	1⅞	1⅞	1⅞	1⅞	2 yd
Interfacing		1⅛ yd of 22–36 in lightweight fusible or non-fusible								
Skirt A	45 in*/**	1¾	1⅞	1⅞	1⅞	2	2	2	2	2⅛ yd
	60 in*/**	1¼	1¼	1⅜	1⅜	1⅜	1⅜	1½	1½	1⅝ yd
Shorts B	45 in*/**	1¾	1¾	1¾	1¾	2	2	2	2	2⅛ yd
	60 in*/**	1¼	1¼	1⅜	1⅜	1⅜	1⅜	1½	1½	1⅝ yd
Pants B	45 in*/**	2⅝	2⅝	2⅝	2⅝	2⅝	2⅝	2⅝	2⅞	2⅞ yd
	60 in*	2⅛	2⅛	2⅛	2⅛	2¼	2¼	2⅜	2½	2½ yd
	60 in **	1¾	1¾	1⅞	2⅛	2⅛	2¼	2⅜	2½	2½ yd

Garment measurements	(6	8	10)	(12	14	16)	(18	20	22)
Jacket bust	36¼	37¼	38¼	39¾	41¾	43¾	45¼	47¾	49¾ in
Jacket waist	31¾	32¾	33¾	35¼	37¼	39¼	41¼	43¼	45¼ in
Jacket back length	28¾	29	29¼	29½	29¾	30	30¼	30½	30¾ in
Skirt A lower edge	39	40	41	42	44	46	48	50	52 in
Skirt A length	24	24	24	24¾	24¾	24¾	25½	25½	25½ in
Shorts B leg width	28	29	30	32	34	37	39	41	43 in
Shorts B side length	19½	19¾	20	20¼	20½	20¾	21	21¼	21½ in
Pants B leg width	21	21	22	22	23	23	24	24	25 in
Pants B side length	40½	40½	40½	40½	40½	40½	40½	40½	40½ in

Outline drawing of garment or item, including back views, showing darts and zip positions

Garment measurements box gives actual size of finished garment

Chart to follow for required fabric quantity, indicating size across top, and chosen view and correct width down the side

Single-size patterns

Some patterns contain a garment or craft project of one size only. If you are using a single-size pattern, cut around the tissue on the thick black cutting line before making any alterations.

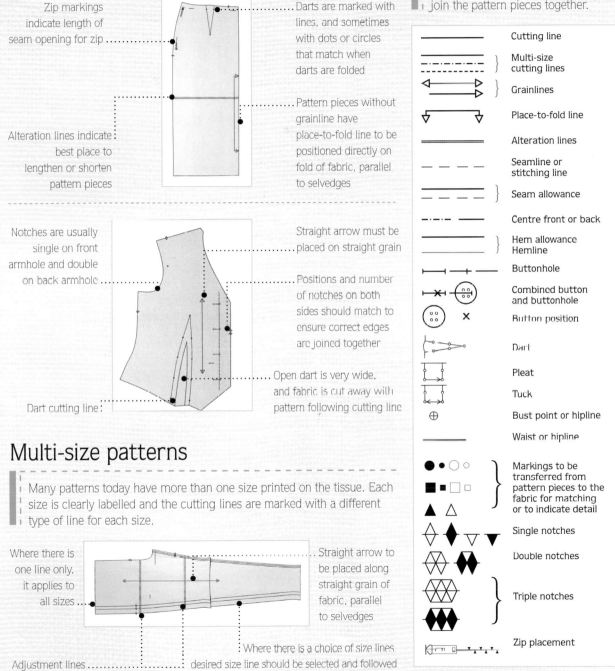

Zip markings indicate length of seam opening for zip ....

Darts are marked with lines, and sometimes with dots or circles that match when darts are folded

Alteration lines indicate best place to lengthen or shorten pattern pieces

Pattern pieces without grainline have place-to-fold line to be positioned directly on fold of fabric, parallel to selvedges

Notches are usually single on front armhole and double on back armhole ....

Straight arrow must be placed on straight grain

Positions and number of notches on both sides should match to ensure correct edges are joined together

Dart cutting line :

Open dart is very wide, and fabric is cut away with pattern following cutting line

Multi-size patterns

Many patterns today have more than one size printed on the tissue. Each size is clearly labelled and the cutting lines are marked with a different type of line for each size.

Where there is one line only, it applies to all sizes ...

Straight arrow to be placed along straight grain of fabric, parallel to selvedges

Adjustment lines ....

Where there is a choice of size lines, desired size line should be selected and followed

Pattern markings

Each pattern piece will have a series of lines, dots, and other symbols printed on it. These symbols are to help you alter the pattern and join the pattern pieces together.

————————	Cutting line
–·–·–·–·–· }	Multi-size cutting lines
◁———————▷ }	Grainlines
▽———————▽	Place-to-fold line
═══════════	Alteration lines
– – – – – –	Seamline or stitching line
— — — — }	Seam allowance
—·—·—·—·	Centre front or back
———————— }	Hem allowance Hemline
⊢—⊣—— ⊣—	Buttonhole
⊢—✕—— ⊙	Combined button and buttonhole
⊙ ✕	Button position
•⋯⋯⋯•⋯⋯⋯	Dart
⫲⫲⫲	Pleat
⫲⫲⫲	Tuck
⊕	Bust point or hipline
————————	Waist or hipline
●•○○ ▪▪□□ ▲△ }	Markings to be transferred from pattern pieces to the fabric for matching or to indicate detail
◇◆▽▼	Single notches
⬡⬢	Double notches
⬡⬡ }	Triple notches
⬢⬢	
⊢——•••••	Zip placement

Body measuring

Accurate body measurements are needed to determine the correct pattern size to use and if any alterations are required. Pattern sizes are usually chosen by the hip or bust measurement; for tops follow the bust measurement, but for skirts or trousers use the hip measurement. If you are choosing a dress pattern, go by whichever measurement is the largest.

TAKING BODY MEASUREMENTS

• You'll need a tape measure and ruler as well as a helper for some of the measuring, and a hard chair or stool.

• Wear close-fitting clothes such as a leotard and leggings.

• Do not wear any shoes.

HOW TO MEASURE YOUR HEIGHT

Most paper patterns are designed for a woman 165 to 168cm (5ft 5in to 5ft 6in). If you are shorter or taller than this you may need to adjust the pattern prior to cutting out your fabric.

1 Remove your shoes.

2 Stand straight, with your back against the wall.

3 Place a ruler flat on your head, touching the wall, and mark the wall at this point.

4 Step away and measure the distance from the floor to the marked point.

CHEST

Measure above the bust, high under the arms, keeping the tape measure flat and straight across the back.

FULL BUST

Make sure you are wearing a good-fitting bra and measure over the fullest part of the bust. If your cup size is in excess of a B, you will probably need to do a bust alteration, although some patterns are now cut to accommodate larger cup sizes.

WAIST

This is the measurement around the smallest part of your waist. Wrap the tape around first to find your natural waist, then measure.

HIPS

This measurement must be taken around the fullest part of the hips, between the waist and legs.

HIGH HIP

Take this just below the waist and just above the hip bones to give a measurement across the tummy.

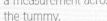

SHOULDER

Hold the end of the tape measure at the base of your neck (where a necklace would lie) and measure to the dent at the end of your shoulder. To find this dent raise your arm slightly.

NECK

Measure around the neck – snugly but not too tight – to determine collar size.

ARM

Bend your elbow and place your hand on your hip, then measure from the end of the shoulder over the elbow to the wrist bone.

BACK WAIST

Take this measurement down the centre of the back, from the lumpy bit at the top of the spine, in line with the shoulders, to the waist.

OUTSIDE LEG

Measure the side of the leg from the waist, over the hip, and straight down the leg to the ankle bone.

INSIDE LEG

Stand with your legs apart and measure the inside of one leg from the crotch to the ankle bone.

CROTCH DEPTH

Sit upright on a hard chair or stool and measure from the waist vertically down to the chair.

Cutting out

Cutting out correctly can make or break your project. But first you need to examine the fabric in the shop, looking for any flaws, such as a crooked pattern, and checking to see if the fabric has been cut properly from the roll – that is at a right angle to the selvedge. If the fabric is creased, press it; if washable, wash it to avoid shrinkage later. After this preparation, you will be ready to lay the pattern pieces on the fabric, pin in place, and cut out.

Fabric grain and nap

It is important that the pattern pieces are cut on the correct grain, as this will make the fabric hang correctly and produce a longer-lasting item. The grain of the fabric is the direction in which the yarns or threads that make up the fabric lie. The majority of pattern pieces need to be placed with the straight of grain symbol running parallel to the warp yarn. Some fabrics have a nap due to the pile, which means the fabric shadows when it is smoothed in one direction. A fabric with a one-way design or uneven stripes is also described as being with nap. Fabrics with nap are generally cut out with the nap running down, whereas those without nap can be cut out at any angle.

GRAIN ON WOVEN FABRICS

The selvedge is the woven, non-frayable edge that runs parallel to the warp grain.

Yarns that run the length of the fabric are called warp yarns. They are stronger than weft yarns and less likely to stretch.

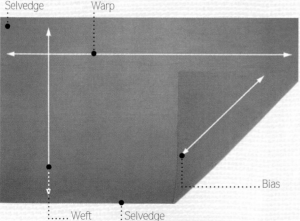

Selvedge   Warp

Bias

Weft   Selvedge

GRAIN ON KNITTED FABRICS

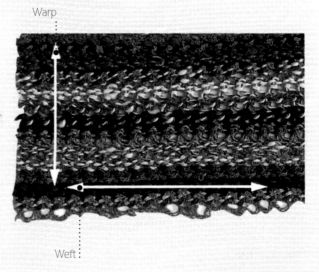

Warp

Weft

Weft yarns run crossways, over and under the warp yarns.

The bias grain is diagonal – running at 45 degrees to the warp and weft. A garment cut on the bias will follow the contours of the body.

A knitted fabric also has a grain. Some knit fabrics stretch only one way while others stretch in both directions. Patterns for knit fabrics often need to be cut following the direction of the greatest stretch.

NAP DUE TO PILE

Fabrics such as velvet, corduroy, and velour will show a difference in colour, depending on whether the nap is running up or down.

NAP IF ONE-WAY DESIGN

A one-way pattern – in this case flowers – that runs lengthways in the fabric will be upside-down on one side when the fabric is folded back on itself.

NAP IF STRIPED

If the stripes do not match on both sides when the fabric is folded back, they are uneven and the fabric will need a nap layout.

Pattern preparation

Before cutting out, sort out all the pattern pieces that are required for the item you are making. Check them to see if any have special cutting instructions. Make pattern alterations, if necessary. If there are no alterations, just trim patterns to your size.

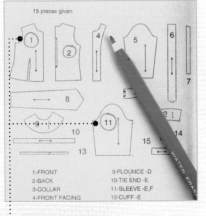

1 Using the pattern instruction sheet, which has drawings of the pattern pieces, select the pieces you require.

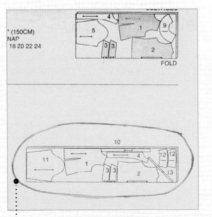

2 The instruction sheet also shows a suggested cutting-out layout for the item you are making, on different widths of fabric, with or without nap.

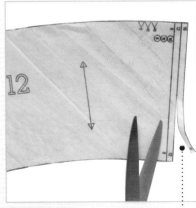

3 Trim multi-size pattern pieces according to the chosen size. Single-size pattern pieces do not need to be cut to shape; just cut around them roughly if there is excess tissue.

Pattern layout

Fabric is usually folded selvedge to selvedge. With the fabric folded, the pattern is pinned on top, and both the right and left-side pieces are cut out at the same time. If pattern pieces have to be cut from single layer fabric, remember to cut matching pairs. For a fabric with a design it is a good idea to have this on the outside so that you can arrange the pattern pieces to show off the design. If you have left and right-side pattern pieces, they are cut on single fabric with the fabric right side up and the pattern right side up.

PINNING THE PATTERN TO THE FABRIC

1 The "to fold" symbol indicates the pattern piece is to be pinned carefully to the folded edge of the fabric. To check the straight of grain on the other pattern pieces, place the grain arrow so that it looks parallel to the selvedge, then pin to secure at one end of the arrow.

2 Measure from the pinned end to the selvedge.

3 Measure from the other end of the arrow to the selvedge.

4 Move the pattern piece slightly until this measurement is the same as the pinned end, then pin in place.

5 Once it is straight, pin around the rest of the pattern piece, placing pins in the seam allowances.

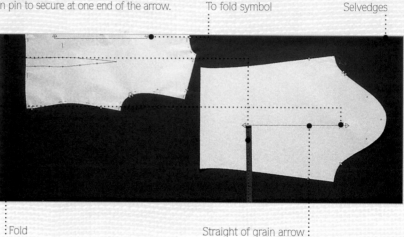

To fold symbol   Selvedges

Fold   Straight of grain arrow

GENERAL GUIDE TO LAYOUT

Place the pattern pieces on the fabric with the printed side uppermost. Some pieces will need to be placed to a fold.

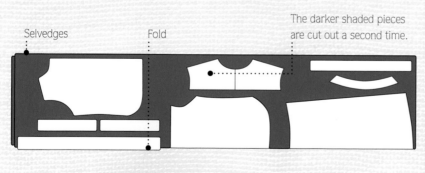

Selvedges   Fold   The darker shaded pieces are cut out a second time.

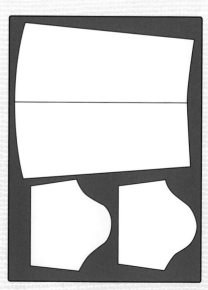

If a piece has to be cut twice in a fold, this will need to be done after the other pieces have been cut and the fabric can be refolded.

If using a single layer of fabric the pieces will need to be cut twice, reversing for the second piece.

LAYOUT FOR FABRICS WITH A NAP OR A ONE-WAY DESIGN

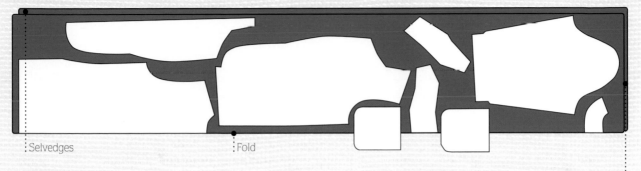

Selvedges   Fold

If your fabric needs to be cut out with a nap, all the pattern pieces need to be placed so the nap will run in the same direction in the made-up garment.

"Top" of fabric, from which direction the nap runs

LAYOUT ON A CROSSWAYS FOLD

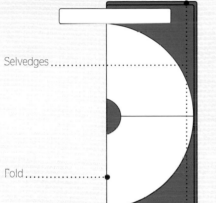

Selvedges ....

Fold ....

Occasionally a fabric is folded across the grain. This is usually done to accommodate very large pattern pieces.

LAYOUT ON A CROSSWAYS FOLD WITH A NAP

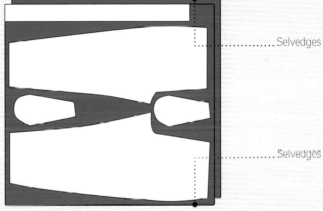

.... Selvedges

.... Selvedges

If a crossways fold is required in a fabric with a nap, fold the fabric with the wrong sides together, then cut into two pieces. Turn one around to make sure that the nap is running in the same direction on both pieces. Place the two pieces of fabric together, wrong side to wrong side.

LAYOUT ON A PARTIAL FOLD

The fabric is folded part way to enable you to cut some pattern pieces on a fold and the remainder from single fabric.

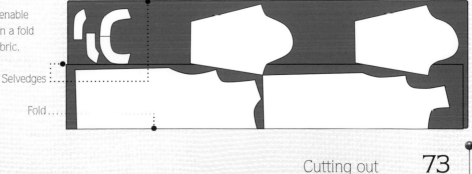

Selvedges :.....................

Fold ....

Stripes and checks

For fabrics with a stripe or check pattern, a little more care is needed when laying out the pattern pieces. If the checks and stripes are running across or down the length of the fabric when cutting out, they will run the same direction in the finished garment. So it is important to place the pattern pieces to ensure that the checks and stripes match and that they run together at the seams. If possible, try to place the pattern pieces so each has a stripe down the centre. With a check, be aware of the hemline placement on the pattern.

EVEN OR UNEVEN STRIPES

Even stripes: When a corner of the fabric is folded back diagonally, the stripes will meet up at the fold.

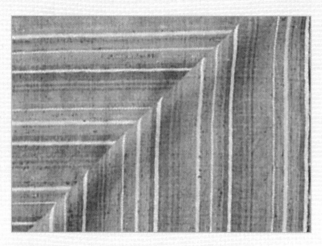

Uneven stripes: When a corner of the fabric is folded back diagonally, the stripes will not match at the fold.

EVEN OR UNEVEN CHECKS

Even checks: When a corner is folded back diagonally, the checks will be symmetrical on both of the fabric areas.

Uneven checks: When a corner of the fabric is folded back diagonally, the checks will be uneven lengthways, widthways, or both.

MATCHING STRIPES OR CHECKS ON A SKIRT

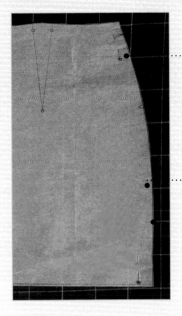

1 Place one of the skirt pattern pieces on the fabric and pin in place.

2 Mark on the tissue the position of the boldest lines of the checks or stripes.

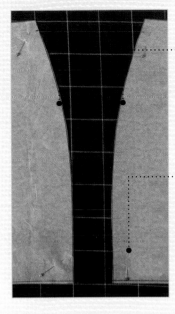

3 Place the adjoining skirt pattern piece alongside, with notches matching and side seams even. Transfer the marks across.

4 Move the second pattern piece away, matching up the bold lines, and pin it in place.

MATCHING STRIPES OR CHECKS AT THE SHOULDER

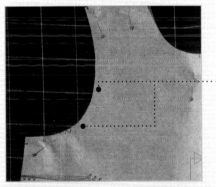

1 Mark the boldest lines of the stripes or checks around the armhole on the front bodice pattern.

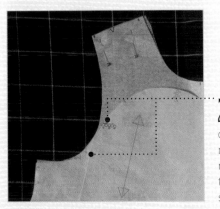

2 Place the sleeve pattern on to the armhole, matching the notches, and copy the marks on to the sleeve pattern.

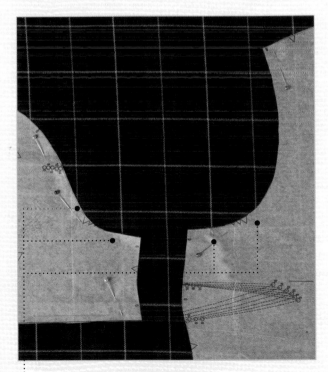

3 Place the sleeve pattern on to the fabric, matching the marks to the corresponding bold lines, and pin in place.

LAYOUT FOR EVEN CHECKS ON FOLDED FABRIC

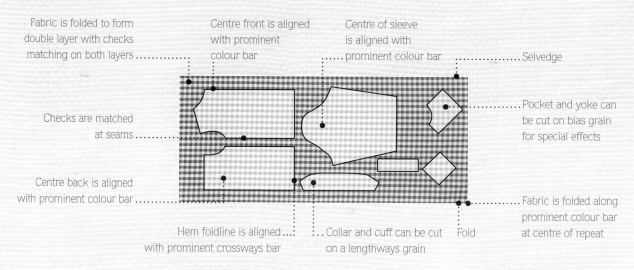

Fabric is folded to form double layer with checks matching on both layers

Centre front is aligned with prominent colour bar

Centre of sleeve is aligned with prominent colour bar

Selvedge

Checks are matched at seams

Pocket and yoke can be cut on bias grain for special effects

Centre back is aligned with prominent colour bar

Fabric is folded along prominent colour bar at centre of repeat

Hem foldline is aligned with prominent crossways bar

Collar and cuff can be cut on a lengthways grain

Fold

LAYOUT FOR EVEN STRIPES ON FOLDED FABRIC

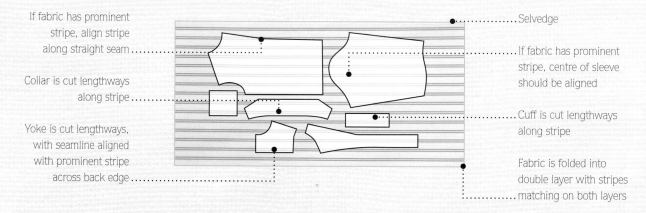

If fabric has prominent stripe, align stripe along straight seam

Selvedge

If fabric has prominent stripe, centre of sleeve should be aligned

Collar is cut lengthways along stripe

Yoke is cut lengthways, with seamline aligned with prominent stripe across back edge

Cuff is cut lengthways along stripe

Fabric is folded into double layer with stripes matching on both layers

LAYOUT FOR UNEVEN CHECKS OR STRIPES ON UNFOLDED FABRIC

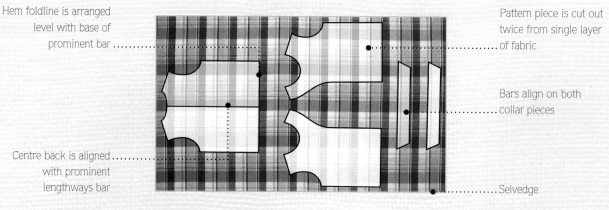

Hem foldline is arranged level with base of prominent bar

Pattern piece is cut out twice from single layer of fabric

Bars align on both collar pieces

Centre back is aligned with prominent lengthways bar

Selvedge

Cutting out accurately

Careful, smooth cutting around the pattern pieces will ensure that they join together accurately. Always cut out on a smooth, flat surface such as a table – the floor is not ideal – and be sure your scissors are sharp. Use the full blade of the scissors on long, straight edges, sliding the blades along the fabric; use smaller cuts around curves. Do not nibble or snip at the fabric.

HOW TO CUT

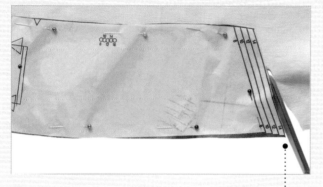

If you are right-handed, place your left hand on the pattern and fabric to hold them in place, and cut cleanly with the scissor blades at a right angle to the fabric.

MARKING DOTS

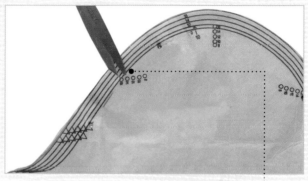

You can cut a small clip into the fabric to mark the dots that indicate the top of the shoulder on a sleeve. Alternatively, these can be marked with tailor's tacks (see page 78).

MARKING NOTCHES

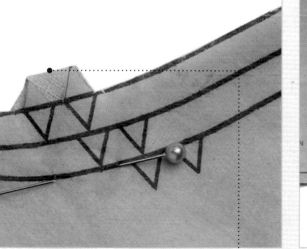

These symbols need to be marked on to the fabric as they are matching points. One of the easiest ways to do this is to cut the mirror image of the notches out into the fabric. Rather than cutting out each notch separately, cut straight across from point to point.

CLIPPING LINES

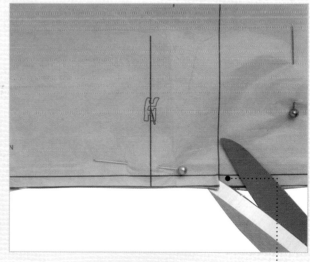

A small clip or snip into the fabric is a useful way to mark some of the lines that appear on a pattern, such as the centre front line and foldlines.

Pattern marking

Once the pattern pieces have been cut out, you will need to mark the symbols shown on the tissue through to the fabric. There are various methods to do this. Tailor's tacks are good for circles and dots, or mark these with a water or air-soluble pen (when using a pen, it's a good idea to test it on a piece of scrap fabric first). For lines, you can use trace tacking or a tracing wheel with dressmaker's carbon paper.

TAILOR'S TACKS

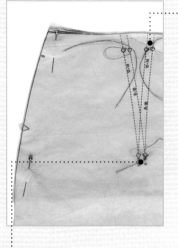

1 As there are often dots of different sizes, it is a good idea to choose a different colour thread for each dot size. It is then easy to match the colours as well as the dots. Have double thread in your needle, unknotted. Insert the needle through the dot from right to left, leaving a tail of thread. Be sure to go through the tissue and both layers of fabric.

2 Now stitch through the dot again, this time from top to bottom to make a loop. Cut through the loop, then snip off excess thread to leave a tail.

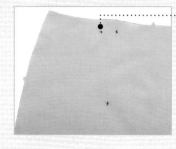

3 Carefully pull the pattern tissue away. On the top side you will have four threads marking each dot. When you turn the fabric over, the dot positions will be marked with an X.

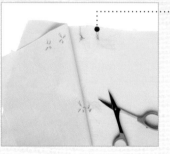

4 Gently turn back the two layers of fabric to separate them, then cut through the threads so that thread tails are left in both pieces of fabric.

TRACING PAPER AND WHEEL

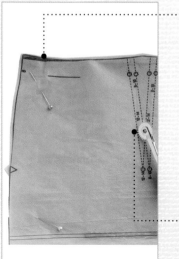

1 This method is not suitable for all fabrics as the marks may not be able to be removed easily. Slide dressmaker's carbon paper against the wrong side of the fabric.

2 Run a tracing wheel along the pattern lines (a ruler will help you make straight lines).

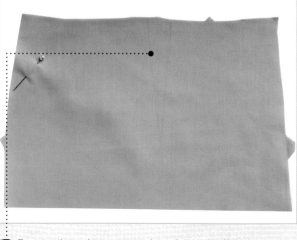

3 Remove the carbon paper and carefully pull off the pattern tissue. You will have dotted lines marked on your fabric.

MARKER PENS

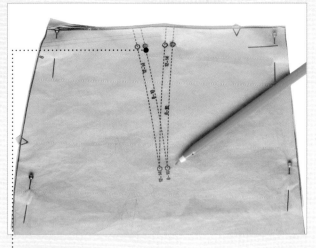

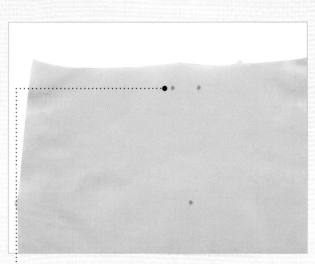

1 This method can only be used with a single layer of fabric. Press the point of the pen into the centre of the dot marked on the pattern piece.

2 Carefully remove the pattern. The pen marks will have gone through the tissue on to the fabric. Be sure not to press the fabric before the pen marks are removed or they may become permanent.

TRACE TACKING

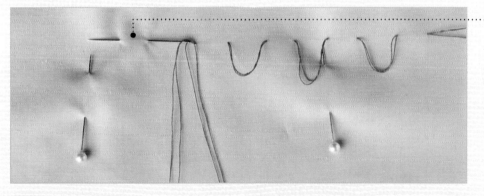

1 This is a really useful technique to mark centre front lines, foldlines, and placement lines. With double thread in your needle, stitch a row of loopy stitches, sewing along the line marked on the pattern.

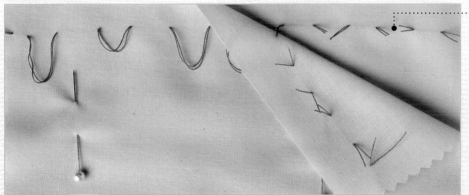

2 Carefully pull away the tissue. Cut through the loops, then gently separate the layers of fabric to show the threads. Snip apart to leave thread tails in both of the fabric layers.

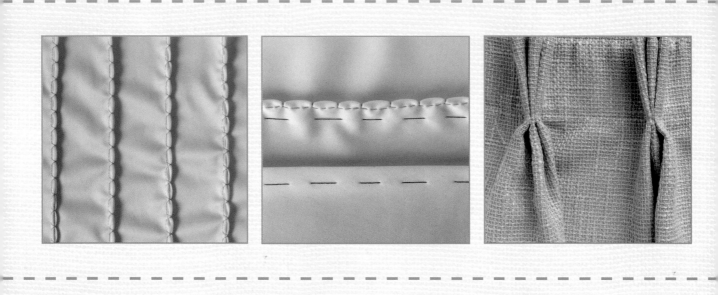

GATHERS, RUFFLES, TUCKS, DARTS, AND PLEATS

GATHERS

Gathers are an easy way to draw up a piece of larger fabric so that it will fit on to a smaller piece of fabric. The gather stitch is inserted after the major seams have been constructed, and it is best worked on the sewing machine using the longest stitch length that is available. On the majority of fabrics two rows of gather stitches are required, but for very heavy fabrics it is advisable to make three rows. Try to stitch the rows so that the stitches line up under one another.

Directory of gathers

GATHERS

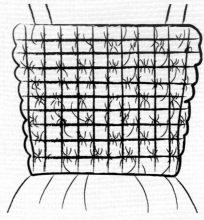

WAFFLE SHIRRING

How to make and fit gathers

Once all the main seams have been sewn, stitch the two rows of gathers so that the stitches are inside the seam allowance. This should avoid the need to remove them because removing gathers after they have been pulled up can damage the fabric.

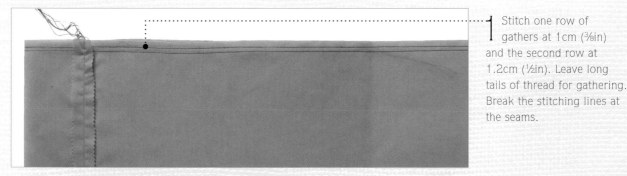

1 Stitch one row of gathers at 1cm (⅜in) and the second row at 1.2cm (½in). Leave long tails of thread for gathering. Break the stitching lines at the seams.

Gathers, ruffles, tucks, darts, and pleats

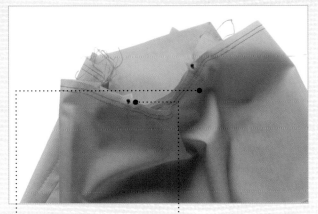

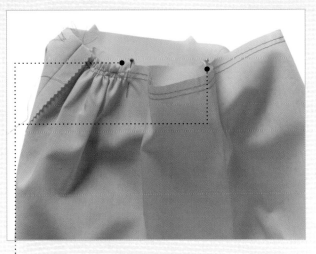

2 Place the piece to be gathered to the other garment section, right side to right side.

3 Match the notches and seams, and pin these first.

4 Gently pull on the two ends of the thread on the wrong side – the fabric will gather along the thread.

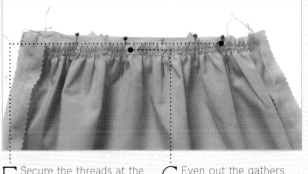

5 Secure the threads at the one end to prevent the stitches from pulling out.

6 Even out the gathers and pin.

7 When all the gathers are in place, use a standard machine stitch to stitch a 1.5cm (⅝in) wide seam.

8 Stitch with the gathers uppermost and keep pulling them to the side to stop them creasing up.

Seam pressed up

9 Turn the bodice of the garment inside. Using a mini iron, press the seam very carefully to avoid creasing the gathers.

10 Neaten the seam by stitching both edges together. Use either a zigzag stitch or a 3-thread overlock stitch.

11 Press the seam up towards the bodice.

12 Press the gathers using the mini iron.

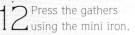

Gathers **83**

Ruffles

Ruffles can be single layer or double layer and are used to give a decorative gathered effect to a garment. The amount of fullness in a ruffle depends on the fabric used – to achieve a similar result, a fine, thin fabric will need twice the fullness of a thicker fabric.

Directory of ruffles

PLAIN RUFFLE

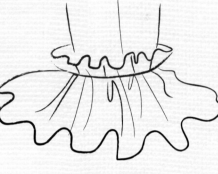

RUFFLE WITH A HEADING

DOUBLE RUFFLE

Plain ruffle

A plain ruffle is normally made from a single layer of fabric cut on the straight of the grain. The length of the fabric needs to be at least two and a half times the length of the seam into which it is to be inserted or of the edge to which it is to be attached. The width of the ruffle depends on where it is to be used.

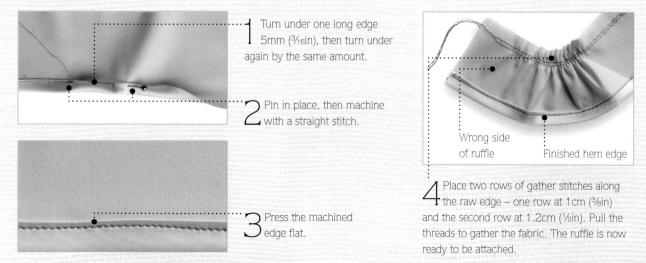

1 Turn under one long edge 5mm (³⁄₁₆in), then turn under again by the same amount.

2 Pin in place, then machine with a straight stitch.

3 Press the machined edge flat.

Wrong side of ruffle

Finished hem edge

4 Place two rows of gather stitches along the raw edge – one row at 1cm (³⁄₈in) and the second row at 1.2cm (½in). Pull the threads to gather the fabric. The ruffle is now ready to be attached.

Double ruffle

This is useful ruffle on a fabric that is prone to fraying.

1 Cut the fabric for the ruffle twice the required depth.

2 Fold the fabric lengthways, wrong side to wrong side.

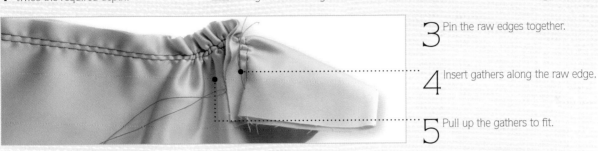

3 Pin the raw edges together.

4 Insert gathers along the raw edge.

5 Pull up the gathers to fit.

Ruffle with a heading

This type of ruffle can give a decorative effect on clothing and soft furnishings.

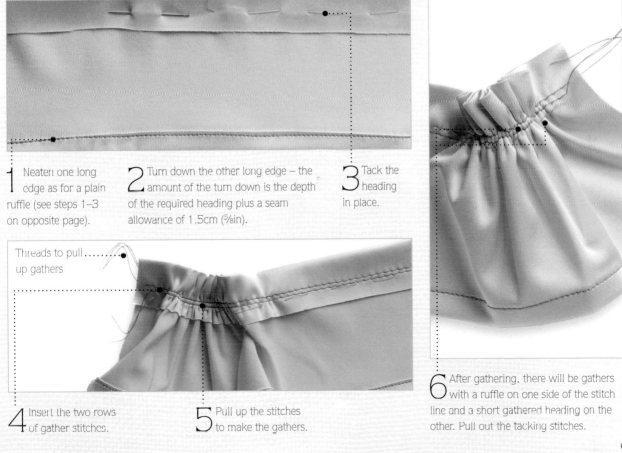

1 Neaten one long edge as for a plain ruffle (see steps 1–3 on opposite page).

2 Turn down the other long edge – the amount of the turn down is the depth of the required heading plus a seam allowance of 1.5cm (⅝in).

3 Tack the heading in place.

Threads to pull up gathers

4 Insert the two rows of gather stitches.

5 Pull up the stitches to make the gathers.

6 After gathering, there will be gathers with a ruffle on one side of the stitch line and a short gathered heading on the other. Pull out the tacking stitches.

Stitching a ruffle to an edge

If a ruffle is not in a seam then it will be attached to an edge. The edge of the seam will require neatening, which is often best done by using a binding method as it is more discreet. A self-bound edge, where the seam is wrapped on to itself, is suitable for fine, delicate fabrics. For thicker fabrics, use a bias binding to finish the edge.

SELF-BOUND FINISH

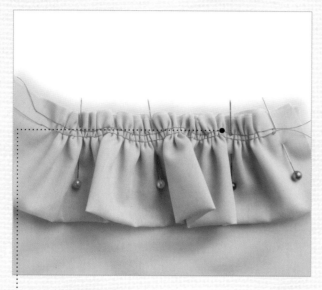

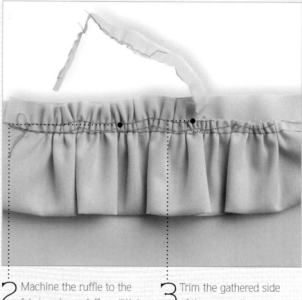

1 Place the gathered ruffle to the edge of the fabric, right side to right side. Pin in place.

2 Machine the ruffle to the fabric using a 1.5cm (⅝in) seam allowance.

3 Trim the gathered side of the seam allowance down to half.

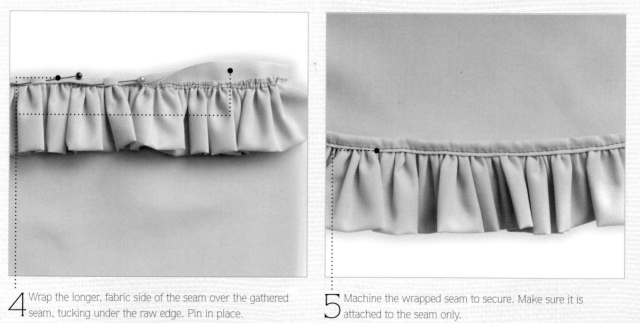

4 Wrap the longer, fabric side of the seam over the gathered seam, tucking under the raw edge. Pin in place.

5 Machine the wrapped seam to secure. Make sure it is attached to the seam only.

BIAS-BOUND FINISH

1 Machine the gathered ruffle to the edge of the fabric, right side to right side, using a 1.5cm (⅝in) seam allowance (see steps 1 and 2, opposite).

Wrong side of fabric

4 Wrap the bias over to the wrong side of the seam. Pin in place.

2 Use 2cm (¾in) wide bias binding. Stitch the crease in the bias over the machine stitching.

3 Trim back both sides of the seam allowance.

Right side of fabric

5 Machine stitch the other side of the bias close to the fold.

Stitching around a corner

It can be difficult to stitch a ruffle to a corner and achieve a sharp point. It is easier to fit the gathers into a tight curve, which can be done as the ruffle is being applied to the corner.

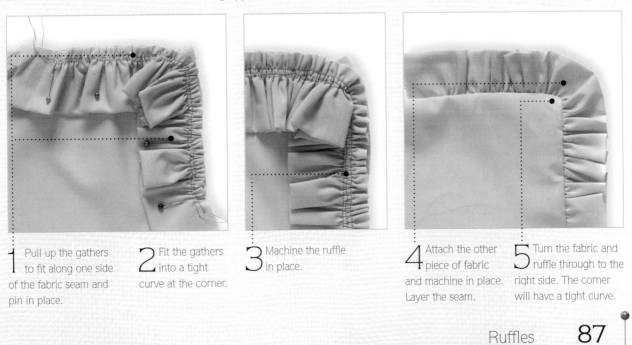

1 Pull up the gathers to fit along one side of the fabric seam and pin in place.

2 Fit the gathers into a tight curve at the corner.

3 Machine the ruffle in place.

4 Attach the other piece of fabric and machine in place. Layer the seam.

5 Turn the fabric and ruffle through to the right side. The corner will have a tight curve.

Stitching into a seam

Once the ruffle has been constructed it can either be inserted into a seam or attached to the edge of the fabric (see page 86). The two techniques below apply to both single and double ruffles.

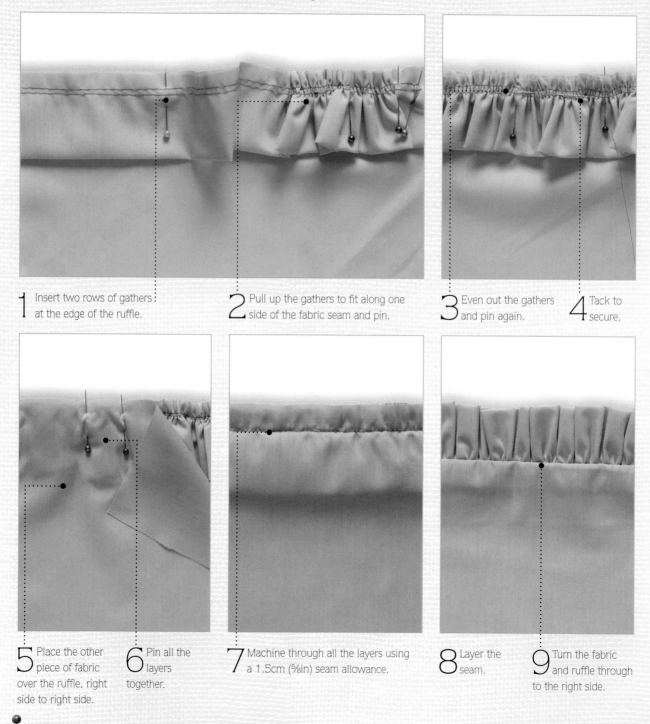

1 Insert two rows of gathers at the edge of the ruffle.

2 Pull up the gathers to fit along one side of the fabric seam and pin.

3 Even out the gathers and pin again.

4 Tack to secure.

5 Place the other piece of fabric over the ruffle, right side to right side.

6 Pin all the layers together.

7 Machine through all the layers using a 1.5cm (⅝in) seam allowance.

8 Layer the seam.

9 Turn the fabric and ruffle through to the right side.

Shirring

Shirring is the name given to multiple rows of gathers. It is an excellent way to give fullness in a garment. If made using shirring elastic in the bobbin, shirring gathers can stretch. On heavier fabrics, such as for soft furnishings, static shirring is more suitable.

MACHINE SHIRRING

1 Hand wind shirring elastic on to the bobbin.

2 Insert the bobbin into the sewing machine and pull the elastic through the tension on the bobbin case.

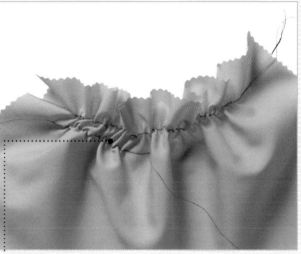

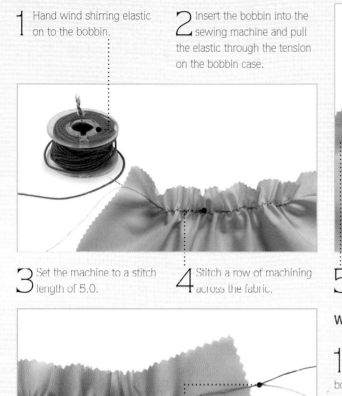

3 Set the machine to a stitch length of 5.0.

4 Stitch a row of machining across the fabric.

5 Stitch a second row of machining. Make sure the rows of stitching are parallel.

WAFFLE SHIRRING

1 For this, two rows of shirring cross each other at right angles. Machine horizontal rows of shirring using shirring elastic in the bobbin (see above). . . . .

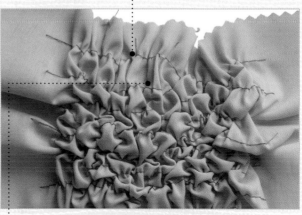

6 Continue stitching as many rows of shirring as required.

7 Knot the ends of the elastic together.

2 Cross these with vertical rows of shirring.

Tucks

A tuck is a decorative addition to any piece of fabric, and can be big and bold or very delicate. Tucks are made by stitching evenly spaced folds into the fabric on the right side, normally on the straight grain of the fabric. As the tucks take up additional fabric, it is advisable to make them prior to cutting out.

Directory of tucks

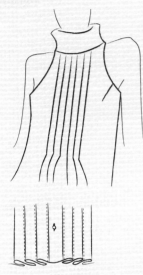

BLIND TUCKS

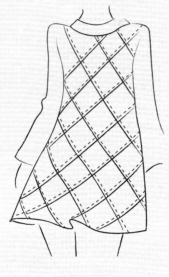

CROSS TUCKS

PLAIN TUCKS

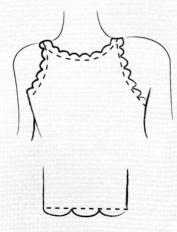

SHELL TUCKS

SPACED TUCKS

Gathers, ruffles, tucks, darts, and pleats

Plain tucks

A plain tuck is made by marking and creasing the fabric at regular intervals. A row of machine stitches are then worked adjacent to the fold.

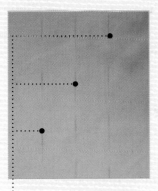

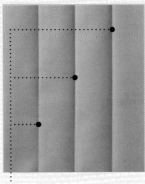

Machine close to the foldline, using the edge of the machine foot as a guide.

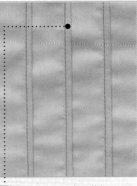

1 Mark the position of the tucks lightly with chalk on the right side of the fabric. Make sure the lines are parallel.

2 Fold along the chalk lines, making sure the folds are straight, and press in place.

4 Repeat along the next fold, and continue until all the folds are stitched.

5 Press the tucks all in the same direction.

Other simple tucks

These tucks are also made by marking and creasing the fabric. The positioning of the machine stitching determines the type of tuck.

SPACED TUCKS

These are similar to a plain tuck but with wider regular spacing. Press the tucks in place along the foldlines and pin. Machine 1cm (⅜in) from the foldline. Press all the tucks in one direction.

PIN TUCKS

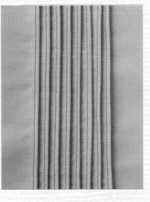

These narrow, regularly spaced tucks are stitched very close to the foldline, which may require moving the machine needle closer to the fold. Use the pintuck foot on the sewing machine.

TWIN NEEDLE TUCKS

For these regularly spaced tucks, stitch along the foldlines using the twin needle on the sewing machine. The twin needle produces a shallow tuck that looks very effective when multiple rows are stitched.

BLIND TUCKS

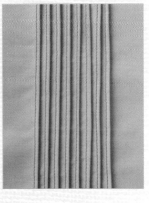

These are stitched so that they touch. Fold back all but one tuck and stitch it in place. Continue stitching the tucks in this way so that the folded edge of each covers the machine line of the previous tuck.

Darted tucks

A tuck that stops to release the fullness is known as a darted tuck. It can be used to give fullness at the bust or hip. The shaped darted tuck is stitched at an angle to release less fabric, while the plain darted tuck is stitched straight on the grainline.

SHAPED DARTED TUCKS

1 Transfer any pattern markings to the fabric.

3 Stop at the point indicated on your pattern.

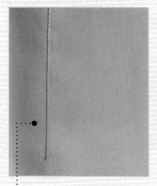

2 Fold the fabric right side to right side. On the wrong side of the fabric, stitch at an angle to the folded edge.

4 Secure the machining.

PLAIN DARTED TUCKS

1 Make similar to the shaped darted tuck (see left), but stitch parallel to the folded edge. Stop as indicated on the pattern.

2 The tuck as seen from the right side.

Cross tucks

These are tucks that cross over each other by being stitched in opposite directions.

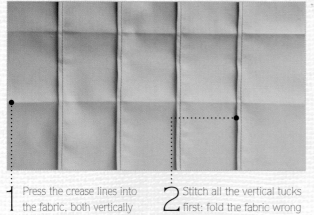

1 Press the crease lines into the fabric, both vertically and horizontally.

2 Stitch all the vertical tucks first: fold the fabric wrong side to wrong side along the crease lines. Stitch 5mm (³⁄₁₆in) from the folded edge.

3 Stitch all the horizontal tucks in the same way.

4 Press all the vertical or horizontal tucks in the same direction.

Shell tucks

A shell tuck is very decorative as it has a scalloped edge. Shell tucks can be easily stitched using the sewing machine. On heavy fabric and delicate fabrics it may be preferable to make the tucks by hand.

MACHINE SHELL TUCKS

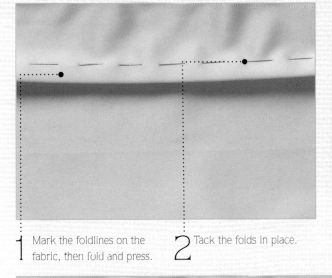

1 Mark the foldlines on the fabric, then fold and press.

2 Tack the folds in place.

3 Use the embroidery foot on the sewing machine and set the machine to a shell hem stitch.

4 Stitch along the fold, keeping the fold close to the inside opening of the machine foot.

5 The finished tucks should be stitched at regular intervals.

SHELL TUCKS BY HAND

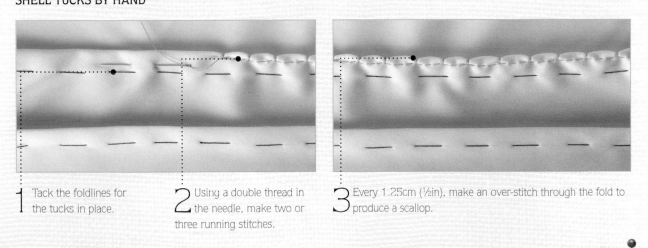

1 Tack the foldlines for the tucks in place.

2 Using a double thread in the needle, make two or three running stitches.

3 Every 1.25cm (½in), make an over-stitch through the fold to produce a scallop.

Darts

A dart is used to give shape to a piece of fabric so that it can fit around the contours of the body. Some darts are stitched using straight stitching lines and other darts are stitched using a slightly curved line. Always stitch a dart from the point to the wide end because you are able to sink the machine needle into the point accurately and securely.

Directory of darts

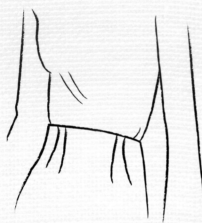

BUST DART

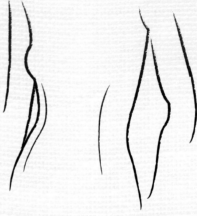

CONTOUR OR DOUBLE-POINTED DART

WAIST DART

ELBOW DART

Plain dart

This is the most common type of dart and is used to give shaping to the bust in the bodice. It is also found at the waist in skirts and trousers to give shape from the waist to the hip.

Point of dart

1 Tailor tack the points of the dart as marked on the pattern, making one tack at the point and two to mark the wide ends.

2 Fold the fabric right side to right side, matching the tailor's tacks.

3 Pin through the tailor's tacks to match them.

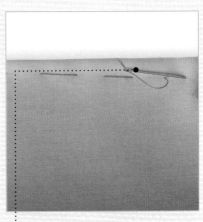

4 Tack along the dart line, joining the tailor's tacks. Remove the pins.

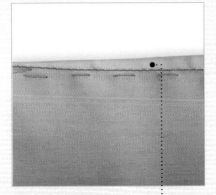

5 Machine stitch alongside the tacking line. Remove the tacks.

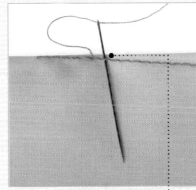

6 Sew the machine threads back into the stitching line of the dart to secure them.

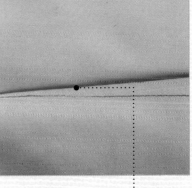

7 Press the dart to one side (see page 97).

8 The finished dart on the right side.

Contour or double-pointed dart

This type of dart is like two darts joined together at the fat end. It is used to give shape at the waist of a garment. It will contour the fabric from the bust into the waist and then out again for the hip.

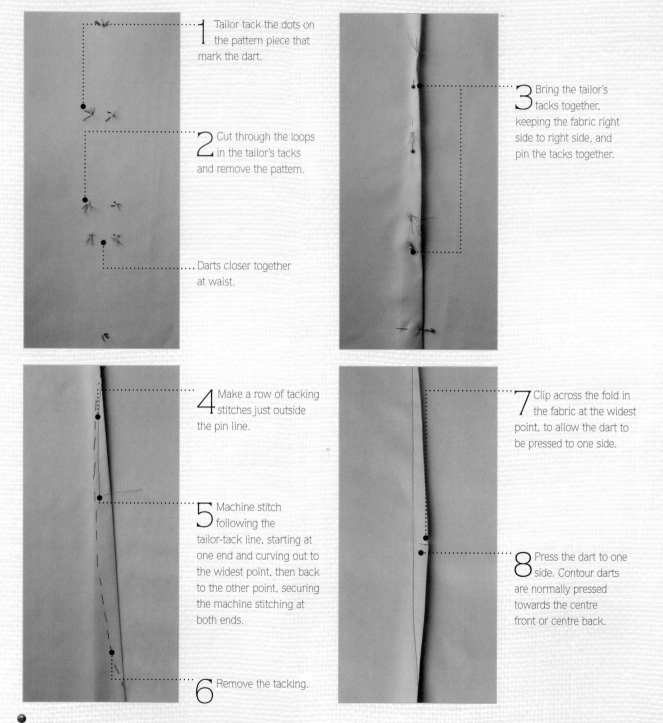

1 Tailor tack the dots on the pattern piece that mark the dart.

2 Cut through the loops in the tailor's tacks and remove the pattern.

Darts closer together at waist.

3 Bring the tailor's tacks together, keeping the fabric right side to right side, and pin the tacks together.

4 Make a row of tacking stitches just outside the pin line.

5 Machine stitch following the tailor-tack line, starting at one end and curving out to the widest point, then back to the other point, securing the machine stitching at both ends.

6 Remove the tacking.

7 Clip across the fold in the fabric at the widest point, to allow the dart to be pressed to one side.

8 Press the dart to one side. Contour darts are normally pressed towards the centre front or centre back.

French dart

A French dart is used on the front of a garment only. It is a curved dart that extends from the side seam at the waist to the bust point. As this is a long dart that is shaped, it will need to be slashed prior to construction, in order for it to fit together and then lie flat when pressed.

1 Mark all the dots on the pattern piece using tailor's tacks.

2 Mark the slash line with trace tacking and a different colour thread.

3 Cut through the loops in the tailor's tacks and remove the pattern.

4 Slash between the tailor's tacks along the slash line.

5 Stop at the end of the slash line.

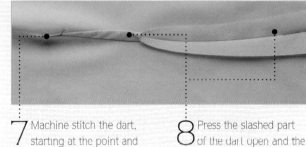

6 Bring the tailor's tacks together, right side to right side, and pin.

7 Machine stitch the dart, starting at the point and securing the stitching, then continue stitching to the fat end.

8 Press the slashed part of the dart open and the non-slashed part of the dart to the one side.

9 On the right side of the piece, the pressed finished dart gives fullness at the point.

Pressing a dart

If a dart is pressed incorrectly, this can spoil the look of a garment. For successful pressing you will need a tailor's ham and a steam iron on a steam setting. A pressing cloth may be required for delicate fabrics such as silk, satin, and chiffon, and for lining fabrics.

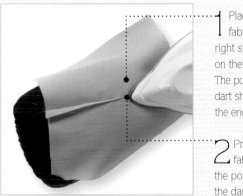

1 Place the fabric piece, right side down, on the tailor's ham. The point of the dart should be over the end of the ham.

2 Press the fabric around the point of the dart.

3 Move the iron from the point towards the wide end of the dart to press the dart flat, open, or to one side, depending on the type of dart.

Pleats

A pleat is a fold or series of folds in fabric. Pleats are most commonly found in skirts where the pleats are made to fit around the waist and hip and then left to fall in crisply pressed folds, giving fullness at the hemline. It is important that pleats are made accurately, otherwise they will not fit the body and will look uneven. Foldlines and placement lines, or foldlines and crease lines, are marked on the fabric from the pattern. It is by using a combination of these lines and the spaces between them that the pleats are made.

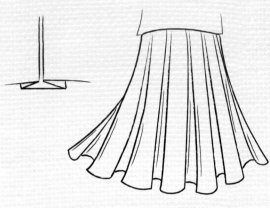

BOX PLEATS

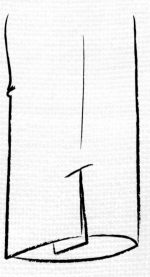

KNIFE PLEATS

INVERTED PLEATS

KICK PLEAT

Gathers, ruffles, tucks, darts, and pleats

Pleats on the right side

Knife pleats are normally formed on the right side of fabric. They can all face the same direction or may face opposite directions from opposite sides of the garment. Knife pleats have foldlines and placement lines.

1 Mark the placement lines and foldlines with trace tacks. Use one colour thread, such as red, for placement lines.

2 Use a contrasting colour thread, such as blue, to mark foldlines.

3 Cut through the thread loops and remove the pattern pieces carefully.

Placement line   Foldline

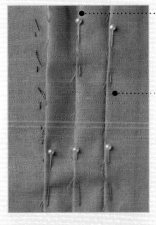

4 Fold the fabric along the foldline, creasing accurately along the trace tacks.

5 Bring the creased line on to the placement line. Pin to secure.

6 Tack along the foldlines about 2mm (¹⁄₁₆in) from the folded edge, through all the layers.

7 Remove the pins and the trace tacking on this part of the pleat.

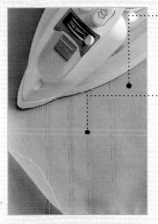

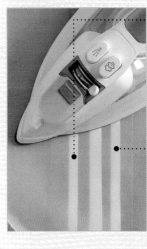

8 With the right side of the fabric uppermost, cover with a silk organza pressing cloth.

9 Using a steam iron on a steam setting, press the pleats in place. Keep the iron still as opposed to moving it around, and eject a shot of steam each time you lift it to a new position. Repeat this action across all of the pleats.

10 Turn the fabric to the wrong side and insert thin strips of manila card or brown paper under the pleat fabric.

11 Press again with the steam iron and a silk organza cloth. The card or paper will prevent the fabric from leaving an imprint on the right side.

Pleats on the wrong side

Some pleats, including box (shown below) and inverted pleats, are formed on the wrong side of the fabric. As the pleats are made on the wrong side, you can mark the crease lines and foldlines with a tracing wheel and dressmaker's carbon paper. Use a ruler to guide the tracing wheel, because these pleats need to be straight lines.

1 Mark the crease lines and foldlines on the wrong side of the fabric, using different colours for the different lines. The lines must be marked down the full length of the fabric.

3 Bring the two crease lines that are either side of the foldline together and pin in place.

5 Tack through the two layers of fabric where the crease lines have been pinned together, along the entire length of the pleat.

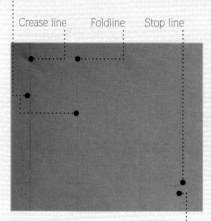

Crease line   Foldline   Stop line

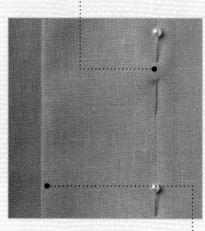

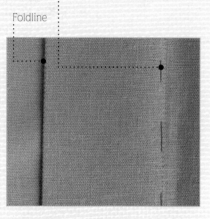

Foldline

2 Also mark the stop line that shows where to stop stitching. Remove the pattern pieces.

4 Be sure the foldline is along the fold in the fabric.

6 Machine along the crease lines.

7 Stop at the stop marking. Secure the machine stitching.

9 Cover the pleats on the wrong side with a silk organza pressing cloth and press, using a steam iron with a shot of steam.

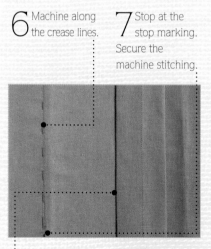

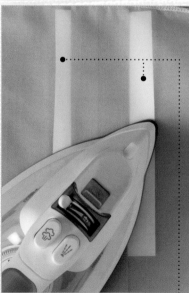

8 Flatten the pleat on the wrong side so that the foldline is lying on top of the machine stitching. Make sure that the fabric on either side of this foldline to the crease line is equal on both sides.

10 Press each section of the pleat in turn, lifting the iron rather than moving it on the fabric.

11 If the fabric is in danger of being marked on the right side with the pleats, place some strips of manila card or brown paper under the pleats on the wrong side, then press again on the wrong side.

Top-stitching and edge-stitching pleats

If a pleat is top-stitched or edge-stitched, it will hang correctly and always look crisp. It will also help the pleats on the skirt to stay in shape when you are sitting.

TOP-STITCHING KNIFE PLEATS

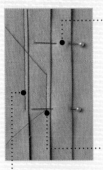

1 Once the knife pleats have been pressed and all tacks and markings removed, place some pins across the pleat to stop it from moving.

2 Machine stitch from the right side approx 2mm (¹⁄₁₆in) from the fold.

3 Start the stitching at the lower end of the pleat and stitch to the waist.

TOP-STITCHING BOX PLEATS THAT HAVE A SQUARE END

1 This requires stitching down on either side of the foldline. Stitch down one side about 5mm (³⁄₁₆in) from the foldline.

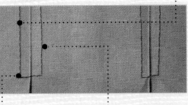

2 Pivot and stitch horizontally across the end of the stitching of the pleat.

3 Pivot again and stitch up the other side of the foldline about 5mm (³⁄₁₆in) from the foldline.

TOP-STITCHING BOX PLEATS THAT HAVE A POINTED END

1 Stitch down one side 5mm (³⁄₁₆in) from the foldline, then pivot and stitch diagonally to the centre.

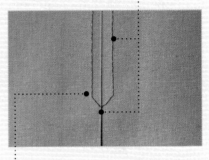

2 Pivot again and stitch diagonally the other side and back to the waist 5mm (³⁄₁₆in) from the foldline.

EDGE-STITCHING KNIFE PLEATS

1 After pressing the pleats into shape, stitch 2mm (¹⁄₁₆in) from the fold.

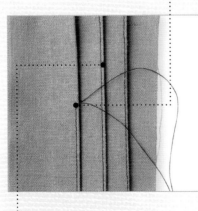

2 Stitch along the entire length of the fold.

EDGE-STITCHING AND TOP-STITCHING PLEATS

1 Edge-stitch first the edge of the pleat about 2mm (¹⁄₁₆in) from the folded edge.

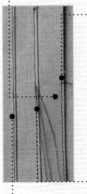

2 Stop the edge-stitching just above the point where the pleat is to be top-stitched.

3 Place the machine needle into the pleat, through all layers, four or five stitches below where the edge-stitching stops.

4 Top-stitch through all the layers, continuing at 2mm (¹⁄₁₆in) from the fold, to the waist.

TOP-STITCHING KICK PLEATS OR INVERTED PLEATS

1 This pleat is pressed to the right. Just below the stitching line that makes the pleat, stitch a line diagonally, to secure the pleat fabric at the back.

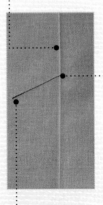

2 Make sure the stitching line finishes exactly on the foldline.

3 Pull the ends of the machine stitching through to the reverse.

Pleats on curtains

Pleats are used in soft furnishings, particularly at the top of curtains, to reduce the fabric so that the curtain will fit on to its track and fit the window. The easiest way to pleat the upper edge of a curtain is to apply a curtain tape. Tapes are available in various depths and will pull the curtain into pencil pleats or goblet pleats. The most common tape used for pencil pleating is 8cm (3¼in) deep. A curtain is normally cut two and a half to three times the width of the window. The curtain tape will reduce the fabric by this much as it pleats up.

PREPARING THE CURTAIN TO TAKE THE TAPE

1 Turn under the two side edges of the curtain by using a double hem of 2.5cm (1in), i.e. turn the fabric 2.5cm (1in) once and then the same again.

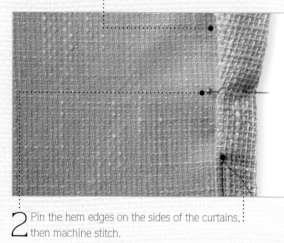

2 Pin the hem edges on the sides of the curtains, then machine stitch.

3 Turn the top of the curtain down by 2.5cm (1in) and pin.

Side edge

4 Reduce the bulk at the top edge on the corners and by trimming away the side hem.

5 Tack the upper edge into place. To ensure the corners are square, pivot and realign the edge of the fabric with the marks on the bobbin cover.

MAKING A POCKET FOR THE STRINGS

1 A small pocket needs to be made to take the strings that are used to pull up the tape. Cut a rectangle of spare fabric 15 x 8cm (6 x 3¼in).

2 Turn one short edge wrong side to wrong side and machine to make a single hem.

3 Fold the rectangle right sides together with a 2cm (¾in) seam at the upper edge free.

4 Stitch down the sides and clip the corners.

5 Turn through to the right side and press.

PENCIL PLEATS

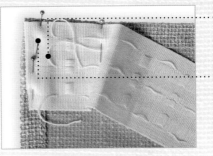

1 Take the curtain tape and release the strings at the one end, making sure they are all visible on the same side.

2 Place the top of the tape 5mm (3/16in) down from the folded edge of the curtain. Pin in place, stretching the tape as you do so. Turn under the short end, avoiding the strings and pin.

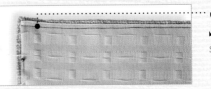

3 Machine the upper edge of the tape to the curtain fabric. Make sure the strings stay free.

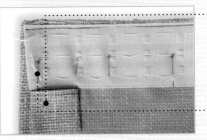

4 Before stitching the lower edge of the tape, place the pocket you made under the end of the tape.

5 Pin the tape and the pocket in place. Machine stitch the tape and pocket.

6 Pull up the strings in the tape from the end with the pocket to make the pleats.

7 Tie the strings together and place in the pocket.

8 At the opposite end of the tape, stitch across each string individually to prevent it from being pulled out.

9 Turn the curtain over to check that the pencil pleats are evenly spaced and will fit the window. Adjust if necessary.

GOBLET PLEATS

1 Goblet pleats are three pleats together at regular intervals. When the tape is pulled up, the pleats are close together at the base and fan out at the top. Prepare the curtain to take the tape and make the pocket (see opposite page).

2 Attach the tape in the same way as for pencil pleats (left).

3 After pulling up the tape, secure it by hand on the right side at the base of the tape.

4 Hand stitch the upper edge of the pleats at the back.

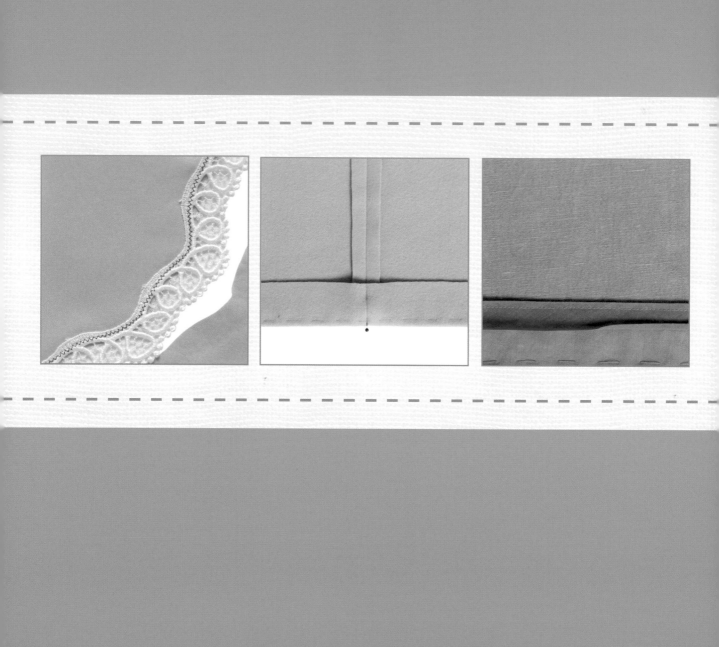

HEMS AND EDGES

Hems and edges

The edge of a piece of fabric can be finished with a hem – which is normally used on garments – or with a decorative edge, which is used for crafts and soft furnishings as well as garments. Sometimes the style of what is being constructed dictates the finish that is used, and sometimes it is the fabric.

Directory of hems

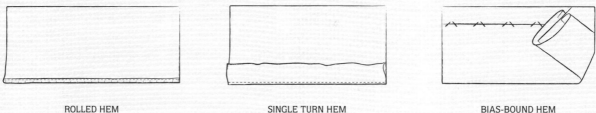

ROLLED HEM

SINGLE TURN HEM

BIAS-BOUND HEM

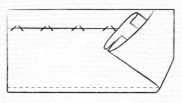

FACED HEM

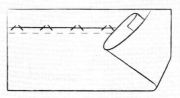

DOUBLE TURN HEM

Marking a hemline

On a garment such as a skirt or a dress it is important that the hemline is level all around. Even if the fabric has been cut straight, some styles of skirt – such as A-line or circular – will "drop", which means that the hem edge is longer in some places. This is due to the fabric stretching where it is not on the straight of the grain. Poor posture will also cause a hem to hang unevenly.

USING A RULER

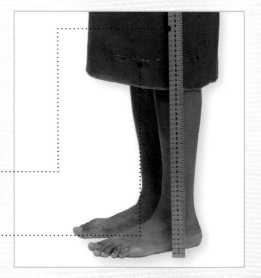

1 You'll need a helper for this method. Put on the skirt or dress (without shoes). With the end of the ruler on the floor, measure straight up on to the skirt.

2 Use pins to mark where the crease line of the hem should be. Mark the hemline all the way around to the same point on the ruler.

Turning up a straight hem

Once the crease line for the hem has been marked by the pins, you need to trim the hem allowance to a reasonable amount. Most straight hems are about 4cm (1½in) deep.

1 Gently press the crease line of the hem with the iron. Don't press too hard as you do not want a sharp crease.

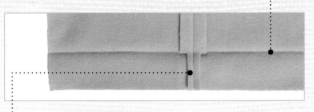

2 Trim the seam allowance back to reduce the bulk. If wished, neaten the raw edge.

3 Turn up the hem at the crease. Match the seams together.

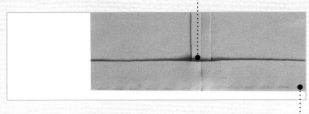

4 Tack the hem into position close to the crease line. The hem is now ready to be stitched in place by hand or machine.

Hand-stitched hems

One of the most popular ways to secure a hem edge is by hand. Hand stitching is discreet and, if a fine hand sewing needle is used, the stitching should not show on the right side of the work.

TIPS FOR SEWING HEMS BY HAND

1 Always use a single thread in the needle – a polyester all-purpose thread is ideal for hemming.
2 Once the raw edge of the hem allowance has been neatened by one of the methods below, secure it using a slip hem stitch. For this, take half of the stitch into the neatened edge and the other half into the wrong side of the garment fabric.

3 Start and finish the hand stitching with a double stitch, not a knot, because knots will catch and pull the hem down.
4 It is a good idea to take a small back stitch every 10cm (4in) or so to make sure that if the hem does come loose in one place it will not all unravel.

CLEAN FINISH

1 This is suitable for fine and lightweight fabrics. Turn the raw edge of the hem allowance to itself, wrong side to wrong side. Tack the edge and then machine.

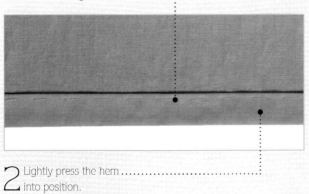

2 Lightly press the hem into position.

3 Tack the hem in place.

4 Roll the edge stitching back and stitch underneath it.

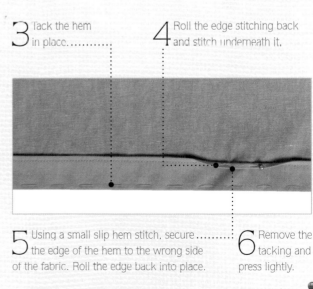

5 Using a small slip hem stitch, secure the edge of the hem to the wrong side of the fabric. Roll the edge back into place.

6 Remove the tacking and press lightly.

BIAS-BOUND FINISH

1 This is a good finish for fabrics that fray or that are
bulky. Turn up the hem on to the wrong side of the
garment and tack close to the crease line.

4 Turn down the bias over the raw edge and press.

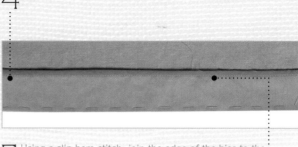

2 Pin the bias binding
to the raw edge of
the hem allowance.

3 Open out the crease in the bias
and stitch along the crease
line, keeping the raw edges level.

5 Using a slip hem stitch, join the edge of the bias to the
wrong side of the fabric. Remove the tacking and
press lightly.

ZIGZAG FINISH

1 Use this to neaten the edge of the hem on fabrics that do not
fray too badly. Set the sewing machine to a zigzag stitch, width
4.0 and length 3.0. Machine along the raw edge. Trim the fabric
edge back to the zigzag stitch.

3 Fold back the zigzag-stitched edge. Using a slip hem stitch,
stitch the hem into place.

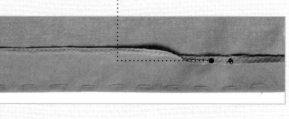

2 Turn the hem on to the wrong side of the garment and tack
in place close to the crease line.

4 Roll the edge back into position. Remove the tacking and
lightly press.

PINKED FINISH

1 Pinking shears can give an excellent hem finish on difficult
fabrics. Machine a row of straight stitching along the raw edge,
1cm (⅜in) from the edge. Pink the raw edge.

3 Fold back the edge along the machine stitching line and hand
stitch the hem in place with a slip hem stitch.

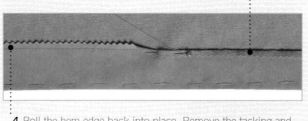

2 Turn up the hem to the wrong side of the garment and tack
in place close to the crease line.

4 Roll the hem edge back into place. Remove the tacking and
lightly press.

Turning up a curved hem

When the hem on a shaped skirt is turned up, it will be fuller at the upper edge. This fullness will need to be eased out before the hem is stitched.

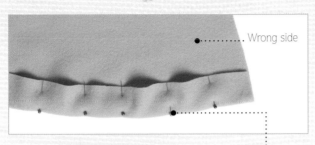

Wrong side

1 Mark the hemline, placing the pins vertically to avoid squashing the fullness out of the upper raw edge.

2 Tack the hem into position close to the crease line. Remove the pins.

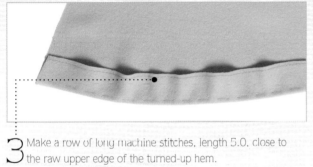

3 Make a row of long machine stitches, length 5.0, close to the raw upper edge of the turned-up hem.

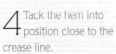

4 Pull on one of the threads of the long stitches to tighten the fabric and ease out the fullness.

5 Use the steam iron to shrink out the remainder of the fullness. The hem is now ready to be stitched in place by hand or machine.

CURVED HEM FINISH

1 With a curved hem on a cotton or firm fabric, it is important that any fullness does not bulge on to the right side. Prior to turning up the hem into position, zigzag the raw edge, using stitch width 4.0 and stitch length 3.0.

4 Tack the hem into position close to the crease line.

5 Pull on the straight stitching to tighten the fabric.

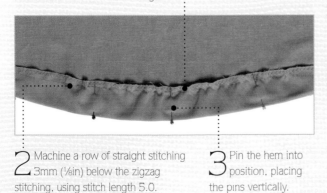

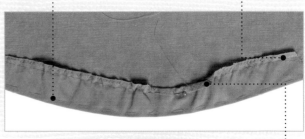

2 Machine a row of straight stitching 3mm (⅛in) below the zigzag stitching, using stitch length 5.0.

3 Pin the hem into position, placing the pins vertically.

6 Roll the zigzagged edge back to the straight stitching line and hand stitch the hem in place using a slip hem stitch. Remove the tacking and press lightly.

Machined hems

On many occasions, the hem or edge of a garment or other item is turned up and secured using the sewing machine. It can be stitched with a straight stitch, a zigzag stitch, or a blind hem stitch.

SINGLE TURN HEM

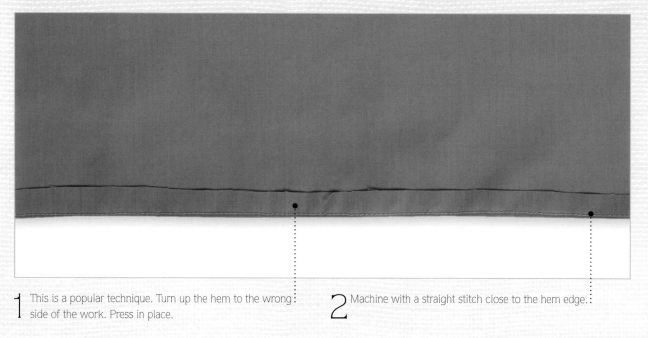

1 This is a popular technique. Turn up the hem to the wrong side of the work. Press in place.

2 Machine with a straight stitch close to the hem edge.

DOUBLE TURN HEM

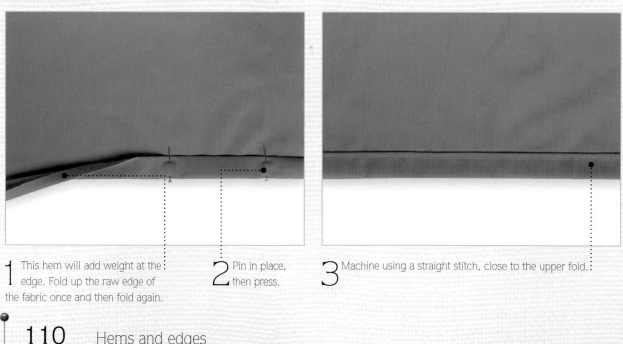

1 This hem will add weight at the edge. Fold up the raw edge of the fabric once and then fold again.

2 Pin in place, then press.

3 Machine using a straight stitch, close to the upper fold.

BLIND HEM STITCH

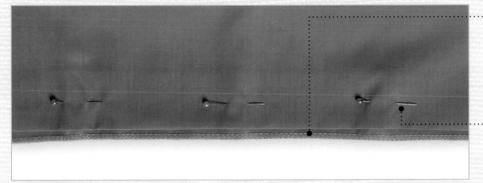

1 This is a single turn hem that is secured using the blind hem stitch on the machine. Neaten the raw edge of the fabric (here an overlock finish has been used).

2 Fold the fabric as indicated for your machine (consult your instruction book). Pin, but not too close to the fold.

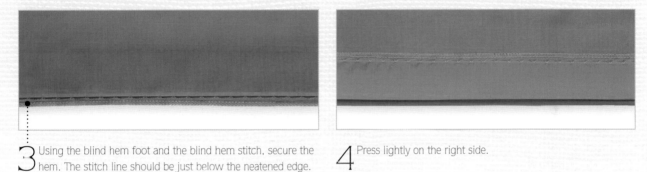

3 Using the blind hem foot and the blind hem stitch, secure the hem. The stitch line should be just below the neatened edge.

4 Press lightly on the right side.

Hems on difficult fabrics

Some very fine fabrics or fabrics that fray badly require more thought when a hem is to be made. This technique works very well on delicate fabrics.

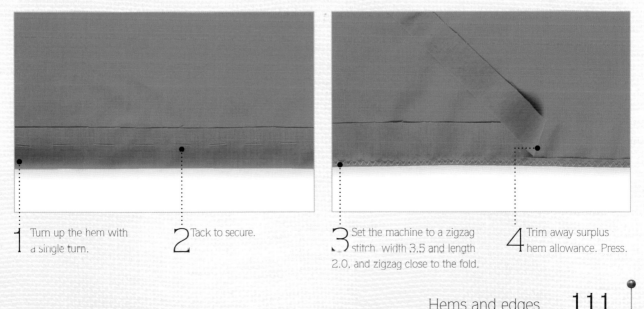

1 Turn up the hem with a single turn.

2 Tack to secure.

3 Set the machine to a zigzag stitch, width 3.5 and length 2.0, and zigzag close to the fold.

4 Trim away surplus hem allowance. Press.

Rolled hems

A rolled hem is used on lightweight fabrics. It is often found on soft furnishings as well as garments. To make it, the fabric is rolled to the wrong side by using the rolled hem foot on the sewing machine.

STRAIGHT-STITCHED ROLLED HEM

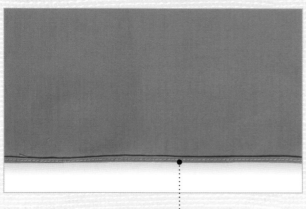

Use the rolled hem foot on the sewing machine and a straight stitch.

ZIGZAG-STITCHED ROLLED HEM

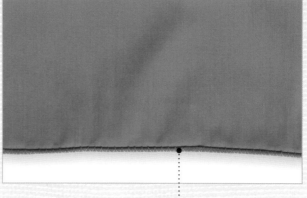

Use the rolled hem foot on the sewing machine and a zigzag stitch.

Fused hem

A fused hem is useful for a fabric that is difficult to hand stitch, as well as for an emergency hem repair. It uses a hemming tape that has a fusible adhesive on both sides.

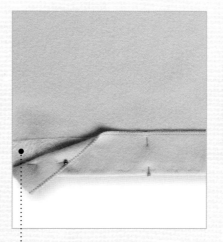

1 Turn up the hem to the wrong side of the fabric. Press. Tack the hem in place close to the crease line.

2 Neaten the raw edge with an overlock or zigzag stitch.

3 Insert the fusible hemming tape between the hem and the wrong side of the garment. Make sure the tape sits just below the overlock or zigzag stitch. Pin the tape in place.

4 Cover the hem allowance with a pressing cloth and, using a steam iron, press the edge of the hem to fuse the tape to the fabric. Once cool the hem will be stuck in place. Remove the tacking stitches.

Bias-bound hems

A bias-bound hem will give a narrow decorative edge to a garment or an item of home furnishing. It is particularly useful for curved shapes, to finish them neatly and securely. On a bulky or chunky fabric a double bias is used so that it will be more substantial and hold its shape better. A double bias is also used on sheer fabrics as there will be no visible raw edges. The bias strip can be made from purchased bias binding or cut from a matching or contrasting fabric.

SINGLE BIAS-BOUND HEM

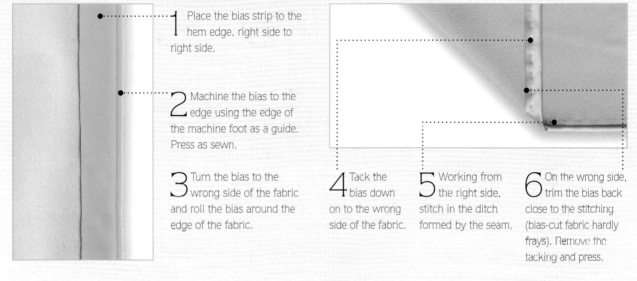

1 Place the bias strip to the hem edge, right side to right side.

2 Machine the bias to the edge using the edge of the machine foot as a guide. Press as sewn.

3 Turn the bias to the wrong side of the fabric and roll the bias around the edge of the fabric.

4 Tack the bias down on to the wrong side of the fabric.

5 Working from the right side, stitch in the ditch formed by the seam.

6 On the wrong side, trim the bias back close to the stitching (bias-cut fabric hardly frays). Remove the tacking and press.

DOUBLE BIAS-BOUND HEM

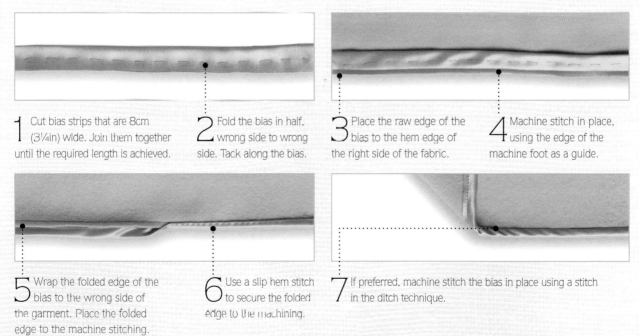

1 Cut bias strips that are 8cm (3¼in) wide. Join them together until the required length is achieved.

2 Fold the bias in half, wrong side to wrong side. Tack along the bias.

3 Place the raw edge of the bias to the hem edge of the right side of the fabric.

4 Machine stitch in place, using the edge of the machine foot as a guide.

5 Wrap the folded edge of the bias to the wrong side of the garment. Place the folded edge to the machine stitching.

6 Use a slip hem stitch to secure the folded edge to the machining.

7 If preferred, machine stitch the bias in place using a stitch in the ditch technique.

Attaching a lace trim

A lace edge can give a look of luxury to any garment. There are many ways of applying lace, depending on how the lace has been made. A heavy lace trim has a definite edge to be sewn on to the fabric. Lace edging has a decorative edge and an unfinished edge, whereas a galloon lace is decorative on both edges.

LACE EDGING

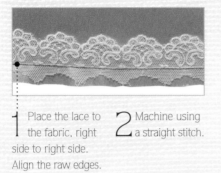 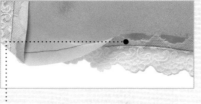 

1 Place the lace to the fabric, right side to right side. Align the raw edges.

2 Machine using a straight stitch.

3 Turn the raw edges to the wrong side of the fabric. Press in place on to the wrong side.

4 Working from the right side of the fabric, zigzag stitch close to the fabric edge.

5 Trim away surplus fabric on the reverse side.

GALLOON LACE

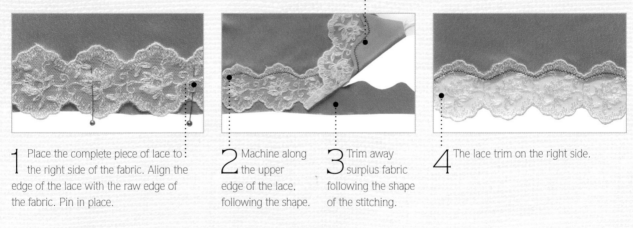

Wrong side

1 Place the complete piece of lace to the right side of the fabric. Align the edge of the lace with the raw edge of the fabric. Pin in place.

2 Machine along the upper edge of the lace, following the shape.

3 Trim away surplus fabric following the shape of the stitching.

4 The lace trim on the right side.

HEAVY LACE TRIM

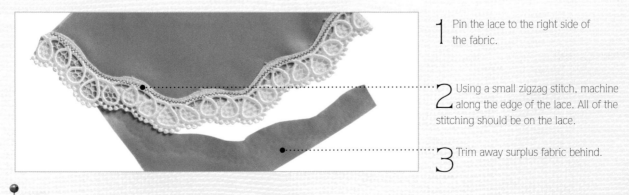

1 Pin the lace to the right side of the fabric.

2 Using a small zigzag stitch, machine along the edge of the lace. All of the stitching should be on the lace.

3 Trim away surplus fabric behind.

Applying a flat trim

On some items a flat trim braid or ribbon is added for a decorative effect. This may be right on the hem or edge, or placed just above it. To achieve a neat finish, any corners should be mitred.

1 Pin the trim to the fabric, wrong side of the trim to right side of the fabric.

2 At the corner point where the trim is to be mitred, fold the trim back on itself and secure with a pin.

3 Stitch across the trim at 45 degrees from the edge of the fold, through all layers.

4 Remove excess trim from the corner.

5 Open the trim out and press.

6 Machine stitch the inner and outer sides of the trim to the fabric, close to the edge. Be sure the stitching at the corners is sharp.

Piped edges

A piped edge can look very effective on a garment, especially if it is made in a contrasting colour or fabric. Piping is also an excellent way of finishing special-occasion wear as well as soft furnishings. The piping may be single, double, or gathered.

SINGLE PIPING

1 Just one piece of piping is used. Cut a bias strip 4cm (1½in) wide.

4 Pin the raw edge of the piping to the raw edge of the right side of the work.

2 Wrap the binding, wrong side to wrong side, around the piping cord. Pin in place.

3 Machine along the binding close to the cord, using the zip foot.

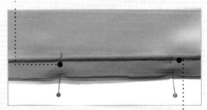

5 Machine close to the stitching line on the piping, using the zip foot.

6 Place the other side of the fabric over the piping, right side to right side.

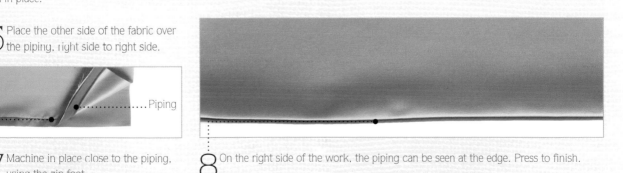

..... Piping

7 Machine in place close to the piping, using the zip foot.

8 On the right side of the work, the piping can be seen at the edge. Press to finish.

DOUBLE PIPING

1 Different thicknesses of piping cord can be used for this. Make up single piping (see steps 1–3, page 115).

2 Cut another bias strip, in a contrasting colour if you like.

4 Place a second piping cord to the wrong side of the contrast strip.

3 Join the bias strip to the single piping, stitching next to the piping.

5 Wrap the contrast strip around the cord and stitch.

6 Attach to the edge of the work as for single piping (see steps 4–7, page 115). On the right side, there is a double row of piping at the edge.

GATHERED PIPING

1 This is a great technique to try on cushions. Cut a bias strip 5cm (2in) wide. Stitch the bias strip loosely around a piece of piping cord. Secure the cord to the bias at one end.

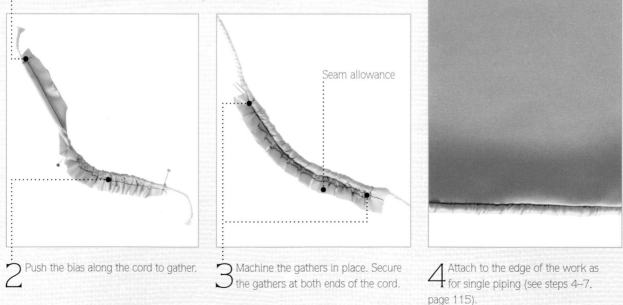

Seam allowance

2 Push the bias along the cord to gather.

3 Machine the gathers in place. Secure the gathers at both ends of the cord.

4 Attach to the edge of the work as for single piping (see steps 4–7, page 115).

Applying other trimmings

There are many kinds of trimmings – ribbons, braids, beads, feathers, sequins, fringes, and so on – that can be applied to a fabric edge. If a trim is made on a narrow ribbon or braid it can often be inserted into a seam during construction. Other trims are attached after the garment or item has been completed.

INSERTING A TRIM IN A SEAM

1 Place the trim to the right side of one piece of fabric, with the beaded or other decorative edge pointing away from the raw edge. The edge of the trim should be on the 1.5cm (⅝in) stitching line. Tack in place.

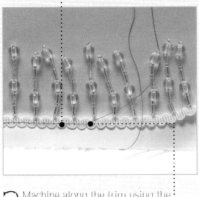

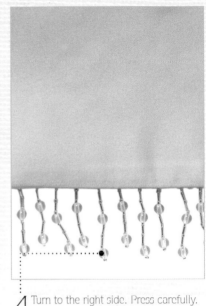

2 Machine along the trim using the zip foot.

3 Place the other piece of fabric to the first one, right side to right side. Machine again to join them.

4 Turn to the right side. Press carefully. The trim should hang free.

ATTACHING A TRIM TO AN EDGE

1 Pin the trim in position along the finished edge of the work. Be sure the trim is aligned to the edge. Tack in place.

2 Using the zip foot, machine in place close to the upper edge, leaving the lower edge of the trim free.

HAND STITCHING A TRIM

Delicate trims are best hand stitched in place because machining the trim may damage it. Place the trim in position and carefully stitch down with a flat fell stitch.

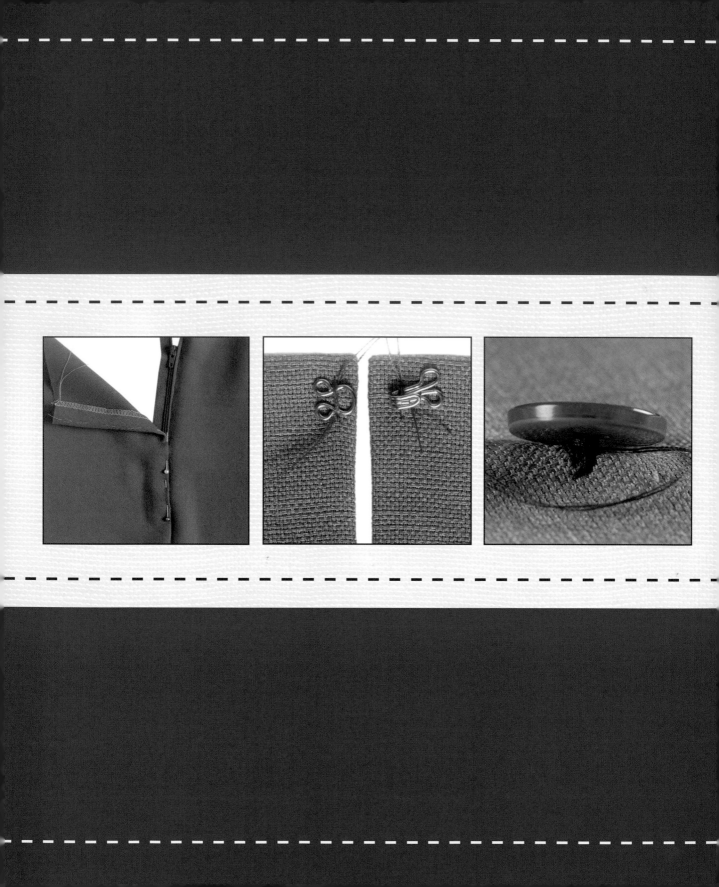

FASTENERS

BUTTONS

Buttons are one of the oldest forms of fastening. They come in many shapes and sizes, and can be made from a variety of materials including shell, bone, plastic, nylon, and metal. Buttons are sewn to the fabric either through holes on their face, or through a hole in a stalk called a shank, which is on the back. Buttons are normally sewn on by hand, although a two-hole button can be sewn on by machine.

Directory of buttons

TWO-HOLE BUTTON

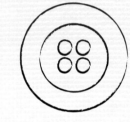

FOUR-HOLE BUTTON

SHANKED BUTTON

NOVELTY BUTTON

COVERED BUTTON

Sewing on a 2-hole button

This is the most popular type of button and requires a thread shank to be made when sewing in place. A cocktail stick will help you to sew on this type of button.

1 Position the button on the fabric. Start with a double stitch and double thread in the needle.

3 Remove the cocktail stick.

5 Take the thread through to the back of the fabric.

2 Place a cocktail stick on top of the button. Stitch up and down through the holes, going over the stick.

4 Wrap the thread around the thread loops under the button to make a shank.

6 Buttonhole stitch over the loop of threads on the back of the work.

Sewing on a 4-hole button

This is stitched in the same way as for a two-hole button except that the threads make an X over the button on the front.

1 Position the button on the fabric. Place a cocktail stick on the button.

3 Remove the cocktail stick.

2 Using double thread, stitch up and down through alternate sets of holes, over the cocktail stick. Make an X shape as you stitch.

4 Wrap the thread around the thread loops under the button to make the shank.

5 On the reverse of the fabric, buttonhole stitch over the thread loops in an X shape.

Sewing on a shanked button

When sewing this type of button in place, use a cocktail stick under the button to enable you to make a thread shank on the underside of the fabric.

1 Position the button on the fabric. Hold a cocktail stick on the other side of the fabric, behind the button.

2 Using double thread, stitch the button to the fabric, through the shank.

3 Be sure each stitch goes through the fabric and around the cocktail stick beneath.

4 Remove the cocktail stick. Work buttonhole stitching over the looped thread shank.

Sewing on a reinforced button

A large, heavy button often features a second button sewn to it on the wrong side and stitched on with the same threads that secure the larger button. The smaller button helps support the weight of the larger button.

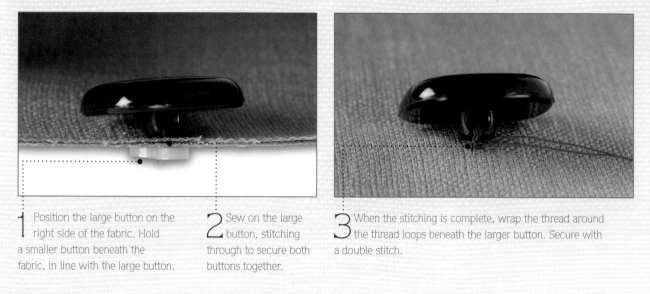

1 Position the large button on the right side of the fabric. Hold a smaller button beneath the fabric, in line with the large button.

2 Sew on the large button, stitching through to secure both buttons together.

3 When the stitching is complete, wrap the thread around the thread loops beneath the larger button. Secure with a double stitch.

Covered buttons

Covered buttons are often found on expensive clothes and will add a professional finish to any jacket or other garment that you make. A purchased button-making gadget will enable you to create covered buttons very easily.

1 On the pattern, select the size of button you want to make.

2 Cut out the button pattern from interfaced fabric.

3 Stitch a gather thread around the edge.

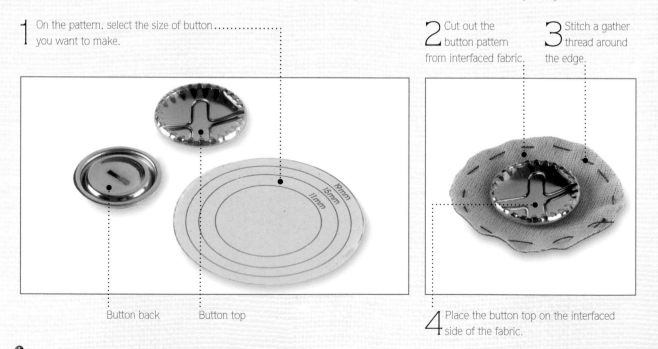

Button back   Button top

4 Place the button top on the interfaced side of the fabric.

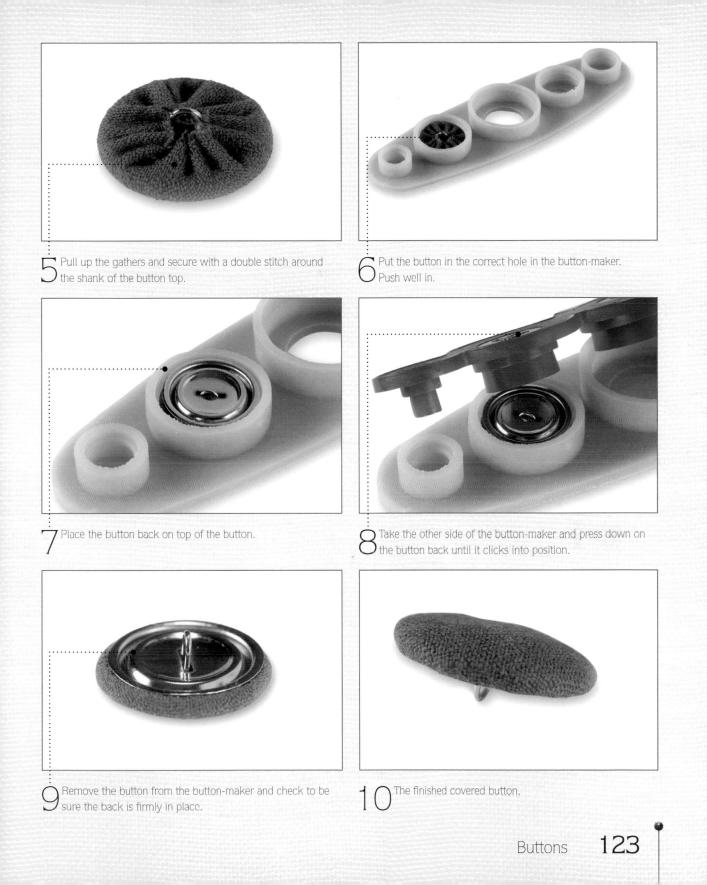

5 Pull up the gathers and secure with a double stitch around the shank of the button top.

6 Put the button in the correct hole in the button-maker. Push well in.

7 Place the button back on top of the button.

8 Take the other side of the button-maker and press down on the button back until it clicks into position.

9 Remove the button from the button-maker and check to be sure the back is firmly in place.

10 The finished covered button.

Buttonholes

A buttonhole is essential if a button is to be truly functional, although for many oversized buttons a snap fastener on the reverse is a better option, because the buttonhole would be just too big and could cause the garment to stretch.

Directory of buttonholes and button loops

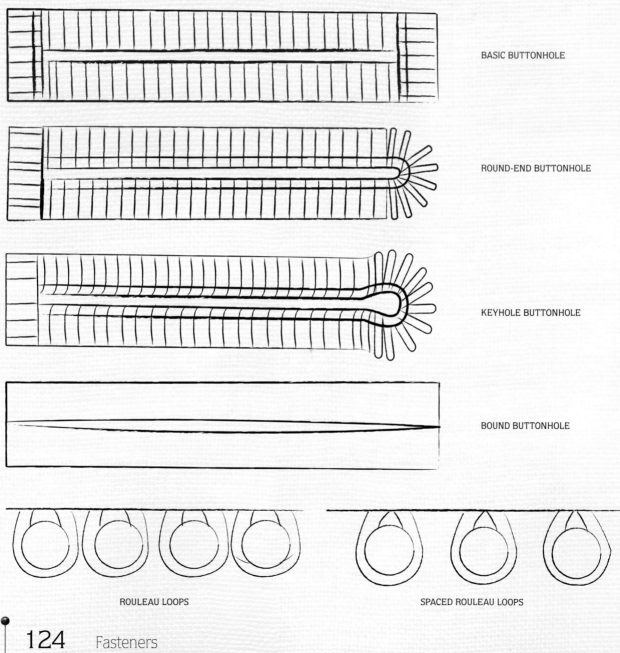

BASIC BUTTONHOLE

ROUND-END BUTTONHOLE

KEYHOLE BUTTONHOLE

BOUND BUTTONHOLE

ROULEAU LOOPS

SPACED ROULEAU LOOPS

Stages of a buttonhole

A sewing machine stitches a buttonhole in three stages. The stitch can be slightly varied in width and length to suit the fabric or item, but the stitches need to be tight and close together.

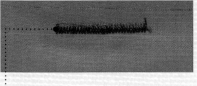

1 Machine the first side of the buttonhole.

2 Stitch a bar tack at one end.

3 Machine the second side and bar tack at the other end.

Positioning buttonholes

Whether the buttonholes are to be stitched by machine or another type of buttonhole is to be made, the size of the button will need to be established in order to work out the position of the button on the fabric.

1 Place the button on a sewing gauge and use the slider to measure the button's diameter.

2 On the right-hand side of the fabric, as the garment will be worn, work a row of tacking stitches along the centre front line.

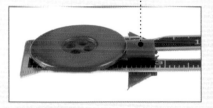

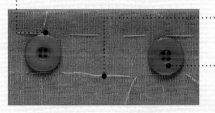

3 Work a second row of tacks the diameter of the button away.

4 Position the buttons between the tack lines. Stitch lines at right angles where the buttonholes are to be placed.

Vertical or horizontal?

As a general rule, buttonholes are only vertical on a garment when there is a placket or a strip into which the buttonhole fits. All other buttonholes should be horizontal. Any strain on the buttonhole will then pull to the end stop and prevent the button from coming undone.

HORIZONTAL BUTTONHOLES

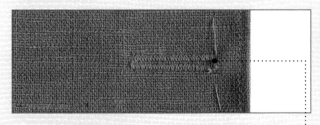

These are positioned with the end stop on the tacked centre line.

VERTICAL BUTTONHOLES

These are positioned with the buttonhole centred on the tacked centre line.

Machine-made buttonholes

Modern sewing machines can stitch various types of buttonholes, suitable for all kinds of garments. On many machines the button fits into a special foot, and a sensor on the machine determines the correct size of buttonhole. The width and length of the stitch can be altered to suit the fabric. Once the buttonhole has been stitched, always slash through with a buttonhole chisel, to ensure that the cut is clean.

BASIC BUTTONHOLE

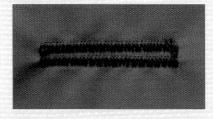

The most popular shape for a buttonhole is square on both ends.

ROUND-END BUTTONHOLE

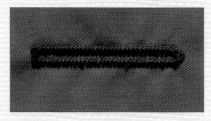

A buttonhole featuring one rounded end and one square end is used on lightweight jackets.

KEYHOLE BUTTONHOLE

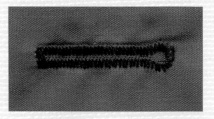

This is also called a tailor's buttonhole. It has a square end and a keyhole end, and is used on jackets and coats.

In-seam buttonhole

This is a buttonhole formed in a seam allowance. It is found down decorative centre fronts that feature seam detailing. It is a very discreet buttonhole.

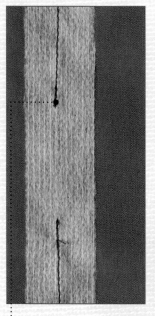

1 Reinforce the seam with a fusible tape on one side.

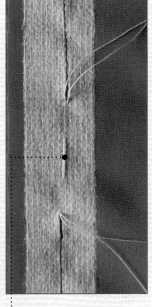

2 Tack the opening closed.

3 Press the seam open. The tacks will show.

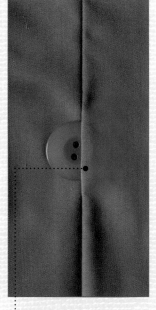

4 Remove the tacking stitches to form the buttonhole.

BUTTON LOOPS

A buttonhole is not the only way of using buttons. Buttons can also be fastened by means of a fabric loop, which is usually attached at the edge of a garment. Fabric loops are often found on the back of special-occasion wear, where multiple loops secure rows of small, often covered buttons.

Rouleau loop

This button loop is formed from a bias strip. Choose a smooth fabric for the strip as it will be easier to turn through. A rouleau loop is used with a round ball type button.

1 Cut a bias strip 4cm (1½in) wide. Fold lengthways, right side to right side, and pin together.

2 Stitch along the strip, keeping the edge of the machine foot against the folded edge.

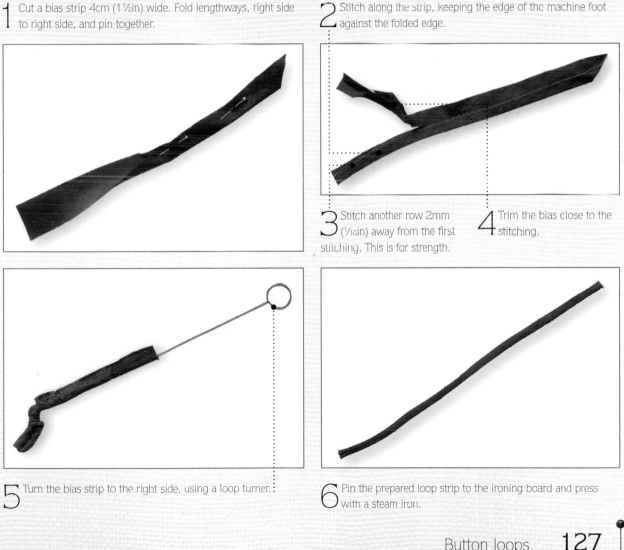

3 Stitch another row 2mm (¹⁄₁₆in) away from the first stitching. This is for strength.

4 Trim the bias close to the stitching.

5 Turn the bias strip to the right side, using a loop turner.

6 Pin the prepared loop strip to the ironing board and press with a steam iron.

Spacing the loops

Once the loops have been made, the next step is to attach them to the garment. It is important that all the loops are the same size and positioned the same distance apart. To achieve this you will need to tack your fabric to mark the placement lines. The loops go on the right-hand front or the left-hand back of the garment or item you are making.

Diameter of button from
..... centre line

Centre
...... front line

Upper seam
...... allowance

1 Mark the placement lines on the fabric using tacking stitches. Be sure the horizontal lines are equally spaced.

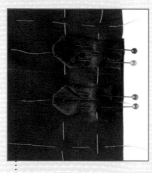

2 Place the loop to the fabric. The folded end of the loop should be on the inner tacking line and the cut ends to the raw edge. Centre the loop over the tack line.

3 Machine the loops just inside the seam allowance at the centre line.

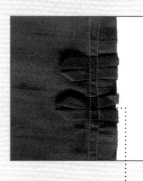

4 Stitch another row to ensure the loops are secure.

5 Place the facing or lining over the loops to finish.

6 The completed loop will extend from the edge of the fabric.

Corded loop

It is possible to make a very fine button loop that has a cord running through it. This type of loop is suitable for lightweight fabrics. Use a shanked button with a corded loop.

1 Cut a bias strip 4cm (1½in) wide. Cut a piece of cord twice the length of the strip.

3 Stitch along the bias strip, next to but not too close to the cord.

4 Machine another row 2mm (1/16in) away from the first stitching.

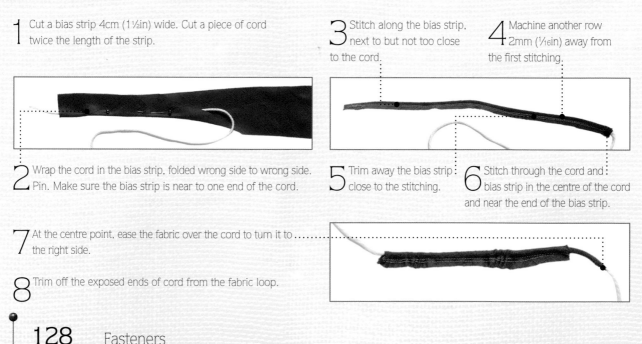

2 Wrap the cord in the bias strip, folded wrong side to wrong side. Pin. Make sure the bias strip is near to one end of the cord.

5 Trim away the bias strip close to the stitching.

6 Stitch through the cord and bias strip in the centre of the cord and near the end of the bias strip.

7 At the centre point, ease the fabric over the cord to turn it to the right side.

8 Trim off the exposed ends of cord from the fabric loop.

Other fastenings

There are many alternative ways to fasten garments, craft projects, and other items, some of which can be used instead of or in conjunction with other fasteners. These include hooks and eyes, snaps, and tape fasteners.

Directory of other fastenings

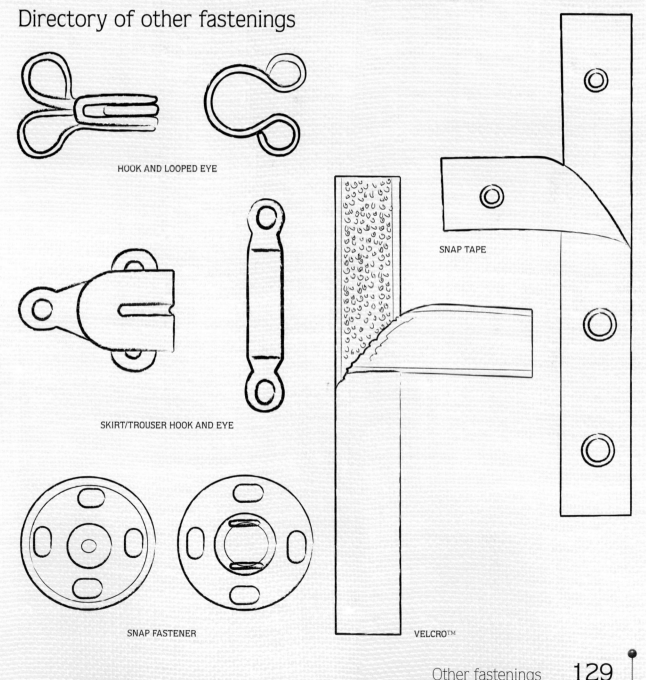

HOOK AND LOOPED EYE

SKIRT/TROUSER HOOK AND EYE

SNAP FASTENER

SNAP TAPE

VELCRO™

Snaps

A snap is a ball and socket fastener that is used to hold two overlapping edges closed. The ball side goes on top and the socket side underneath. Snaps can be round or square and can be made from metal or plastic.

1 Tack the ball and socket halves of the snap in place......

2 Secure permanently using a buttonhole stitch through each hole in the outer edge of the snap half.

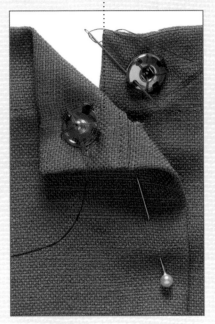

3 Remove the tacks.

PLASTIC SNAPS

A **plastic snap** may be white or clear plastic and is usually square in shape. Stitch in place as for a metal snap (see above).

Hooks and eyes

There are a multitude of different types of hook and eye fasteners. Purchased hooks and eyes are made from metal and are normally silver or black in colour. Different shaped hooks and eyes are used on different garments – large, broad hooks and eyes can be decorative and stitched to show on the outside, while the tiny fasteners are meant to be discreet. A hook that goes into a hand-worked eye produces a neat, close fastening.

ATTACHING HOOKS AND EYES

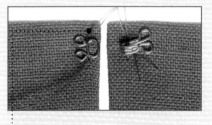  

1 Secure the hook and eye in place with a tacking stitch. Make sure they are in line with each other.

2 Stitch around each circular end with a buttonhole stitch.

3 Place a few over-stitches under the hook to stop it moving.

HAND-WORKED EYE

1 Using a double thread, work several small loops into the edge of the fabric.

2 Buttonhole stitch over these loops.

3 The completed loop will have a neat row of tight buttonhole stitches.

TROUSER HOOK AND EYE

1 The hook and eye fastener for trouser and skirt waistbands is large and flat. Tack the hook and eye in position. Do not tack through the holes that are used for securing.

2 Buttonhole stitch through each hole on the hook and eye.

Tape fasteners

In addition to individual small fasteners, there are fastenings in the form of tapes that can be sewn on or stuck on. Velcro™, a hook and loop tape, is available in many colours and types. Sewn-on Velcro™ is ideal for both clothing and soft furnishings, while the stick-on variety can be used to fix curtain pelmets and blinds to battens on windows. Plain cotton tape with snap fasteners is used primarily in soft furnishings. Hook and eye tape is found in underwear or down the front of a shirt or jacket, where it can be very decorative.

VELCRO™

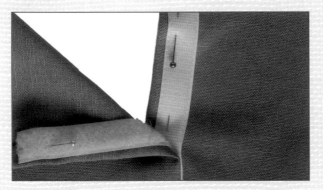

1 Pin the Velcro™ in place. The loop side should be underneath and the hook side on top.

2 Stitch around all the edges.

Eyelets

An eyelet fastening can be very decorative and is often found on bridal wear and prom dresses. A piece of boning needs to be inserted into the fabric between the edge and the eyelets, to give strength. You will require eyelet pliers to punch the holes and then insert the eyelets.

1 Using the pliers, punch out the holes for the eyelets at 3–4cm (1¼–1½in) intervals...............

3 Insert a row of eyelets on either side of the back opening.

............Boning channel

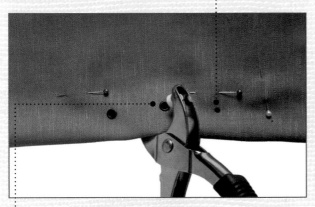

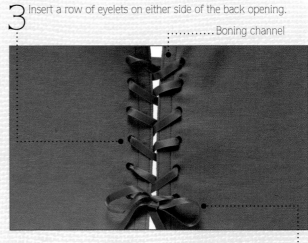

2 Place an eyelet in each hole. Change the heads on the pliers and squeeze the eyelet in place.

4 To close, lace ribbon across from eyelet to eyelet and finish with a bow.

Zips

The zip is probably the most used of all fastenings. There are a great many types available, in a variety of lengths, colours, and materials, but they all fall into one of five categories: skirt or trouser zips, metal or jeans zips, concealed zips, open-ended zips, and decorative zips.

Directory of zips

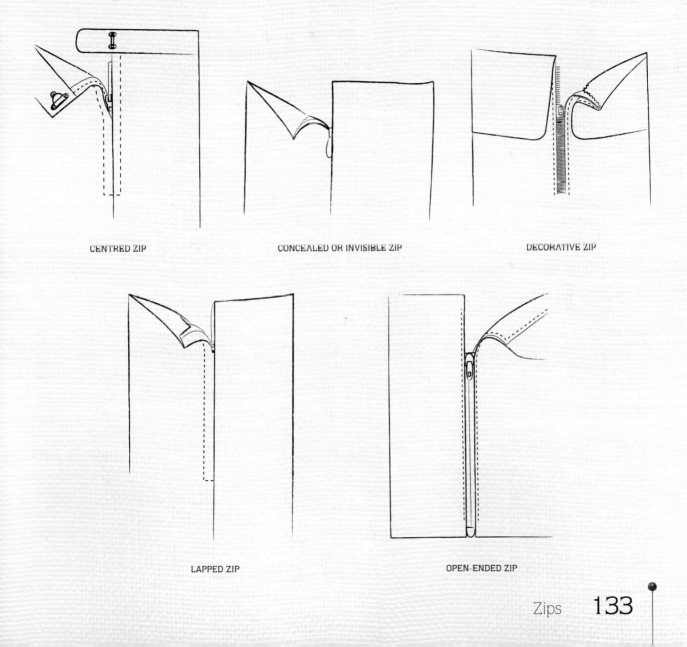

CENTRED ZIP

CONCEALED OR INVISIBLE ZIP

DECORATIVE ZIP

LAPPED ZIP

OPEN-ENDED ZIP

How to shorten a zip

Zips do not always come in the length that you need, but it is easy to shorten them. Skirt or trouser zips and concealed zips are all shortened by stitching across the teeth or coils, whereas an open-ended zip is shortened at the top and not at the bottom.

SHORTENING A SKIRT/TROUSER OR CONCEALED ZIP

SHORTENING AN OPEN-ENDED ZIP

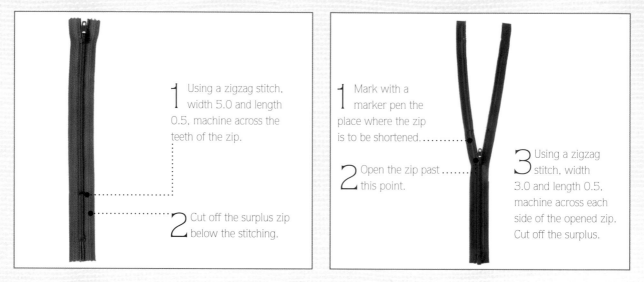

1 Using a zigzag stitch, width 5.0 and length 0.5, machine across the teeth of the zip.

2 Cut off the surplus zip below the stitching.

1 Mark with a marker pen the place where the zip is to be shortened..........

2 Open the zip past this point.

3 Using a zigzag stitch, width 3.0 and length 0.5, machine across each side of the opened zip. Cut off the surplus.

Marking for zip placement

For a zip to sit accurately in the seam, the seam allowances where the zip will be inserted need to be marked. The upper seam allowance at the top of the zip also needs marking to ensure the zip pull sits just fractionally below the stitching line.

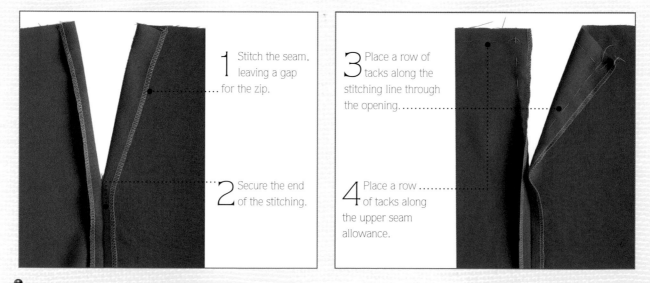

1 Stitch the seam, leaving a gap for the zip.

2 Secure the end of the stitching.

3 Place a row of tacks along the stitching line through the opening..........

4 Place a row of tacks along the upper seam allowance.

Lapped zip

A skirt zip in a skirt or a dress is usually put in by means of a lapped technique or a centred zip technique (see page 137). For both of these techniques you will require the zip foot on the sewing machine. A lapped zip features one side of the seam – the left-hand side – covering the teeth of the zip to conceal them.

1 Stitch the seam, leaving enough of the seam open to accommodate the zip.........

2 Secure the end............... of the stitching.

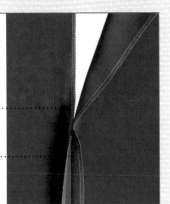

3 Insert the right hand side of the zip first. Fold back the right-hand seam allowance by 1.3cm (½in). This folded edge is not in line with the seam...................

4 Place the folded............. edge against the zip teeth. Tack.

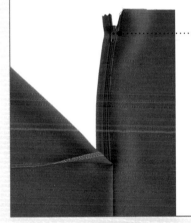

5 Using the zip foot, stitch along the tack line to secure the zip tape to the fabric. Stitch from the bottom of the zip to the top.

6 Fold back the left-hand seam allowance by 1.5cm (⅝in). Place the folded edge over the machine line of the other side. Pin and then tack.

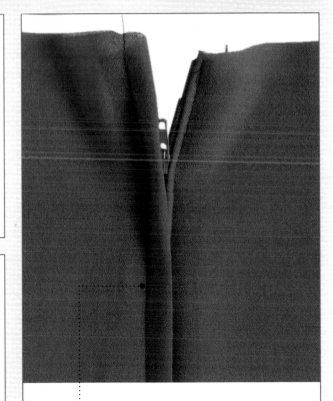

7 Starting at the bottom of the zip, stitch across from the centre seamline and then up the side of the zip. The finished zip should have the teeth covered by the fabric.

Open-ended zip

The open-ended zip is used on garments where the two halves need to be fully opened in order to put the garment on – for example, on a jacket or cardigan.

1 On both pieces of fabric, turn under the seam allowance at the centre front and tack.

3 Place the folded edge of the centre front about 3mm (⅛in) from the zip teeth to allow for the puller to move up and down. Pin in place.

5 Using the zip foot, machine the zip in place. Start with the zip open. Stitch 5cm (2in), then place the machine needle in the work, raise the zip foot, and close the zip.

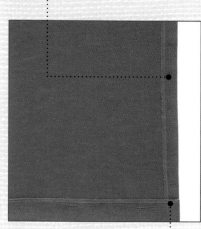

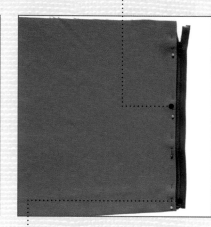

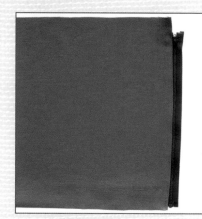
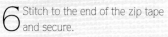

2 Turn up the hem allowance and tack in place.

4 Place the bottom of the zip at the hem edge.

6 Stitch to the end of the zip tape and secure.

7 Pin the other side of the zip in place on the other piece of fabric. Make sure the fabric lines up top and bottom.

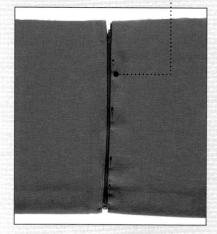

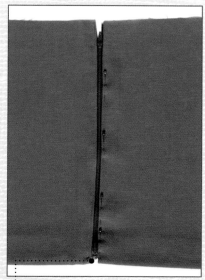

8 Undo the zip and, using the zip foot, machine in place as you did on the first side.

9 Once the zip is machined in place, check that the hems line up. If they do not, you will have to unpick and start again.

10 The zip should open completely.

Centred zip

With a centred zip, the two folded edges of the seam allowances meet over the centre of the teeth, to conceal the zip completely.

1 Stitch the seam, leaving a gap for the zip.

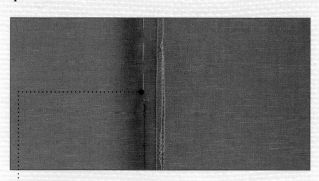

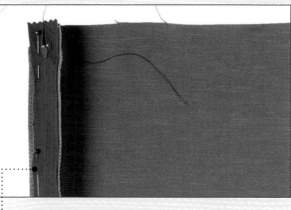

2 Tack the rest of the seam allowance.

3 Press the seam open lightly.

4 Centre the zip behind the tacked part of the seam. Pin and then tack in place along both sides.

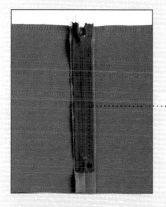

5 On the wrong side, lift the seam allowance and the zip tape away from the main fabric. Pin.

6 Machine the zip tape to the seam allowance. Make sure both sides of the zip tape are secured to the seam allowances. Stitch through to the end of the zip tape.

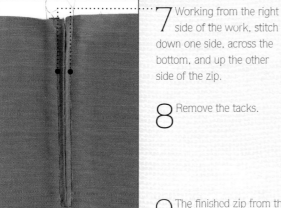

7 Working from the right side of the work, stitch down one side, across the bottom, and up the other side of the zip.

8 Remove the tacks.

9 The finished zip from the right side.

Concealed or invisible zip

This type of zip looks different from other zips because the teeth are on the reverse and nothing except the pull is seen on the front. The zip is inserted before the seam is stitched. A special concealed zip foot is required.

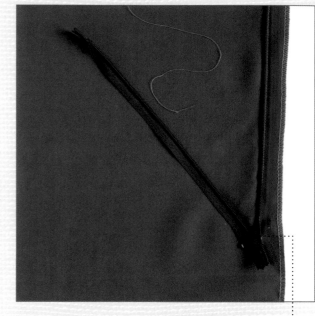

1 Mark the seam allowance with tacking stitches.

2 Place the centre of the zip over the tack line, right side of zip to right side of fabric. Pin in place.

3 Undo the zip. Using the concealed zip foot, stitch from the top of the zip down as far as possible. Stitch under the teeth. The machine will stop when the foot hits the zip pull.

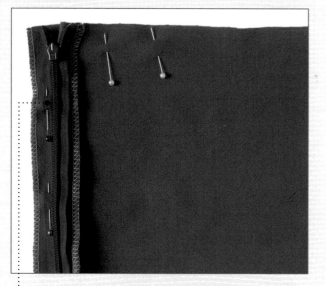

4 Do the zip up. Place the other piece of fabric to the zip. Match along the upper edge. Pin the other side of the zip tape in place.

5 Open the zip again. Using the concealed zip foot, stitch down the other side of the zip to attach to the second piece of fabric. Remove any tacking stitches.

6 Close the zip. On the wrong side at the bottom of the zip, the two rows of stitching that hold in the zip should be finishing at the same place.

Free end of zip tape

7 Stitch the seam below the zip. Use the normal machine foot for this. There will be a small gap of about 3mm (⅛in) between the stitching line for the zip and that for the seam.

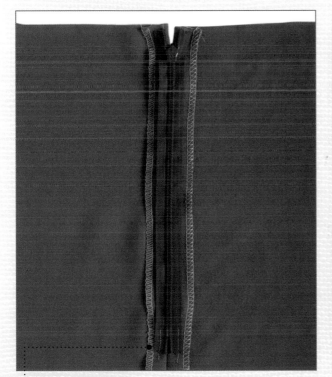

8 Stitch the last 3cm (1¼in) of the zip tape to just the seam allowances. This will stop the zip pulling loose.

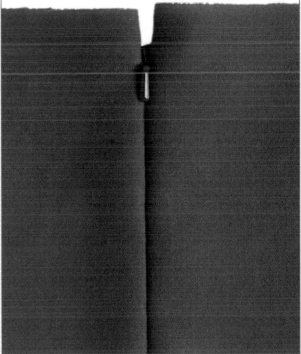

9 On the right side, the zip is completely concealed, with just the pull visible at the top. Apply waistband or facing.

POCKETS

Pockets

Pockets come in lots of shapes and formats. Some, such as patch pockets are external and can be decorative, while others, including front hip pockets, are more discreet and hidden from view. They can be made from the same fabric as the garment or from a contrasting fabric. Whether casual or tailored, all pockets are functional.

Directory of pockets

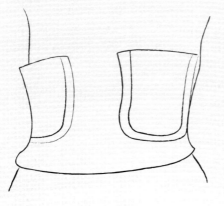

PATCH POCKET

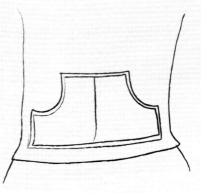

KANGAROO POCKET

Unlined patch pocket

An unlined patch pocket is one of the most popular types of pocket. It can be found on garments of all kinds and be made from a wide variety of fabrics. On lightweight fabrics, such as used for a shirt pocket, interfacing is not required, but on medium and heavier fabrics it is advisable to apply a fusible interfacing.

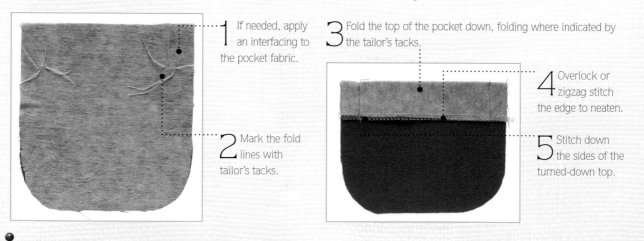

1 If needed, apply an interfacing to the pocket fabric.

2 Mark the fold lines with tailor's tacks.

3 Fold the top of the pocket down, folding where indicated by the tailor's tacks.

4 Overlock or zigzag stitch the edge to neaten.

5 Stitch down the sides of the turned-down top.

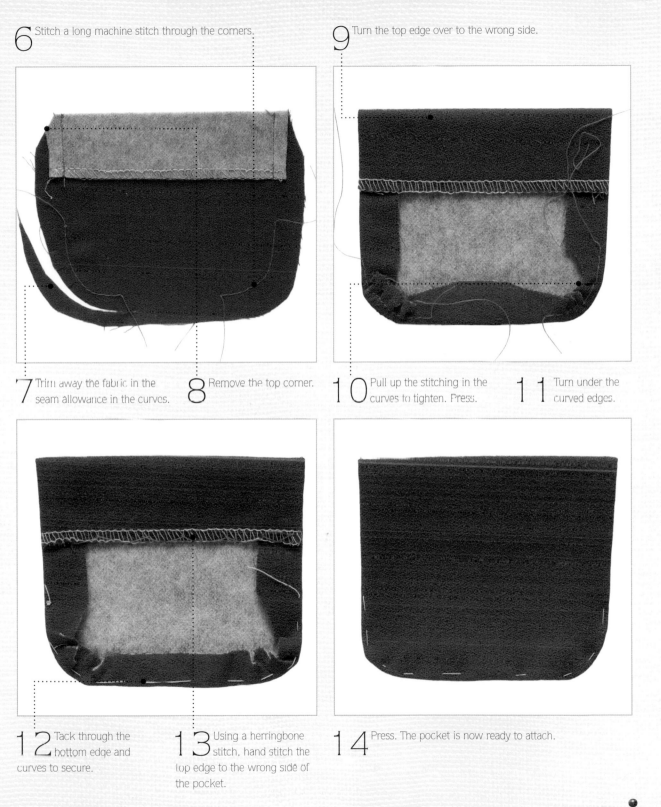

6 Stitch a long machine stitch through the corners.

9 Turn the top edge over to the wrong side.

7 Trim away the fabric in the seam allowance in the curves.

8 Remove the top corner.

10 Pull up the stitching in the curves to tighten. Press.

11 Turn under the curved edges.

12 Tack through the bottom edge and curves to secure.

13 Using a herringbone stitch, hand stitch the top edge to the wrong side of the pocket.

14 Press. The pocket is now ready to attach.

Self-lined patch pocket

If a patch pocket is to be self-lined, it needs to be cut with the top edge of the pocket on a fold. Like an unlined pocket, if you are using a lightweight fabric an interfacing may not be required, whereas for medium-weight fabrics a fusible interfacing is advisable. A self-lined patch pocket is not suitable for heavy fabrics.

1 Cut the pocket fabric and apply a fusible interfacing, if needed.

2 Fold the pocket in half, right side to right side. Pin to secure.

3 Machine around the three open sides of the pocket. Leave a gap of about 3cm (1¼in) for turning through.

4 Remove bulk from the corners by trimming.

5 Trim one side of the seam allowance down to half its width.

6 Use pinking shears to trim the corners.

7 Turn the pocket through the gap to the right side. Press.

8 Hand stitch the gap in the seam using a flat fell or blind hem stitch. The pocket is now ready to be attached.

Square patch pocket

It is possible to have a patch pocket with square corners. This requires mitring the corners to reduce the bulk. Use a fusible interfacing on medium-weight fabrics.

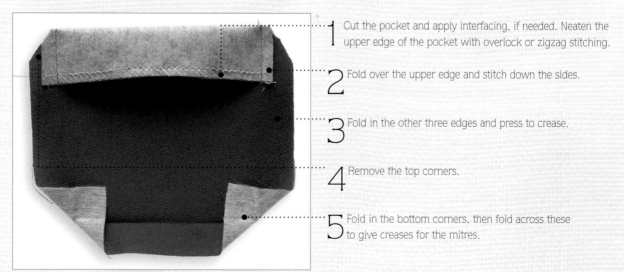

1 Cut the pocket and apply interfacing, if needed. Neaten the upper edge of the pocket with overlock or zigzag stitching.

2 Fold over the upper edge and stitch down the sides.

3 Fold in the other three edges and press to crease.

4 Remove the top corners.

5 Fold in the bottom corners, then fold across these to give creases for the mitres.

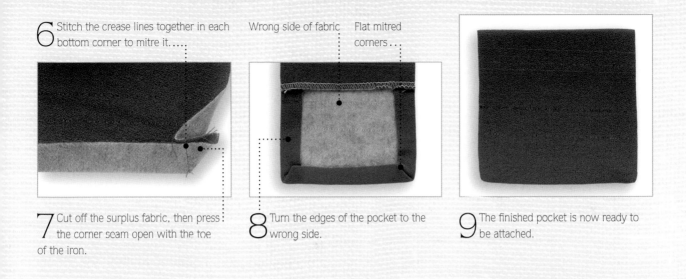

6 Stitch the crease lines together in each bottom corner to mitre it.....

Wrong side of fabric   Flat mitred corners...

7 Cut off the surplus fabric, then press the corner seam open with the toe of the iron.

8 Turn the edges of the pocket to the wrong side.

9 The finished pocket is now ready to be attached.

Attaching a patch pocket

To attach a pocket successfully, accurate pattern marking is essential. It is best to do this by means of tailor's tacks or even trace tacking. If you are using a check or stripe fabric, the pocket fabric must align with the checks or stripes on the garment.

1 Mark the pocket placement lines on the garment with tailor's tacks.....................

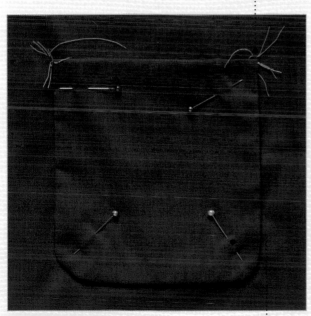

2 Take the completed pocket and place it to the fabric, matching the corners with the tailor's tacks. Pin in position.

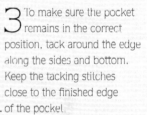

3 To make sure the pocket remains in the correct position, tack around the edge along the sides and bottom. Keep the tacking stitches close to the finished edge .... of the pocket.

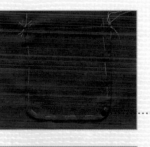

4 Machine stitch about 1mm (1/32in) from the edge of the pocket.

5 Remove the tacking stitches. Press.

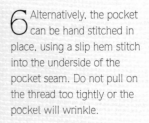

6 Alternatively, the pocket can be hand stitched in place, using a slip hem stitch into the underside of the pocket seam. Do not pull on the thread too tightly or the pocket will wrinkle.

Reinforcing pocket corners

On any patch pocket it is essential to reinforce the upper corners as these take all the strain when the pocket is being used. There are several ways to do this, some of which are quite decorative.

REVERSE STITCH

1 Reinforce the corner with a reverse stitch. Make sure the stitches lie on top of one another.

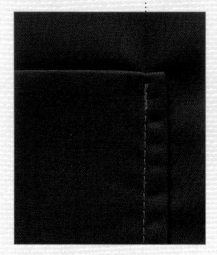

2 Pull the threads to the reverse to tie off.

DIAGONAL STITCH

1 This technique is used primarily on shirts. When machining the pocket in place, stitch along horizontally for four stitches.

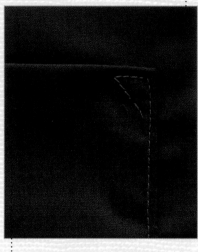

2 Turn and stitch diagonally back to the side, to create a triangular shape in the corner.

ZIGZAG STITCH

1 Using a small zigzag stitch, width 1.0 and length 1.0, stitch diagonally across the corner.

2 Make a feature of this stitch by using a thread in a contrasting colour.

PARALLEL ZIGZAG STITCH

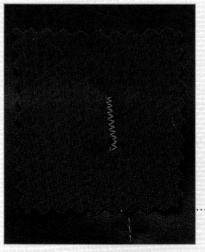

1 Place a patch on the wrong side of the garment, behind the pocket corner, to stitch into for strength.

2 Using a small zigzag stitch, width 1.0 and length 1.0, machine a short vertical line next to the straight stitching.

Making a pocket flap

Some styles of garment have no pocket, just a flap for decorative purposes. The flap is sewn where the pocket would be, but there is no opening under the flap. This is to reduce the bulk that would arise from having the rest of the pocket.

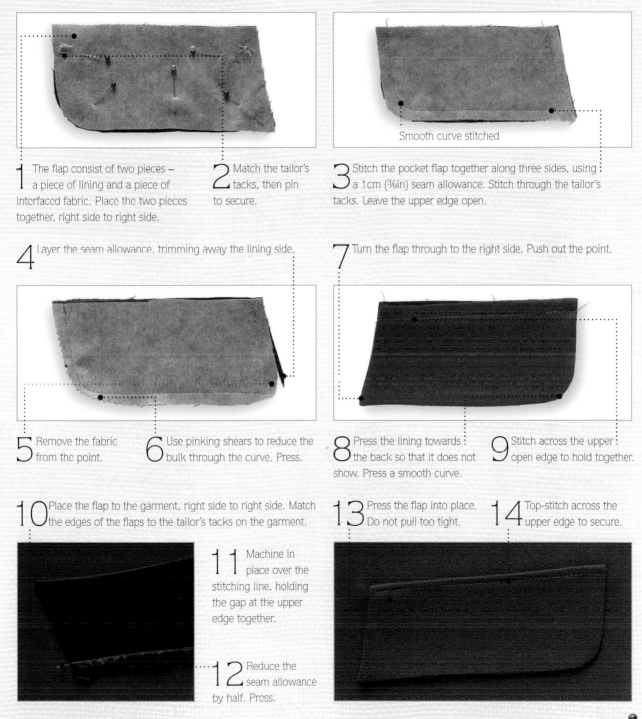

Smooth curve stitched

1 The flap consist of two pieces – a piece of lining and a piece of interfaced fabric. Place the two pieces together, right side to right side.

2 Match the tailor's tacks, then pin to secure.

3 Stitch the pocket flap together along three sides, using a 1cm (⅜in) seam allowance. Stitch through the tailor's tacks. Leave the upper edge open.

4 Layer the seam allowance, trimming away the lining side.

7 Turn the flap through to the right side. Push out the point.

5 Remove the fabric from the point.

6 Use pinking shears to reduce the bulk through the curve. Press.

8 Press the lining towards the back so that it does not show. Press a smooth curve.

9 Stitch across the upper open edge to hold together.

10 Place the flap to the garment, right side to right side. Match the edges of the flaps to the tailor's tacks on the garment.

11 Machine in place over the stitching line, holding the gap at the upper edge together.

12 Reduce the seam allowance by half. Press.

13 Press the flap into place. Do not pull too tight.

14 Top-stitch across the upper edge to secure.

Front hip pocket

On many trousers and casual skirts, the pocket is placed on the hipline. It can be low on the hipline or cut quite high as on jeans. The construction is the same for all types of hip pockets. When inserted at an angle, hip pockets can slim the figure.

1 Apply a piece of fusible tape on the garment along the line of the pocket.

Wrong side of garment front

2 Place the pocket lining to the front, right side to right side. Match any notches that are on the seam. Pin in place.

3 Machine the lining in place taking a 1.5cm (⅝in) seam allowance.

4 Trim the lining side of the seam allowance down to half its width.

5 Open out the pocket and press the seam towards the lining.

6 Turn the lining to the inside. Press so that the lining is not visible on the outside.

7 Top-stitch 5mm (³⁄₁₆in) from the edge.

8 On the right side of the garment, pin the pocket bag along the pocket opening.

Wrong side of garment

9 Take the side front section that incorporates the pocket bag and place to the lining pocket section, right side to right side. Match any seams and tailor's tacks. Pin in place.

10 Machine the pocket bag together using a 1.5cm (⅝in) seam allowance. Press.

11 Neaten the raw edges of the seam allowance around the pocket.

12 Neaten the side seam allowance, stitching from the top down. Make sure the fabric lies flat where it joins the side seam.

13 The angled front hip pocket from the right side.

Kangaroo pocket

This is a variation on a patch pocket. It is a large pocket that is often found on aprons and the front of children's pinafore dresses. A half version of this pocket also features on casual jackets.

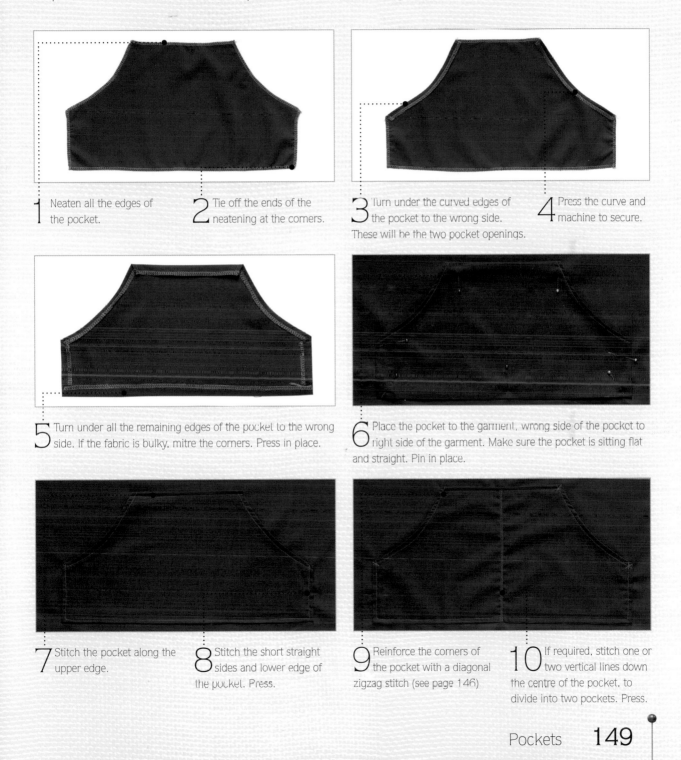

1 Neaten all the edges of the pocket.

2 Tie off the ends of the neatening at the corners.

3 Turn under the curved edges of the pocket to the wrong side. These will be the two pocket openings.

4 Press the curve and machine to secure.

5 Turn under all the remaining edges of the pocket to the wrong side. If the fabric is bulky, mitre the corners. Press in place.

6 Place the pocket to the garment, wrong side of the pocket to right side of the garment. Make sure the pocket is sitting flat and straight. Pin in place.

7 Stitch the pocket along the upper edge.

8 Stitch the short straight sides and lower edge of the pocket. Press.

9 Reinforce the corners of the pocket with a diagonal zigzag stitch (see page 146)

10 If required, stitch one or two vertical lines down the centre of the pocket, to divide into two pockets. Press.

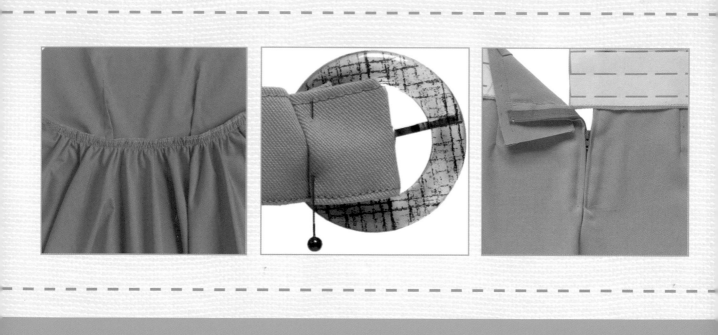

WAISTLINES, BELTS, AND TIE-BACKS

Waistlines

Waistlines can be formed where a bodice and skirt join together or at the waist edge of a skirt or pair of trousers. Some waistlines are attached separately to the garment to create a feature and others are more discreet. They may be shaped to follow the contours of the body.

Directory of waistlines

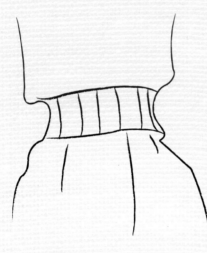

WAISTLINE WITH A CASING

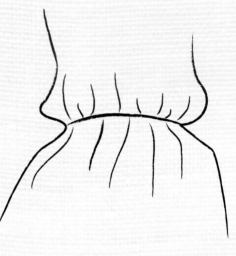

GATHERED WAISTLINE

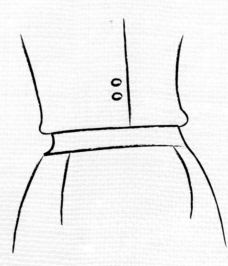

BASIC STRAIGHT WAISTBAND

Joining a fitted skirt to a bodice

Many dresses feature a straight fitted skirt attached to a fitted dress bodice. When joining them together, it is important that the darts or seamlines on the bodice line up with those on the skirt.

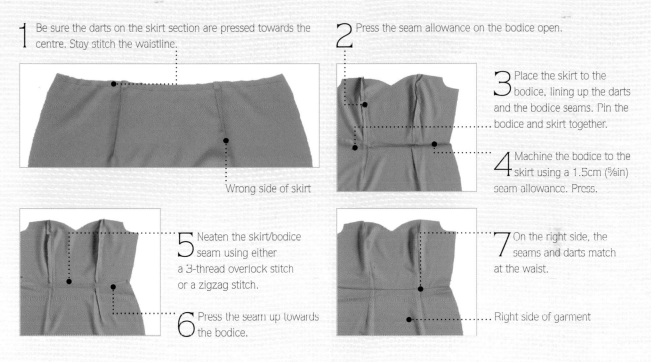

1 Be sure the darts on the skirt section are pressed towards the centre. Stay stitch the waistline.

Wrong side of skirt

2 Press the seam allowance on the bodice open.

3 Place the skirt to the bodice, lining up the darts and the bodice seams. Pin the bodice and skirt together.

4 Machine the bodice to the skirt using a 1.5cm (⅝in) seam allowance. Press.

5 Neaten the skirt/bodice seam using either a 3-thread overlock stitch or a zigzag stitch.

6 Press the seam up towards the bodice.

7 On the right side, the seams and darts match at the waist.

Right side of garment

Joining a gathered skirt to a bodice

When attaching a gathered skirt to a fitted bodice, the gathers must be distributed evenly around the waist. If there are seams on the gathered skirt these must be matched to the bodice seams and darts.

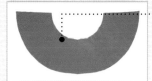

1 Machine a double row of gather stitches around the waistline of a half circle skirt.

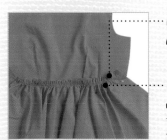

2 Pull up the gathers to fit the bodice waist.

3 Pin the gathered skirt to the bodice, making sure the bodice darts face towards the centre.

4 Machine the gathered skirt to the bodice using a 1.5cm (⅝in) seam allowance. Neaten the seam using either a 3-thread overlock stitch or a zigzag stitch.

5 Press the seam up towards the bodice. On the right side the skirt seam is gathered into a smooth bodice seam.

Making a casing at the waist edge

An elasticated waist edge is featured on both skirts and trousers and also at the waist edge on casual jackets. The casing can be made by using a deep waist seam or by attaching a facing. The facing will form a complete circle that will be attached to the waist edge.

USING A DEEP WAIST SEAM AS A CASING

1 Turn under a 1.5cm (⅝in) seam allowance to the wrong side and press.

2 Turn again by 3cm (1¼in). Pin in place.

Wrong side

3 Stitch 2mm (¹⁄₁₆in) from the top folded edge.

Wrong side

4 Machine the lower edge of the fold 2mm (¹⁄₁₆in) from the edge. Leave a gap of about 3cm (1¼in) to insert the elastic through.

5 Cut a piece of non-roll elastic the length required to go around the waist comfortably.

6 Pin one end of the elastic to the fabric just below the opening.

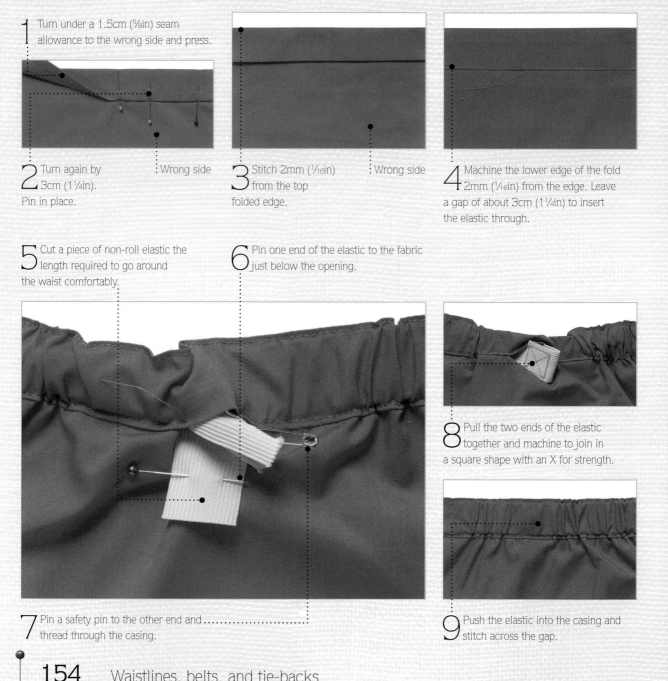

8 Pull the two ends of the elastic together and machine to join in a square shape with an X for strength.

7 Pin a safety pin to the other end and thread through the casing.

9 Push the elastic into the casing and stitch across the gap.

USING A FACING AS A CASING

1 Cut the facing, and join the facing sections together at the side seams. Press open. Do not join the remaining seam but press back the seam allowances.

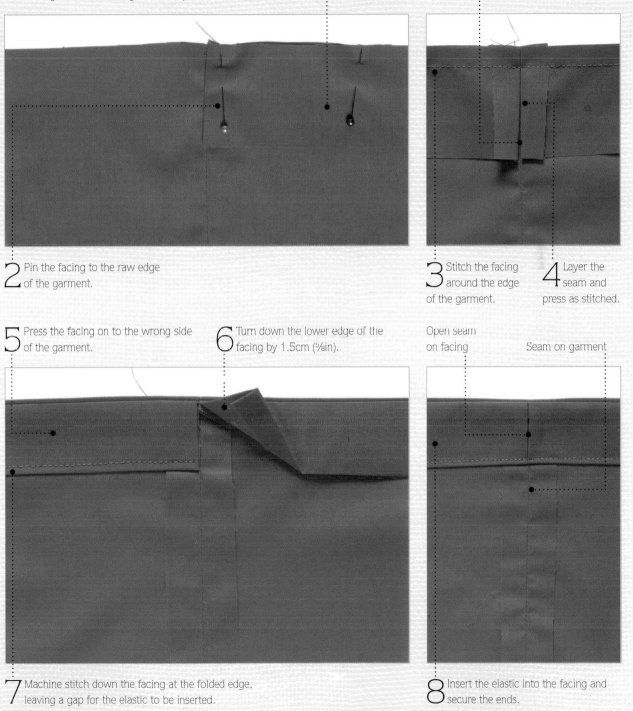

Gap where facing seam has been left open

2 Pin the facing to the raw edge of the garment.

3 Stitch the facing around the edge of the garment.

4 Layer the seam and press as stitched.

5 Press the facing on to the wrong side of the garment.

6 Turn down the lower edge of the facing by 1.5cm (⅝in).

Open seam on facing

Seam on garment

7 Machine stitch down the facing at the folded edge, leaving a gap for the elastic to be inserted.

8 Insert the elastic into the facing and secure the ends.

Applied casings

Some elasticated waist edges will require the application of extra fabric to make a casing into which the elastic can be inserted. The casing may be applied to the inside or the outside of the garment. A quick way is to make the casing with bias binding. The casing can also be made from the same fabric as the garment or from a facing.

INTERNAL CASING

1 This type of casing is often used on a shirt-waisted dress or on a blouson-style jacket. Cut a strip of fabric on the straight of grain wide enough to accommodate your elastic and turnings.

2 Turn under the edge at one end by 1.5cm (⅝in) and then the same along the sides. Press.

3 Mark the waist with a row of tacks.

4 Place the casing over the tacks with the finished short end towards the centre front. Pin in place.

5 Machine to attach the casing to the waist.

6 Insert the elastic into the casing. Secure the elastic at both ends.

INTERNAL CASING USING BIAS BINDING

1 Be sure to use bias binding that will be wide enough to insert an elastic through after it has been stitched down. Apply the bias to the waistline and stitch at 2mm (¹⁄₁₆in) from either edge.

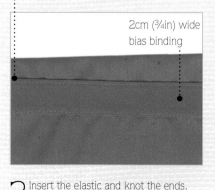

2cm (¾in) wide bias binding

2 Insert the elastic and knot the ends.

EXTERNAL CASING

1 Cut a strip of straight grain fabric 3.5cm (1⅜in) wide x the waist measurement on the garment. Turn under all raw edges by 5mm (³⁄₁₆in) and press.

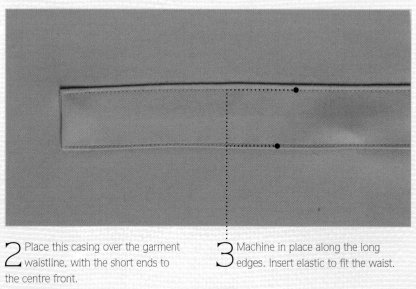

2 Place this casing over the garment waistline, with the short ends to the centre front.

3 Machine in place along the long edges. Insert elastic to fit the waist.

Mock casings

There are several ways to construct mock casings. The simplest is to stitch on elastic at the waist. An alternative, if a bodice and skirt have a waist seam joining them together, is to insert elastic between the seam allowances. On many garments, there is elastic at the back only, in a partial casing, and a waistband interfacing at the front.

STITCHING ON ELASTIC TO MAKE A WAISTLINE

1 Cut a piece of elastic to the required length. Mark the waistline on the garment with a row of tacking stitches.

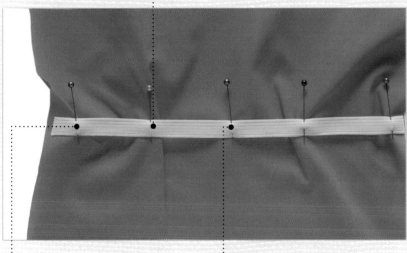

2 Secure the elastic at one end with a pin

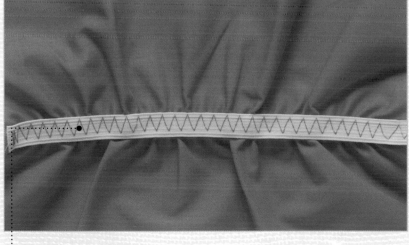

6 The elastic stitched in place.

3 Stretch the elastic across the fabric, pinning at regular intervals. The fabric will be loose under the elastic.

4 Secure the elastic at one end with a few machine stitches.

5 Place under the sewing machine and join the elastic to the fabric using a 3-step zigzag stitch, stretching the fabric and elastic together as you do so.

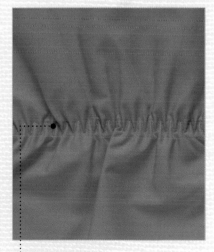

7 On the right side there is a neat elasticated waistline.

CASING IN A WAIST SEAM ALLOWANCE

1 Join the fabric together using a 2cm (¾in) seam allowance.

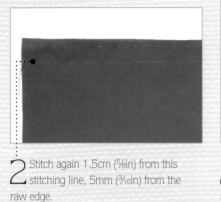

2 Stitch again 1.5cm (⅝in) from this stitching line, 5mm (³⁄₁₆in) from the raw edge.

3 Neaten the edge of the seam using a 3-thread overlock stitch or a zigzag stitch.

4 Insert elastic into the casing that you have made, with the help of a safety pin.

ALTERNATIVE CASING USING A SEAM ALLOWANCE

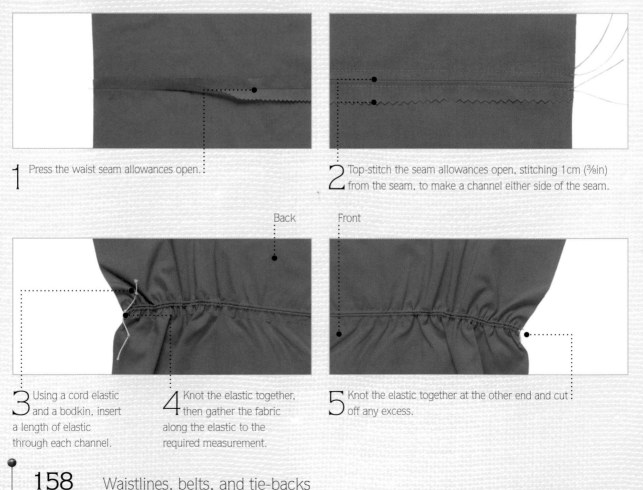

1 Press the waist seam allowances open.

2 Top-stitch the seam allowances open, stitching 1cm (⅜in) from the seam, to make a channel either side of the seam.

Back

Front

3 Using a cord elastic and a bodkin, insert a length of elastic through each channel.

4 Knot the elastic together, then gather the fabric along the elastic to the required measurement.

5 Knot the elastic together at the other end and cut off any excess.

PARTIAL CASING

1 The front waist is made by using a grown-on waistband. This means the waistband has been cut in one piece together with the skirt front. Apply a fusible interfacing to the waistband allowance.

4 On the back of the skirt, fold down the waist allowance.

5 Top-stitch close to the fold at the upper edge.

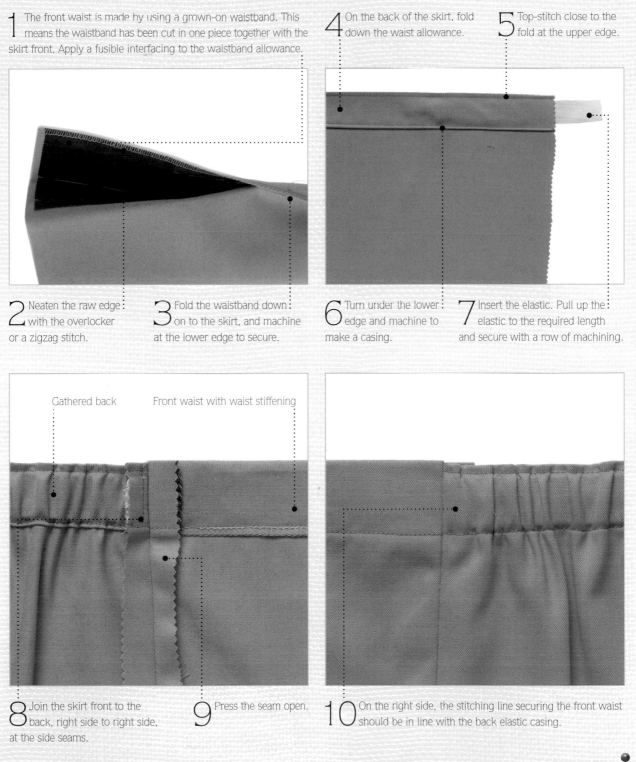

2 Neaten the raw edge with the overlocker or a zigzag stitch.

3 Fold the waistband down on to the skirt, and machine at the lower edge to secure.

6 Turn under the lower edge and machine to make a casing.

7 Insert the elastic. Pull up the elastic to the required length and secure with a row of machining.

Gathered back

Front waist with waist stiffening

8 Join the skirt front to the back, right side to right side, at the side seams.

9 Press the seam open.

10 On the right side, the stitching line securing the front waist should be in line with the back elastic casing.

Attaching a straight waistband

A waistband is designed to fit snugly but not tight to the waist. Whether it is shaped or straight or slightly curved, it will be constructed and attached in a similar way. Every waistband will require a fusible interfacing to give it structure and support. Special waistband interfacings are available, usually featuring slot lines that will guide you where to fold the fabric. Make sure the slots on the outer edge correspond to a 1.5cm (⅝in) seam allowance. If a specialist waistband fusible interfacing is not available you can use a medium-weight fusible interfacing.

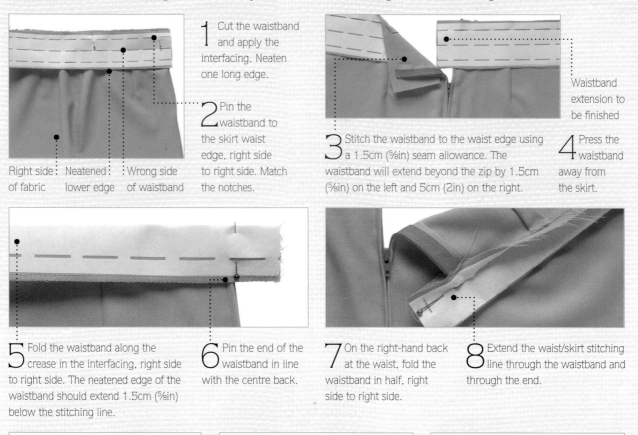

1 Cut the waistband and apply the interfacing. Neaten one long edge.

2 Pin the waistband to the skirt waist edge, right side to right side. Match the notches.

Right side of fabric   Neatened lower edge   Wrong side of waistband

Waistband extension to be finished

3 Stitch the waistband to the waist edge using a 1.5cm (⅝in) seam allowance. The waistband will extend beyond the zip by 1.5cm (⅝in) on the left and 5cm (2in) on the right.

4 Press the waistband away from the skirt.

5 Fold the waistband along the crease in the interfacing, right side to right side. The neatened edge of the waistband should extend 1.5cm (⅝in) below the stitching line.

6 Pin the end of the waistband in line with the centre back.

7 On the right-hand back at the waist, fold the waistband in half, right side to right side.

8 Extend the waist/skirt stitching line through the waistband and through the end.

9 Turn the ends of the waistband to the right side. The extension on the waistband should be on the right-hand back. Add your chosen fasteners.

10 To complete the waistband, stitch through the band to the skirt seam. This is known as stitching in the ditch.

11 The finished straight waistband.

A waist with a facing

Many waistlines on skirts and trousers are finished with a facing, which will follow the contours of the waist but will have had the dart shaping removed to make it smooth. A faced waistline always sits comfortably to the body. The facing is attached after all the main sections of the skirt or trousers have been constructed.

1 Apply a fusible interfacing to the facing. Neaten the lower edge of the facing with bias binding.

4 Layer the seam allowance on the facing side of the seam to reduce it by half.

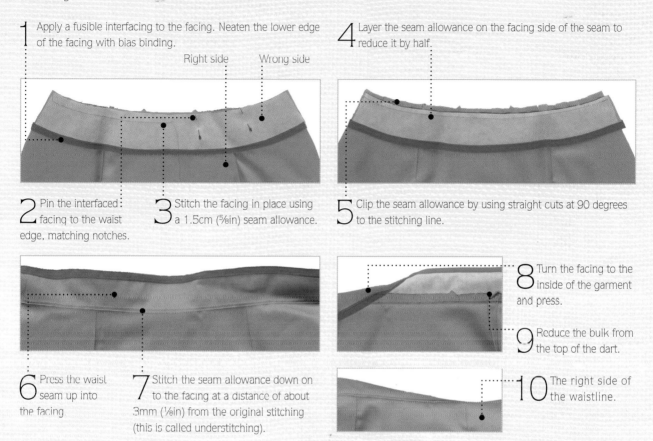

Right side   Wrong side

2 Pin the interfaced facing to the waist edge, matching notches.

3 Stitch the facing in place using a 1.5cm (⅝in) seam allowance.

5 Clip the seam allowance by using straight cuts at 90 degrees to the stitching line.

8 Turn the facing to the inside of the garment and press.

9 Reduce the bulk from the top of the dart.

6 Press the waist seam up into the facing

7 Stitch the seam allowance down on to the facing at a distance of about 3mm (⅛in) from the original stitching (this is called understitching).

10 The right side of the waistline.

Finishing the edge of a waistband

One long edge of the waistband will be stitched to the garment waist. The other edge will need to be finished, to prevent fraying and reduce bulk inside.

TURNING UNDER

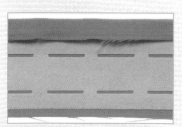

This method is suitable for fine fabrics only. Turn under 1.5cm (⅝in) along the edge of the waistband and press in place. After the waistband has been attached to the garment, hand stitch the pressed-under edge in place.

BIAS BINDING

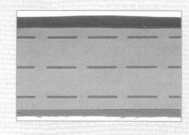

This method is ideal for fabrics that fray badly and can add a feature inside the garment. It is left flat inside the garment after construction. Apply a 2cm (¾in) bias binding to one long edge of the waistband.

Belts

A belt in a fabric that matches the garment can add the perfect finishing touch. Whether it be a soft tie belt or a stiff structured belt, it will be best if it has an interfacing of some kind – the firmer and more structured the belt, the firmer the interfacing should be. A belt will also need belt carriers to support it and prevent it from drooping.

Directory of belts and tie-backs

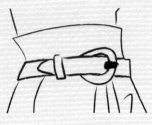

STRAIGHT BELT

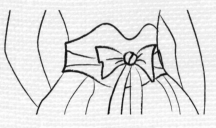

OBI SASH

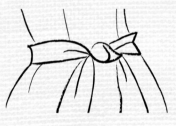

TIE BELT

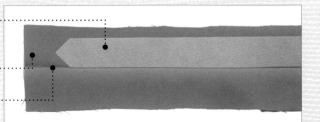

STRUCTURED CURTAIN TIE-BACK

Reinforced straight belt

This is a straightforward way to make a belt to match a garment. It can be of any width as it is reinforced with a very firm fusible interfacing, such as a craft interfacing. If one layer of interfacing is not firm enough, try adding another layer. The interfacing should be cut along its length to avoid joins.

1 Cut the interfacing to the dimensions of the finished belt. Cut the fabric to twice the width of the interfacing plus seam allowances.

3 Fuse the cut interfacing to the fabric.

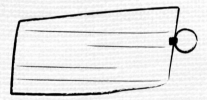

2 Fold the fabric in half lengthways and press to mark the centre line. Place the interfacing along the crease, leaving the fabric longer at the pointed end of the interfacing.

4 At the centre line on the pointed end, cut through to the side of the interfacing point.

5 Press the fabric edges over the interfacing. Press the point carefully.

6 Fold one long raw edge of the belt under and press.

7 Press under the remaining edge to match and pin in place.

8 Tack along the pressed-under edges to sew them together.

9 Use short tacking stitches around the point.

10 Machine stitch along both long sides of the belt, stitching on the right side of the fabric. Keep the machine stitching close to the edge – 2mm (¹⁄₁₆in) from it. Make sure the stitching is accurate through the point.

11 Measure the positioning of the eyelets towards the pointed end of the belt.

12 Punch the hole for each eyelet with pliers.

13 Insert a 4mm (³⁄₁₆in) eyelet into the hole.

14 Change the heads in the pliers and squeeze the eyelets around the hole.

15 Insert one eyelet at the other end of the belt about 5cm (2in) from the end, placing it centrally on the right side of the belt.

16 Push the buckle prong through the eyelet.

17 Fold the surplus fabric over on itself under the buckle and pin.

18 Secure with a machine or hand stitch, then turn the belt over.

19 When the belt is placed around the waist, check that the fit is correct. Add extra eyelets if required.

Tie belt

A tie belt is the easiest of all the belts to make. It can be any width and made of most fabrics, from cottons for summer dresses to satin and silks for bridal wear. Most tie belts will require a light to medium-weight interfacing for support. A fusible interfacing is the best choice as it will stay in place when tied repeatedly. If a very long tie belt is required, the belt can be joined at the centre back.

1 Cut fabric for the belt, with a point at each end. Cut a fusible interfacing the same length but half the width.

3 Fold the belt in half, right side to right side so the fusible is showing. Pin.

5 Layer the seam by removing half of the seam allowance on the fused side.

8 Once the belt has been turned to the right side, press the seam carefully so that it is on the very edge.

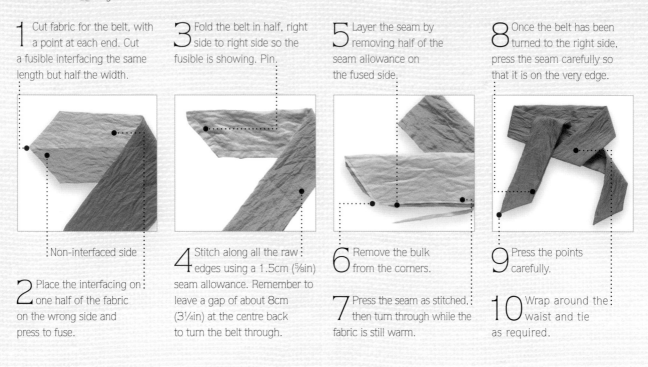

Non-interfaced side

4 Stitch along all the raw edges using a 1.5cm (⅝in) seam allowance. Remember to leave a gap of about 8cm (3¼in) at the centre back to turn the belt through.

6 Remove the bulk from the corners.

9 Press the points carefully.

2 Place the interfacing on one half of the fabric on the wrong side and press to fuse.

7 Press the seam as stitched, then turn through while the fabric is still warm.

10 Wrap around the waist and tie as required.

Obi sash

An obi sash is a variation of the traditional sash that is worn with a kimono. This type of sash has a stiffened centre piece with softer ties that cross at the back and then wrap to the front and tie. If you are using a firm fabric, such as silk dupion or heavy cotton, interfacing will not be required for the ties.

1 Make the ties first. Cut long strips of fabric of the required length and width.

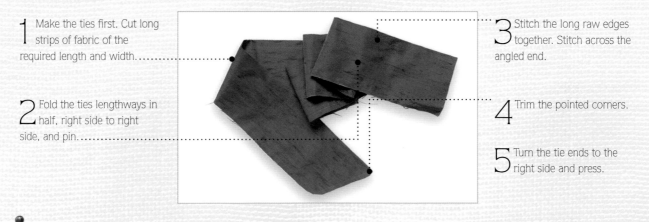

3 Stitch the long raw edges together. Stitch across the angled end.

2 Fold the ties lengthways in half, right side to right side, and pin.

4 Trim the pointed corners.

5 Turn the tie ends to the right side and press.

6 Next make the centre section. Cut out two shaped pieces of fabric and a matching piece of very firm fusible interfacing.

Right side

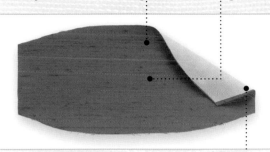

7 Fuse the interfacing to the wrong side of one piece of fabric. If one layer of interfacing does not make the fabric stiff enough, add another layer.

8 Centre the tie ends to the short ends of the stiffened centre piece on the right side. Machine stitch to secure, using a 1cm (⅜in) seam allowance.

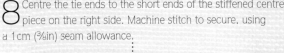

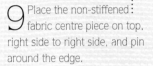

9 Place the non-stiffened fabric centre piece on top, right side to right side, and pin around the edge.

10 Fold up and tuck the tie ends inside, between the two layers of fabric.

11 Machine stitch around the centre section, leaving a gap at the lower edge for turning through.

12 Remove the surplus fabric from the corners.

13 Clip the curved edges of the centre section in the seam allowance.

14 Pull the tie ends through the gap at the lower edge.

15 Turn the centre section through to the right side and press.

16 Hand stitch the gap at the lower edge with a flat fell or blind hem stitch.

17 The finished obi sash.

Curtain tie-backs

Tie-backs are used to hold the drape of a curtain in position. Some are structured, with an interfacing, and follow a predetermined shape, while others are softer and more decorative. The construction of a tie-back is similar to that of a tie belt.

STRUCTURED TIE-BACK

1 Cut out two pieces of fabric for the tie-back. Use a heavy fusible interfacing and cut it to the same size as the fabric, minus the seam allowances of 1.5cm (⅝in) on all sides.

3 Pin the non-interfaced piece of fabric to the interfaced piece, right side to right side.

4 Stitch around the two pieces, taking a 1.5cm (⅝in) seam allowance. The machining should follow the edge of the interfacing, but not go through it.

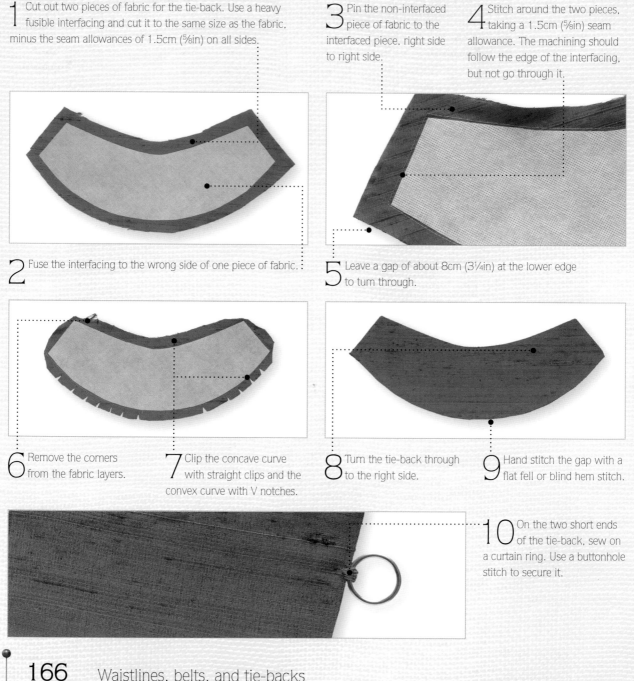

2 Fuse the interfacing to the wrong side of one piece of fabric.

5 Leave a gap of about 8cm (3¼in) at the lower edge to turn through.

6 Remove the corners from the fabric layers.

7 Clip the concave curve with straight clips and the convex curve with V notches.

8 Turn the tie-back through to the right side.

9 Hand stitch the gap with a flat fell or blind hem stitch.

10 On the two short ends of the tie-back, sew on a curtain ring. Use a buttonhole stitch to secure it.

DECORATIVE RUCHED TIE-BACK

1 Cut a piece of curtain interlining 25cm (10in) wide and to the required tie-back length.

2 Roll up the interlining like a sausage but not too tight, and pin in place.

3 Using a bold thread, herringbone stitch the raw edge down to hold it in position. Make sure the rolled interlining is the same thickness throughout.

4 For the outer decorative layer, cut a piece of fabric 12cm (5in) wide and three times the required length.

5 Fold lengthways in half, right side to right side.

6 Machine stitch the long raw edges together using a 1cm (⅜in) seam allowance.

7 Stitch again, between the stitching line and the raw edge. The double stitching is for strength.

8 Turn the decorative top layer fabric through to the right side and press.

9 Tie the thread ends from the herringbone stitch on the interlining to a loop turner.

10 Using the loop turner, pull the interlining sausage through the decorative layer. This is difficult as it will stick. Work the decorative fabric gently down the interlining.

11 Ruche the decorative fabric up around the interlining, evening out the fabric with your fingers. Remove the loop turner.

12 Hand stitch with a small, straight running stitch about every 3cm (1¼in) to secure the ruching on the tie-back.

13 Sew on a curtain ring at each end, using a buttonhole stitch to secure the rings.

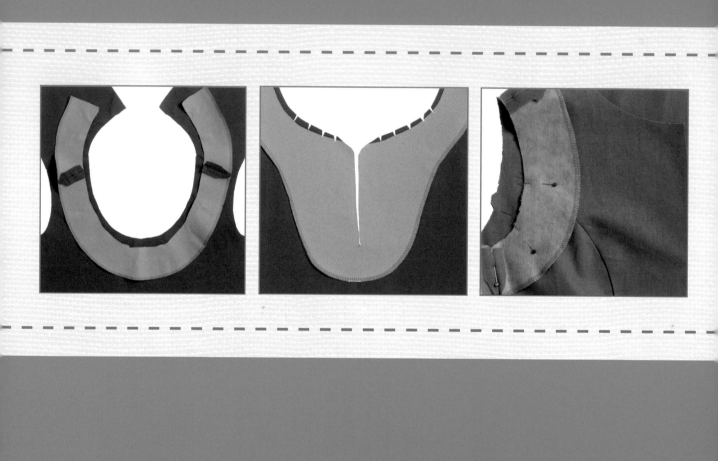

FACINGS AND NECKLINES

Facings and necklines

The simplest way to finish the neck or armhole of a garment is to apply a facing. The neckline can be any shape to have a facing applied, from a curve to a square to a V, and many more. Some facings and necklines can add interest to the centre back or centre front of a garment.

Directory of necklines

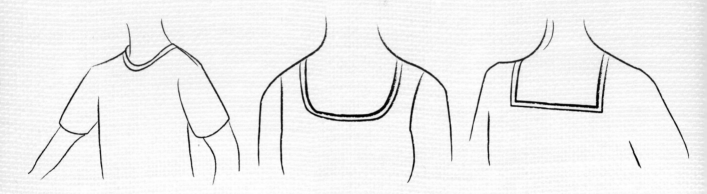

ROUND NECK
SCOOP NECK
SQUARE NECK

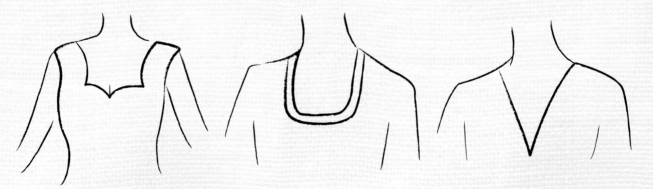

SWEETHEART NECK
U-NECK
V-NECK

Applying interfacing to a facing

All facings require interfacing. The interfacing is to give structure to the facing and to hold it in shape. A fusible interfacing is the best choice and it should be cut on the same grain as the facing. Choose an interfacing that is lighter in weight than the main fabric.

INTERFACING FOR HEAVY FABRIC

Right side of facing

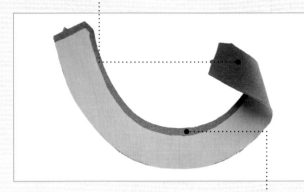

For a heavy-weight fabric use a medium-weight fusible interfacing. Remove the seam allowance on the interfacing on the inner curve to reduce bulk.

INTERFACING FOR LIGHT FABRIC

Right side of facing

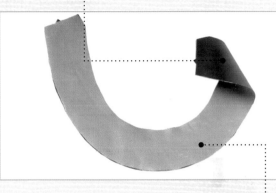

For a light to medium-weight fabric, choose a lightweight interfacing and fuse it over the complete facing.

Construction of a facing

The facing may be in two or three pieces in order to fit around a neck or armhole edge. The facing sections need to be joined together prior to being attached. The photographs here show an interfaced neck facing in three pieces.

1 Tack together the pieces of the facing at the shoulder seams.

2 Stitch the shoulder seams and press open.

3 Stay stitch around the edge of the inner curve, to prevent stretch.

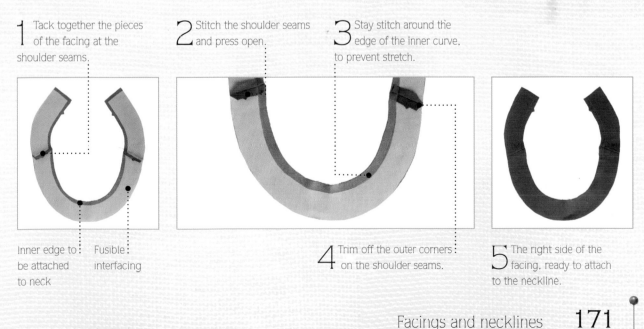

Inner edge to be attached to neck

Fusible interfacing

4 Trim off the outer corners on the shoulder seams.

5 The right side of the facing, ready to attach to the neckline.

Neatening the edge of a facing

The outer edge of a facing will require neatening to prevent it from fraying, and there are several ways to do this. Binding the lower edge of a facing with a bias strip makes the garment a little more luxurious and can add a designer touch inside the garment. Alternatively, the edge can be stitched or pinked (see opposite page).

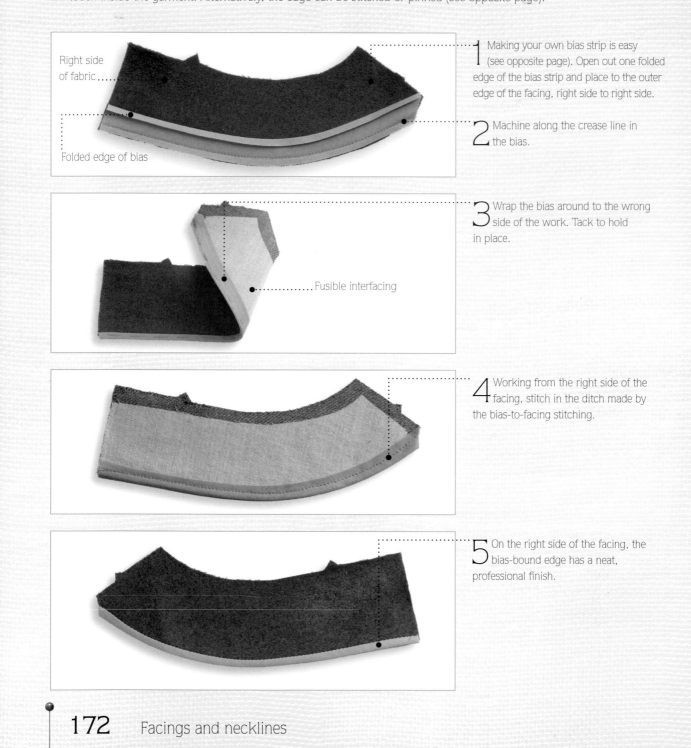

Right side of fabric

Folded edge of bias

1 Making your own bias strip is easy (see opposite page). Open out one folded edge of the bias strip and place to the outer edge of the facing, right side to right side.

2 Machine along the crease line in the bias.

3 Wrap the bias around to the wrong side of the work. Tack to hold in place.

Fusible interfacing

4 Working from the right side of the facing, stitch in the ditch made by the bias-to-facing stitching.

5 On the right side of the facing, the bias-bound edge has a neat, professional finish.

HOW TO CUT BIAS STRIPS

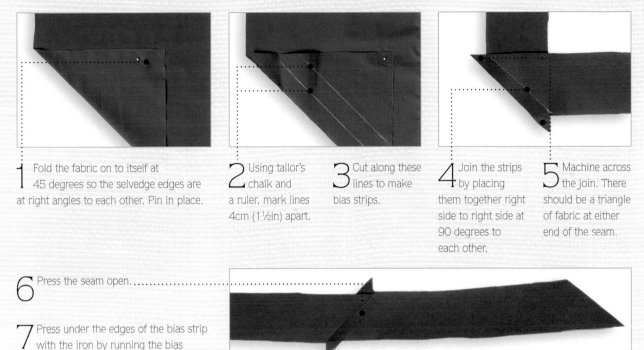

1 Fold the fabric on to itself at 45 degrees so the selvedge edges are at right angles to each other. Pin in place.

2 Using tailor's chalk and a ruler, mark lines 4cm (1½in) apart.

3 Cut along these lines to make bias strips.

4 Join the strips by placing them together right side to right side at 90 degrees to each other.

5 Machine across the join. There should be a triangle of fabric at either end of the seam.

6 Press the seam open.

7 Press under the edges of the bias strip with the iron by running the bias strip through a 25mm (1in) tape maker.

Other neatening methods

The following techniques are alternative popular ways to neaten the edge of a facing. The one you choose depends upon the garment being made and the fabric used.

OVERLOCKED

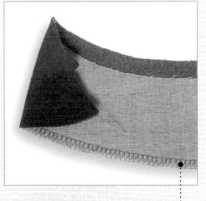

Neaten the outer edge with a 3-thread overlock stitch.

PINKED

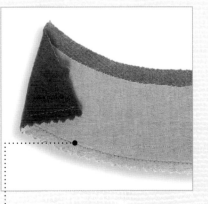

Machine stitch 1cm (³/₈in) from the edge and trim the raw edge with pinking shears.

ZIGZAGGED

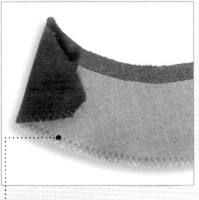

Neaten the outer edge with a zigzag stitch.

Facing a slashed neckline

A slashed neckline occurs at either the centre front or the centre back neck edge. It enables a close-fitting neckline to open sufficiently to go over the head.

1 Apply a fusible interfacing to the facing (see page 171). Place the facing to the neckline, right side to right side.

3 Stitch the facing at the neck edge, pivoting to stitch along both sides of the slash between the tailor's tacks. Take one stitch horizontally at the bottom edge of the slash line.

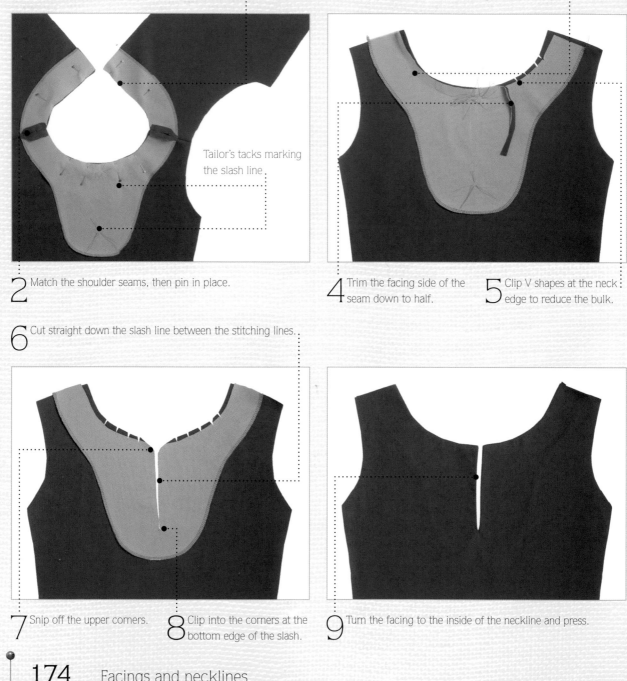

Tailor's tacks marking the slash line

2 Match the shoulder seams, then pin in place.

4 Trim the facing side of the seam down to half.

5 Clip V shapes at the neck edge to reduce the bulk.

6 Cut straight down the slash line between the stitching lines.

7 Snip off the upper corners.

8 Clip into the corners at the bottom edge of the slash.

9 Turn the facing to the inside of the neckline and press.

Attaching a neck facing

▌ This technique applies to all shapes of neckline, from round to square to sweetheart.

1 Apply a fusible interfacing to the facing (see page 171).

4 Pin the facing in place, matching around the neck edge.

6 Machine in place using a 1.5cm (⅝in) seam allowance.

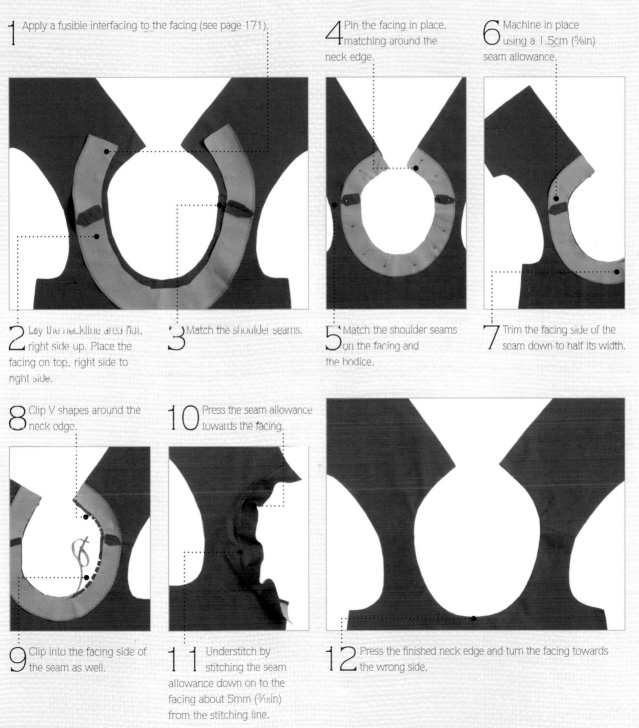

2 Lay the neckline area flat, right side up. Place the facing on top, right side to right side.

3 Match the shoulder seams.

5 Match the shoulder seams on the facing and the bodice.

7 Trim the facing side of the seam down to half its width.

8 Clip V shapes around the neck edge.

10 Press the seam allowance towards the facing.

9 Clip into the facing side of the seam as well.

11 Understitch by stitching the seam allowance down on to the facing about 5mm (³⁄₁₆in) from the stitching line.

12 Press the finished neck edge and turn the facing towards the wrong side.

Bound neck edge

Binding is an excellent way to finish a raw neck edge. It has the added advantage of being a method that can be used if you are short of fabric or you would like a contrast or decorative finish. You can use bought bias binding or a bias strip cut from the same or a contrasting fabric (see page 173). A double bias strip is used on fine fabrics.

BIAS-BOUND NECK EDGE VERSION 1

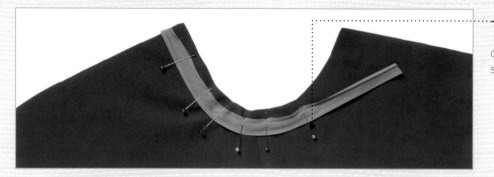

1 Open out one edge of the bias strip and place the crease line on the 1.5cm (⅝in) stitching line. Pin in place.

2 Machine in place along the crease line.

3 Trim away the surplus fabric from the seam allowance.

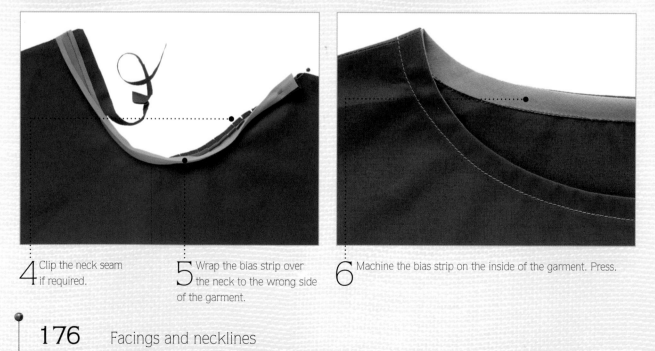

4 Clip the neck seam if required.

5 Wrap the bias strip over the neck to the wrong side of the garment.

6 Machine the bias strip on the inside of the garment. Press.

BIAS-BOUND NECK EDGE VERSION 2

1 This technique is used on bulkier fabrics. Cut a bias strip 7cm (2¾in) wide.

2 Pin to the neck edge.

3 Machine along the neck edge using a 1.5cm (⅝in) seam allowance.

4 Trim the seam allowance to half on the garment side.

5 Clip the seam allowance on the bias strip.

6 Fold the raw edge of the bias to the wrong side, to touch the machine stitches.

7 Fold again to bring the folded edge of the bias to the same place, and pin.

8 Stitch permanently in position using a flat fell stitch.

Armhole facing

On sleeveless garments, a facing is an excellent way of neatening an armhole because it is not bulky. Also, as the facing is made in the same fabric as the garment, it does not show.

1 Construct the interfaced armhole facing (see page 171) and neaten the edge by your preferred method.

Armhole

2 Place the facing to the armhole, right side to right side. Match at the shoulder seams and at the underarm seam.

3 Match the notches, one at the front and two at the back. Pin the facing in place.

4 Machine around the armhole to attach the facing, taking a 1.5cm (⅝in) seam allowance.

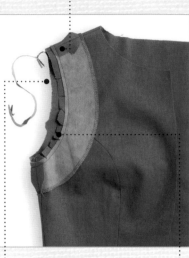

5 Trim the facing side of the seam allowance down to half.

6 Clip out some V shapes in the seam allowance to reduce bulk.

7 Turn the facing into position on the wrong side Understitch by pressing the seam allowance on to the facing and machining down.

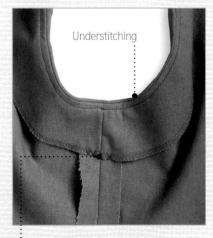

Understitching

8 On the underarm and shoulder seams, secure the facing to the seam allowance with cross stitches.

9 Press the stitched edge. On the right side the armhole will have a neat finish.

Grown-on facing

A facing is not always a separate unit. Many garments, especially blouses, feature what is known as a grown-on facing, which is where the facing is an extension of the front of the garment, cut out at the same time.

1 Mark the foldline that divides off the facing area and crease by pressing.

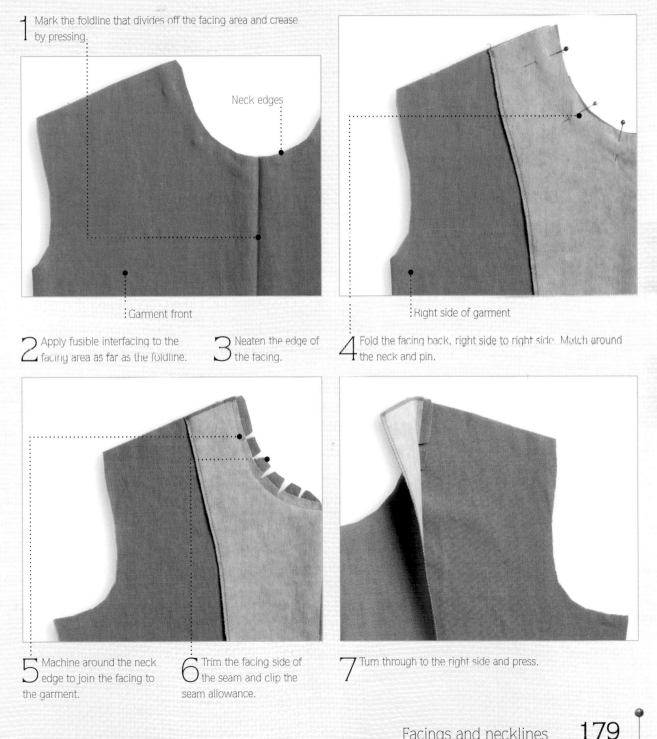

Neck edges

Garment front

Right side of garment

2 Apply fusible interfacing to the facing area as far as the foldline.

3 Neaten the edge of the facing.

4 Fold the facing back, right side to right side. Match around the neck and pin.

5 Machine around the neck edge to join the facing to the garment.

6 Trim the facing side of the seam and clip the seam allowance.

7 Turn through to the right side and press.

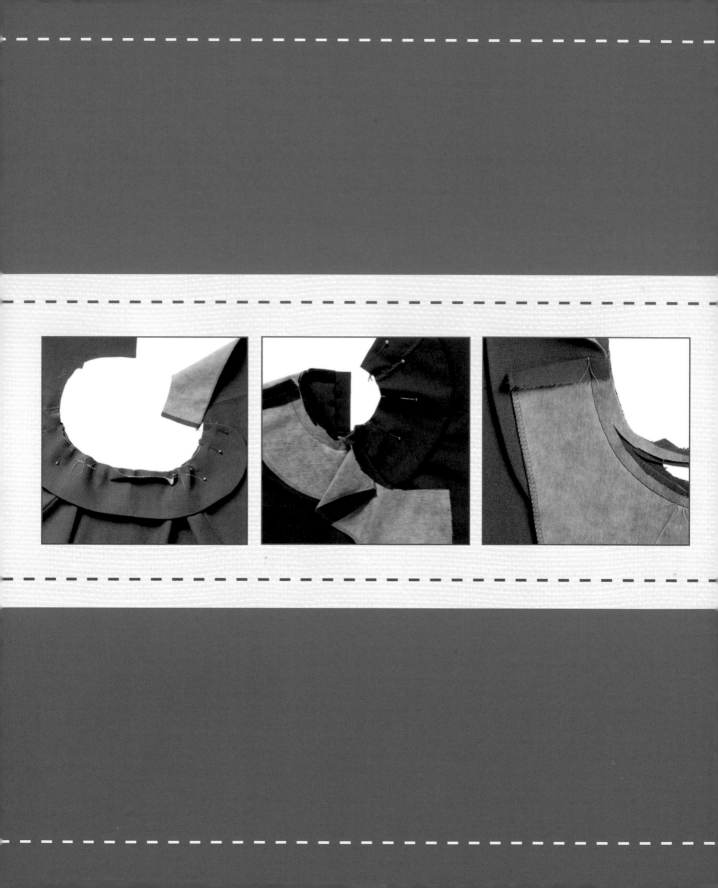

COLLARS

Collars

All collars consist of a minimum of two pieces, the upper collar (which will be on the outside) and the under collar. Interfacing, which is required to give the collar shape and structure, is often applied to the upper collar to give a smoother appearance to the fabric.

Directory of collars

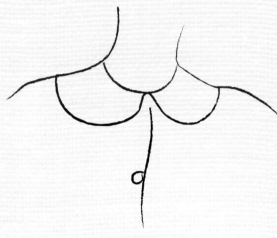

FLAT COLLAR

PETER PAN COLLAR

BLOUSE COLLAR

STAND COLLAR

Flat collar

A flat collar is the easiest of all the collars to construct, and the techniques used are the same for most other shapes of flat collar and facings.

1 Cut out the fabric for the collar accurately. Make sure the two halves match.

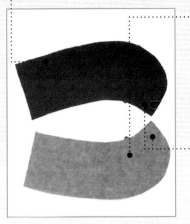

2 Cut out a fusible interfacing, being sure to cut on the same grain as the collar. Apply the interfacing to the upper collar.

3 Insert tailor's tacks at the centre front point of the collar where indicated by a dot on the pattern piece.

4 Pin the upper collar and under collar together, right side to right side. Match any notches and make sure the cut edges match.

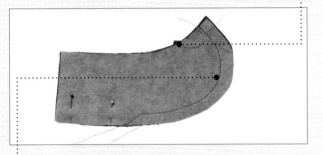

5 Machine stitch 1.5cm (⅝in) along the raw outer curved edge to the lower edge of the collar. Make sure the machining at the centre front goes through the tailor's tack. If you have problems stitching a curve, mark the fabric first with chalk.

6 Trim the under collar seam allowance to half of its width, which will reduce the bulk.

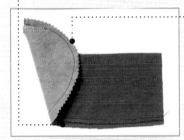

7 Trim around the curve with pinking shears, reducing both layers. This will allow the fabric to turn.

8 Clip the curve on the collar using small cuts at 90 degrees to the stitching line, clipping through the pinked seam.

9 Press the seam allowance of the upper collar on to the collar.

10 While the collar is still warm from the steam iron, turn to the right side.

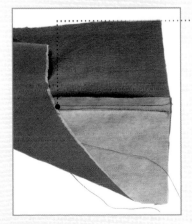

11 Working from the inside of the collar, push all the seam allowance towards the under collar and machine it to the under collar. This is called understitching and will hold the collar in shape.

12 Understitch as far through the curve as you can.

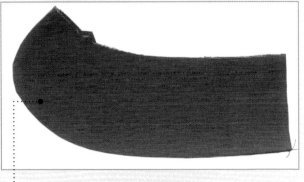

13 Press the curved edge flat on the right side, making sure the seam is pushed out completely.

Attaching a flat collar

A flat collar can be attached to the neckline by means of a facing. Depending upon the style of the garment, the facing may go all around the neck, which is usually found on garments with centre back openings, or just be at the front. The collar with no back facing has to be attached to the garment in stages.

FLAT ROUND COLLAR WITH NO BACK FACING

1 Construct the collar (see page 183).

2 Mark the centre front points on the garment and the collar with tailor's tacks.

3 Place the collar to the neckline, right side to right side. Match the notches.

Grown-on front facing, interfaced to foldline

4 Pin in place, pinning just to the tailor's tacks.

5 Snip the collar at the tailor's tacks. The collar should be loose across the back neck.

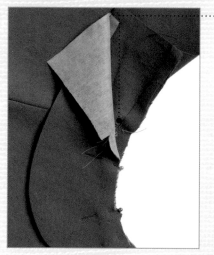

6 Machine the under collar across the back of the neck first, stitching from tailor's tack to tailor's tack. Keep the upper collar clear of stitching.

7 Fold back the shoulder seam allowance on the grown-on facing and press. Then fold the facing over the front edge of the collar.

8 Match the tailor's tacks in the collar and facing, and match the notches.

9 Machine from the centre front to the tailor's tack at the shoulder point.

Shoulder point

10 Trim the seam allowance.

11 Turn through to the right side and press.

12 At the centre back, turn under the seam allowance on the upper collar and hand stitch across the back neck with a flat fell or blind hem stitch.

FLAT ROUND COLLAR WITH A FULL FACING

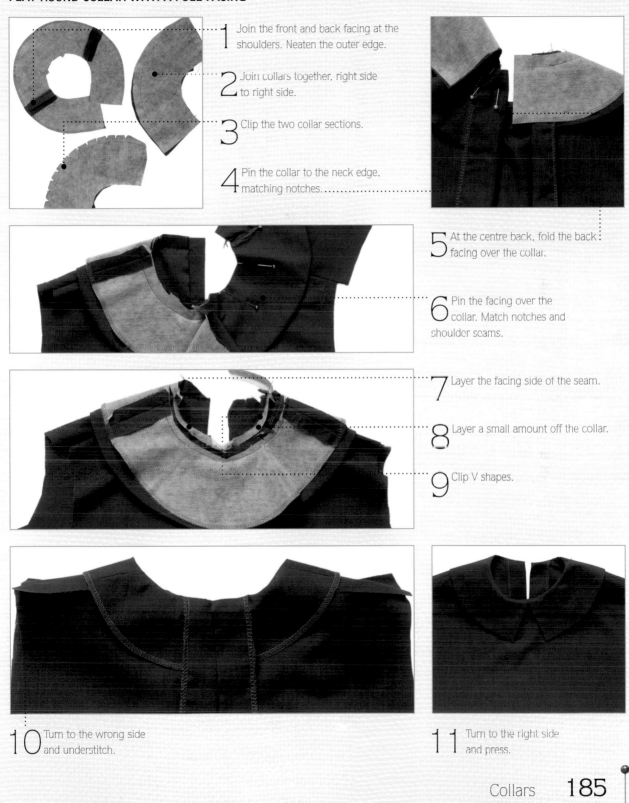

1 Join the front and back facing at the shoulders. Neaten the outer edge.

2 Join collars together, right side to right side.

3 Clip the two collar sections.

4 Pin the collar to the neck edge, matching notches.

5 At the centre back, fold the back facing over the collar.

6 Pin the facing over the collar. Match notches and shoulder seams.

7 Layer the facing side of the seam.

8 Layer a small amount off the collar.

9 Clip V shapes.

10 Turn to the wrong side and understitch.

11 Turn to the right side and press.

Stand collar

Also called a mandarin collar, this collar stands upright around the neck. It is normally cut from a straight piece of fabric, with shaping at the centre front edges. For a very close-fitting stand collar, the collar is cut with a slight curve.

1 Apply a fusible interfacing to the upper collar (see page 183). Insert any tailor's tacks as indicated on the pattern.

2 Pin the upper collar, interfacing side out, to the neckline of the garment, matching any notches and tailor's tacks at the centre front edge.

3 Machine the upper collar to the neckline using a 1.5cm (⅝in) seam allowance. Make sure the stitching stops at the tailor's tack at the front edge.

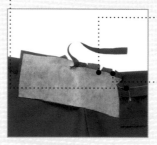

4 Reduce the seam allowance on the upper collar by half.

5 Clip though the seam allowances – this will allow the fabric to relax into shape when pressed later.

Wrong side of collar

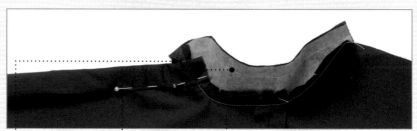

6 Working from the wrong side of the garment, turn in the centre front edge as indicated by the pattern. This will leave the front edge of the collar proud of the garment.

7 Pin the under collar to the upper collar, right side to right side, along the top edge.

8 Machine the two pieces together using a 1.5cm (⅝in) seam allowance.

9 At the centre front, the reduced neck seam allowance needs to be pointing up into the collar, so that the machining attaching the two collar sections together goes over it. Be sure the machining is in line with the centre front of the garment.

Wrong side

10 Reduce the seam allowance to half its width on the under collar side of the seam (the non-interfaced side).

11 Clip V shapes out of the seam allowance to reduce the bulk. Be careful not to cut through the stitching.

12 Press the seam as it has been stitched, and while warm turn to the right side.

13 Turn under the lower edge seam allowance on the under collar and tack in place around the neck edge.

14 Make sure the two leading front edges of the collar are symmetrical.

15 Use a flat fell stitch to secure the under collar at the neck edge.

Shawl collar

A shawl collar, which is a deep V-neck shape that combines both collar and rever in one, gives a flattering neckline that is often found on blouses and jackets. Although the collar looks complicated, it is straightforward to make. The under collar is usually part of the front of the garment.

1 Join the garment fronts together at the centre back and press the seam open.

2 Stay stitch the corner of the neck/shoulder at the top of the dart through the tailor's tack.

3 Slash to the tailor's tack.

4 Make the darts in the front – these will form the roll line of the collar.

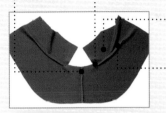

5 Join the back sections of the garment together at the centre back and press the seam open.

6 Join the front to the back across the shoulder seams, stopping at the slash.

7 Join the front of the garment to the back across the back neck, working from slash line to slash line. Press open.

Centre back

8 Apply a fusible interfacing to the upper collar (see page 183). Tailor tack to mark the shoulder/neck point.

9 Join the two upper collar sections together at the centre back.

10 Pin the upper collar to the garment, matching the centre back seams and any notches. Machine in place using a 1.5cm (⅝in) seam.

11 Trim the seam allowance on the under collar side (the non-interfaced side) by half. Clip V shapes into the seam to reduce the bulk.

12 Press the seam as it has been stitched and turn to the right side while still warm.

13 Press on the right side so the seam falls slightly to the wrong side, to avoid it showing on the right side.

14 At the back neck, turn under the raw edge and hand stitch in place with a flat fell stitch. Neaten the other raw edges of the upper collar by your preferred technique.

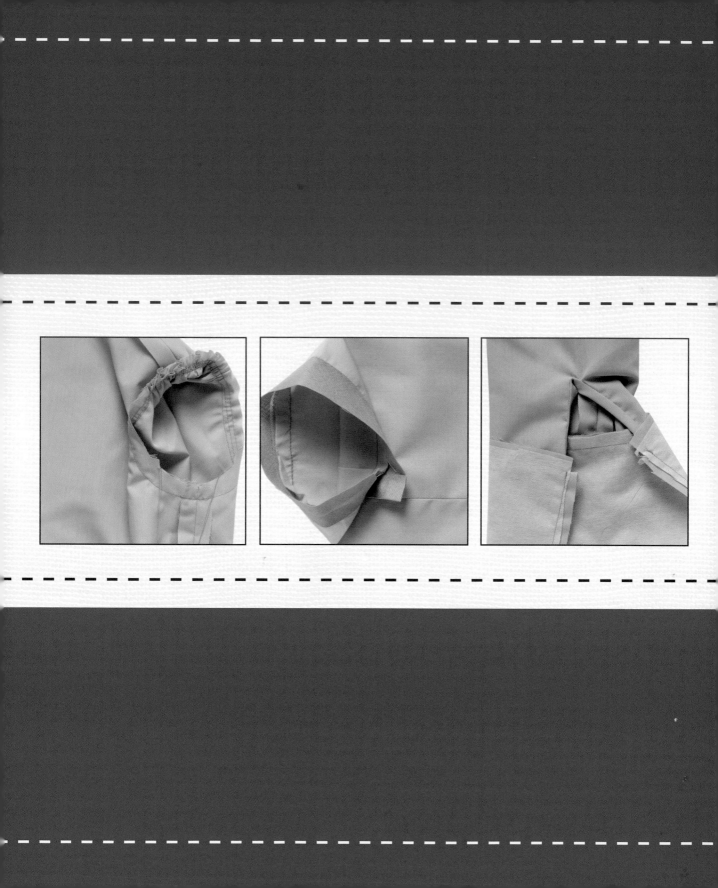

SLEEVES AND SLEEVE FINISHES

Sleeves

A few sleeves, such as the dolman, are cut as part of the garment, but most sleeves, including set-in and raglan, are made separately and then inserted into the armhole. Whichever type of sleeve is being inserted, always place it to the armhole and not the armhole to the sleeve – in other words, always work with the sleeve facing you.

Directory of sleeves

SET-IN SLEEVE (SHORT)

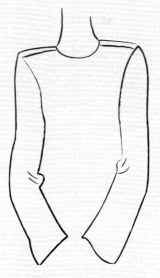

SET-IN SLEEVE (LONG)

CAP SLEEVE

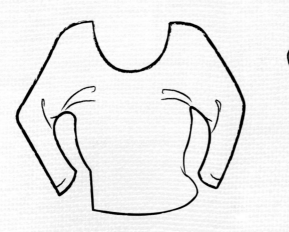

DOLMAN SLEEVE

PUFF SLEEVE

Inserting a set-in sleeve

A set-in sleeve should feature a smooth sleeve head that fits on the end of your shoulder accurately. This is achieved by the use of ease stitches, which are long stitches used to tighten the fabric but not gather it.

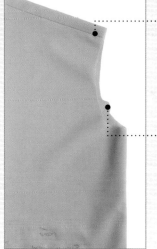

1 Machine the side seams and the shoulder seams on the garment and press them open.

Armhole with notches

Single notch denotes front of the sleeve

2 Machine the seam of the sleeve and press open. Turn the sleeve to the right side.

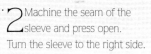
Double notch denotes back of the sleeve

3 Around the sleeve head, work two rows of long stitches between the notches – one row at 1cm (⅜in) from the edge and the second row at 1.2cm (½in). These are the ease stitches.

4 Place the sleeve into the armhole, right side to right side. Match the underarm seams and the notches.

5 Match the highest point of the sleeve to the shoulder.

6 Pull up the ease stitches until the sleeve fits neatly in the armhole.

7 Pin from the sleeve side.

8 Machine the sleeve in, starting at the underarm seam, using a 1.5cm (⅝in) seam allowance. Machine so that the sleeve is uppermost and keep the machining straight over the shoulder.

9 Overlap the machining at the underarm to reinforce the stitching.

10 Stitch around the sleeve again inside the seam allowance.

11 Trim the raw edges of the sleeve.

Right side of the garment

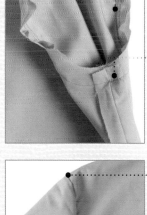

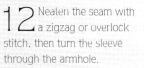
Smooth sleeve head

12 Neaten the seam with a zigzag or overlock stitch, then turn the sleeve through the armhole.

Flat sleeve construction

On shirts and children's clothes, sleeves are inserted flat prior to the side seams being constructed. This technique can be difficult on some fabrics, such as those firmly woven, because no ease stitches are used.

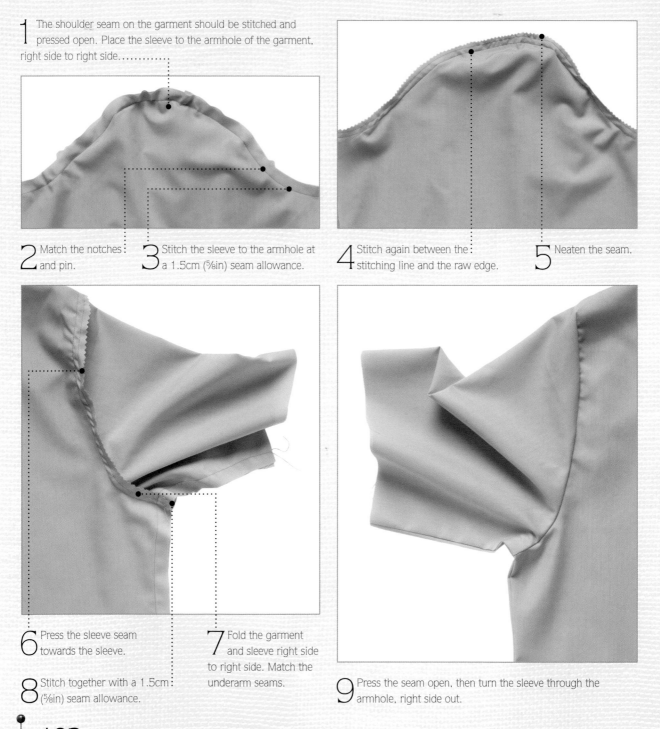

1 The shoulder seam on the garment should be stitched and pressed open. Place the sleeve to the armhole of the garment, right side to right side.

2 Match the notches and pin.

3 Stitch the sleeve to the armhole at a 1.5cm (⅝in) seam allowance.

4 Stitch again between the stitching line and the raw edge.

5 Neaten the seam.

6 Press the sleeve seam towards the sleeve.

7 Fold the garment and sleeve right side to right side. Match the underarm seams.

8 Stitch together with a 1.5cm (⅝in) seam allowance.

9 Press the seam open, then turn the sleeve through the armhole, right side out.

Puff sleeve

A sleeve that has a gathered sleeve head is referred to as a puff sleeve or gathered sleeve. It is one of the easiest sleeves to insert because the gathers take up any spare fabric.

1 Machine stitch the sleeve, right side to right side, using a 1.5cm (⅝in) seam allowance. Press the seam open.

3 Place the sleeve into the armhole, right side to right side.

4 Match the notches and the underarm seams.

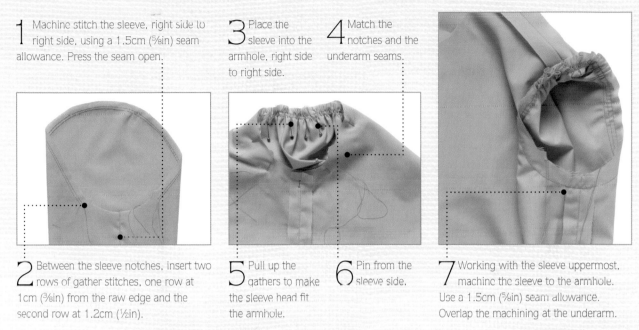

2 Between the sleeve notches, insert two rows of gather stitches, one row at 1cm (⅜in) from the raw edge and the second row at 1.2cm (½in).

5 Pull up the gathers to make the sleeve head fit the armhole.

6 Pin from the sleeve side.

7 Working with the sleeve uppermost, machine the sleeve to the armhole. Use a 1.5cm (⅝in) seam allowance. Overlap the machining at the underarm.

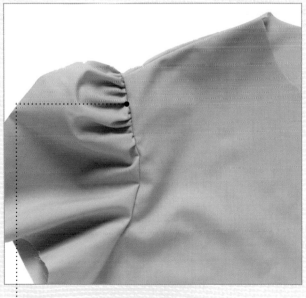

8 Stitch around the sleeve seam again between the seam stitching and the raw edge.

9 Trim away the surplus fabric by 5mm (³⁄₁₆in).

10 Neaten the seam.

11 Turn right side out – all the gathers will be at the top of the sleeve.

Raglan sleeve

A raglan sleeve can be constructed as a one-piece sleeve or a two-piece sleeve. The armhole seam on a raglan sleeve runs diagonally from the armhole to the neck.

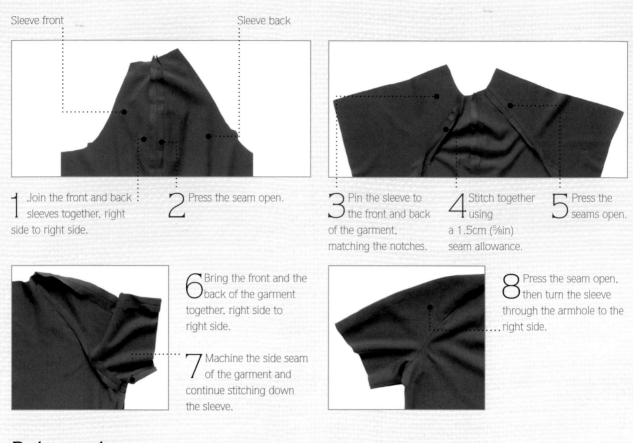

Sleeve front

Sleeve back

1 Join the front and back sleeves together, right side to right side.

2 Press the seam open.

3 Pin the sleeve to the front and back of the garment, matching the notches.

4 Stitch together using a 1.5cm (⅝in) seam allowance.

5 Press the seams open.

6 Bring the front and the back of the garment together, right side to right side.

7 Machine the side seam of the garment and continue stitching down the sleeve.

8 Press the seam open, then turn the sleeve through the armhole to the right side.

Dolman sleeve

A dolman sleeve is cut as an extension to a garment. As the armhole is very loose, it is ideal for a coat or jacket. The dolman sleeve often has a raglan shoulder pad to define the shoulder end.

1 The back and the front of the garment feature the same shape from neck to sleeve end. Stitch the back and front together along the shoulder/sleeve seam.

2 Stitch the underarm/side seam.

3 Clip V shapes under the arm.

4 Press the seams open, then turn the sleeve through the armhole to the right side.

Sleeve edge finishes

The lower edge of a sleeve has to be finished according to the style of the garment being made. Some sleeves are finished tight into the arm or wrist, while others may have a more decorative or functional finish.

Directory of sleeve edge finishes

EDGE WITH BIAS-BOUND HEM

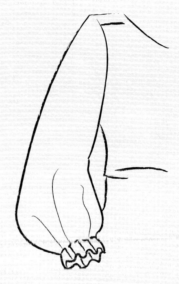

ELASTICATED EDGE

EDGE WITH RUFFLE

ELASTICATED EDGE WITH A HEADING

EDGE WITH SELF HEM

Sleeve hems

The simplest way to finish a sleeve is to make a small hem, which can be part of the sleeve or additional fabric that is attached to turn up. A self hem is where the edge of the sleeve is turned up on to itself. If there is insufficient fabric to turn up, a bias binding can be used to create the hem. You can use purchased bias binding or make your own bias strips.

SELF HEM

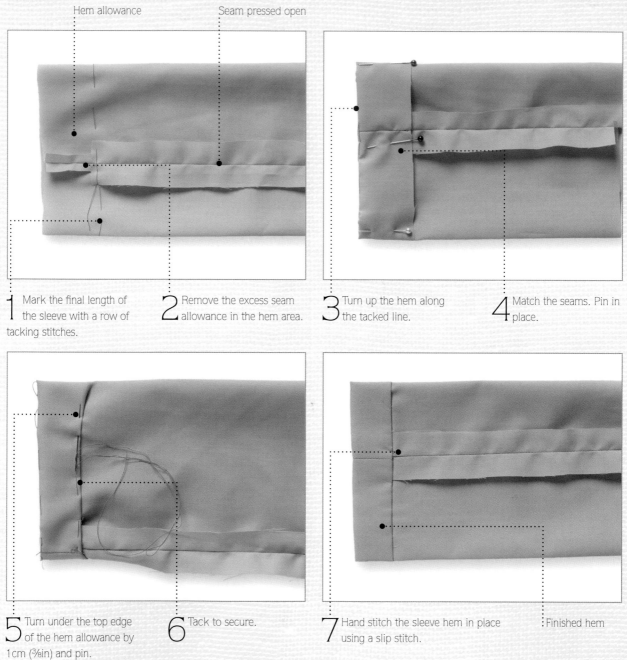

Hem allowance

Seam pressed open

1 Mark the final length of the sleeve with a row of tacking stitches.

2 Remove the excess seam allowance in the hem area.

3 Turn up the hem along the tacked line.

4 Match the seams. Pin in place.

5 Turn under the top edge of the hem allowance by 1cm (⅜in) and pin.

6 Tack to secure.

7 Hand stitch the sleeve hem in place using a slip stitch.

Finished hem

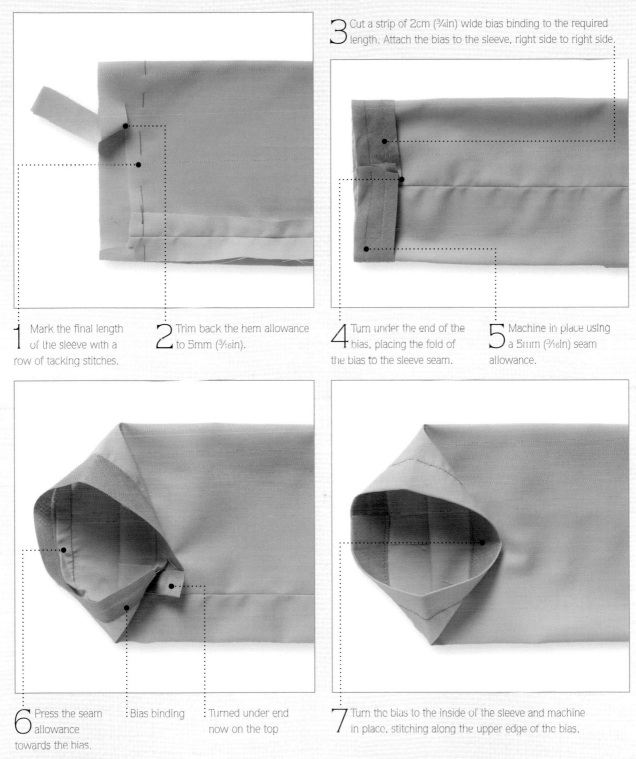

3 Cut a strip of 2cm (¾in) wide bias binding to the required length. Attach the bias to the sleeve, right side to right side.

1 Mark the final length of the sleeve with a row of tacking stitches.

2 Trim back the hem allowance to 5mm (³⁄₁₆in).

4 Turn under the end of the bias, placing the fold of the bias to the sleeve seam.

5 Machine in place using a 5mm (³⁄₁₆in) seam allowance.

6 Press the seam allowance towards the bias.

Bias binding

Turned under end now on the top

7 Turn the bias to the inside of the sleeve and machine in place, stitching along the upper edge of the bias.

Elasticated sleeve edge

The ends of sleeves on workwear and children's clothes are often elasticated to produce a neat and functional finish. Elastic that is 12mm (½in) or 25mm (1in) wide will be most suitable.

1 Make up the sleeve and press the seam open.

3 Turn up 5mm (³⁄₁₆in) at the raw edge and press.

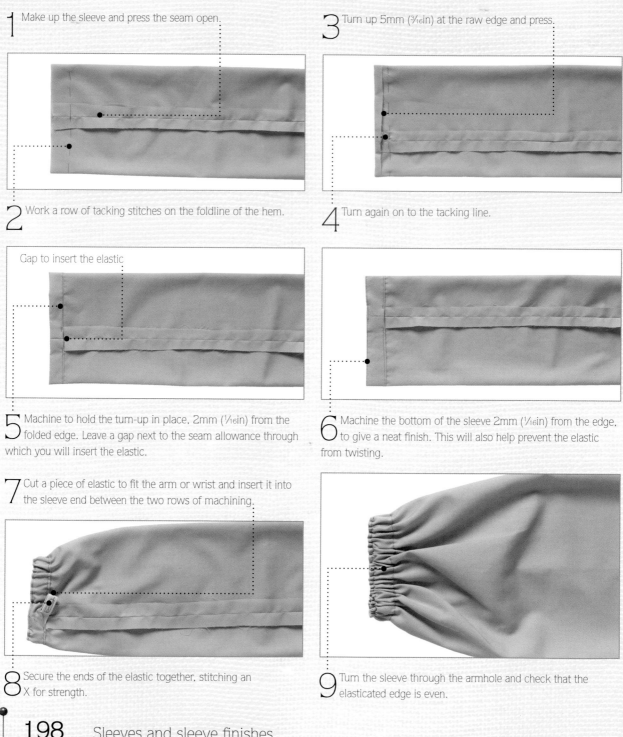

2 Work a row of tacking stitches on the foldline of the hem.

4 Turn again on to the tacking line.

Gap to insert the elastic

5 Machine to hold the turn-up in place, 2mm (¹⁄₁₆in) from the folded edge. Leave a gap next to the seam allowance through which you will insert the elastic.

6 Machine the bottom of the sleeve 2mm (¹⁄₁₆in) from the edge, to give a neat finish. This will also help prevent the elastic from twisting.

7 Cut a piece of elastic to fit the arm or wrist and insert it into the sleeve end between the two rows of machining.

8 Secure the ends of the elastic together, stitching an X for strength.

9 Turn the sleeve through the armhole and check that the elasticated edge is even.

A casing on a sleeve edge

A casing is often used on the edge of a sleeve to insert elastic into, which will allow you to gather the sleeve in a specific place. The casing may be grown-on, which means it is part of the sleeve, or it may be applied separately. The photographs below show an applied casing of bias binding.

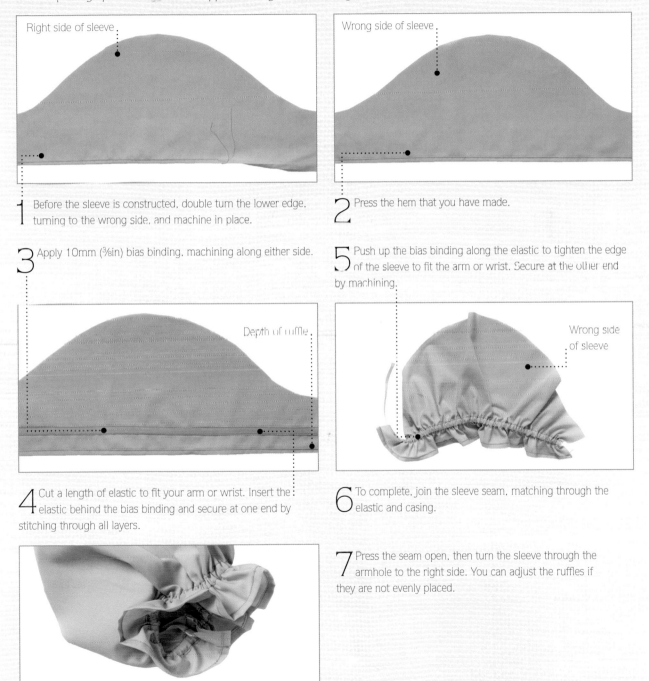

Right side of sleeve

Wrong side of sleeve

1 Before the sleeve is constructed, double turn the lower edge, turning to the wrong side, and machine in place.

2 Press the hem that you have made.

3 Apply 10mm (⅜in) bias binding, machining along either side.

Depth of ruffle

5 Push up the bias binding along the elastic to tighten the edge of the sleeve to fit the arm or wrist. Secure at the other end by machining.

Wrong side of sleeve

4 Cut a length of elastic to fit your arm or wrist. Insert the elastic behind the bias binding and secure at one end by stitching through all layers.

6 To complete, join the sleeve seam, matching through the elastic and casing.

7 Press the seam open, then turn the sleeve through the armhole to the right side. You can adjust the ruffles if they are not evenly placed.

Cuffs and openings

A cuff and an opening are ways of producing a sleeve finish that will fit neatly around the wrist. The opening enables the hand to fit through the end of the sleeve, and it allows the sleeve to be rolled up. There are various types of cuffs – single or double, and with pointed or curved edges. All cuffs are interfaced, with the interfacing attached to the upper cuff. The upper cuff is sewn to the sleeve.

Directory of cuffs and openings

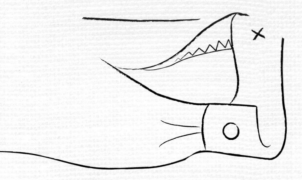

SINGLE CUFF WITH FACED OPENING

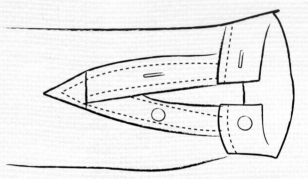

SINGLE CUFF WITH PLACKET OPENING

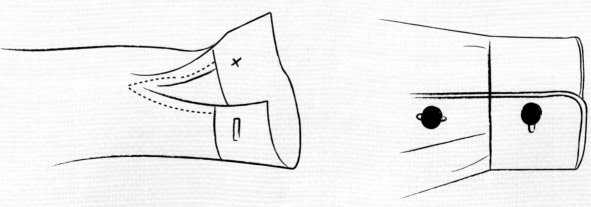

SINGLE CUFF WITH BOUND OPENING

SHIRT CUFF

Faced opening

Adding a facing to the area of the sleeve where the opening is to be is a neat method of finishing. This type of opening is appropriate to use with a one-piece cuff.

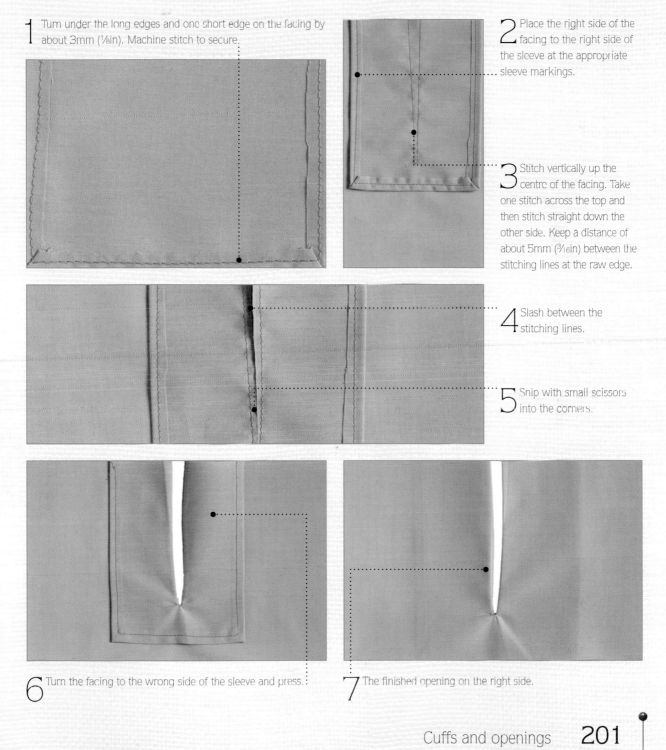

1 Turn under the long edges and one short edge on the facing by about 3mm (⅛in). Machine stitch to secure.

2 Place the right side of the facing to the right side of the sleeve at the appropriate sleeve markings.

3 Stitch vertically up the centre of the facing. Take one stitch across the top and then stitch straight down the other side. Keep a distance of about 5mm (³⁄₁₆in) between the stitching lines at the raw edge.

4 Slash between the stitching lines.

5 Snip with small scissors into the corners.

6 Turn the facing to the wrong side of the sleeve and press.

7 The finished opening on the right side.

Bound opening

On a fabric that frays badly or a sleeve that may get a great deal of wear, a strong bound opening is a good idea. It involves binding a slash in the sleeve with a matching bias strip.

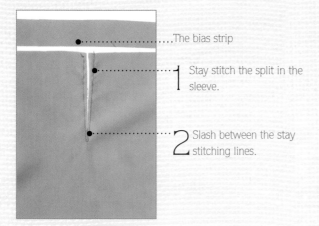

The bias strip

1 Stay stitch the split in the sleeve.

2 Slash between the stay stitching lines.

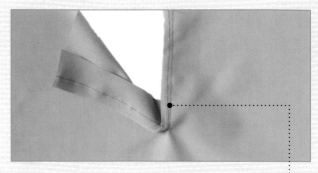

3 Working on the right side of the sleeve, pin the bias strip along the stay stitching lines. To stitch around the top of the split, open the split out into a straight line.

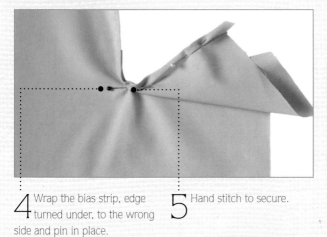

4 Wrap the bias strip, edge turned under, to the wrong side and pin in place.

5 Hand stitch to secure.

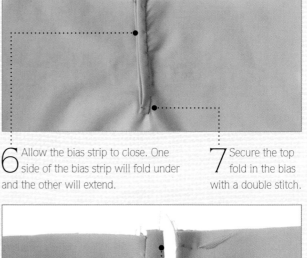

6 Allow the bias strip to close. One side of the bias strip will fold under and the other will extend.

7 Secure the top fold in the bias with a double stitch.

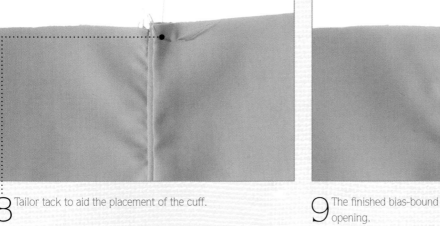

8 Tailor tack to aid the placement of the cuff.

9 The finished bias-bound opening.

Bias strip folded and secured at top

One-piece cuff

> A one-piece cuff is cut out from the fabric in one piece, and in most cases only half of it is interfaced. The exception is the one-piece double cuff (see page 207).

1 Apply fusible interfacing to the half of the cuff that will be the upper cuff.

3 Fold the cuff in half, right side to right side.

Seam allowance free on interfaced side of cuff.

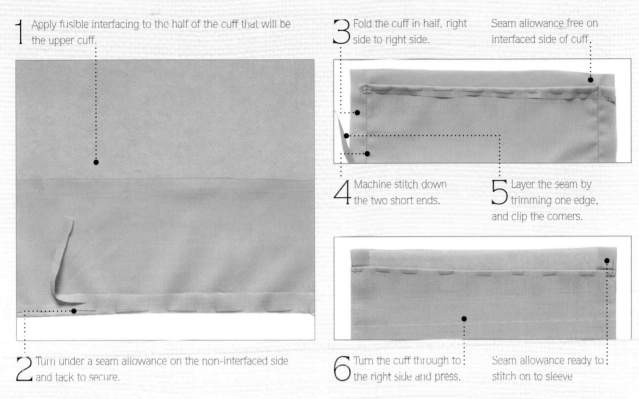

4 Machine stitch down the two short ends.

5 Layer the seam by trimming one edge, and clip the corners.

2 Turn under a seam allowance on the non-interfaced side and tack to secure.

6 Turn the cuff through to the right side and press.

Seam allowance ready to stitch on to sleeve

Two-piece cuff

> Some cuffs are cut in two pieces: an upper cuff and an under cuff. The upper cuff piece is interfaced.

1 Apply fusible interfacing to the upper cuff.

2 Turn under a seam allowance on the under cuff and tack in place.

Seam allowance on upper cuff free

4 Machine stitch the two short ends together. Also machine together along the lower edge.

5 Layer the seam and clip the corner.

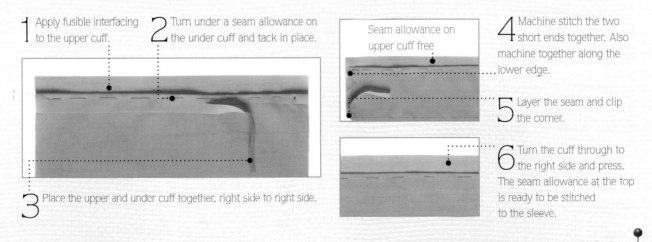

3 Place the upper and under cuff together, right side to right side.

6 Turn the cuff through to the right side and press. The seam allowance at the top is ready to be stitched to the sleeve.

Shirt sleeve placket

This is the opening that is found on the sleeves of men's shirts and tailored ladies' shirts. It looks complicated but is straightforward if you take it one step at a time.

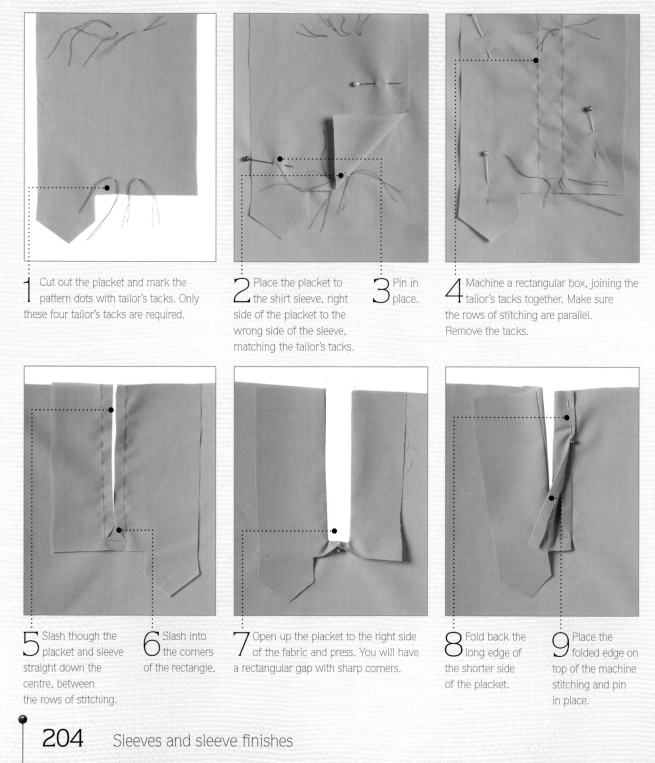

1 Cut out the placket and mark the pattern dots with tailor's tacks. Only these four tailor's tacks are required.

2 Place the placket to the shirt sleeve, right side of the placket to the wrong side of the sleeve, matching the tailor's tacks.

3 Pin in place.

4 Machine a rectangular box, joining the tailor's tacks together. Make sure the rows of stitching are parallel. Remove the tacks.

5 Slash though the placket and sleeve straight down the centre, between the rows of stitching.

6 Slash into the corners of the rectangle.

7 Open up the placket to the right side of the fabric and press. You will have a rectangular gap with sharp corners.

8 Fold back the long edge of the shorter side of the placket.

9 Place the folded edge on top of the machine stitching and pin in place.

10 Machine the folded edge. Stop the machining at the top of the gap.

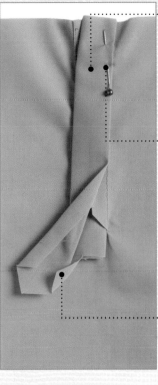

11 Fold the other side of the placket across the shorter side.

12 Press under the long edge. Fold back so that the pressed under edge is on the machining line. Pin in place.

13 Fold under the top pointed end, following the cut edge, and press.

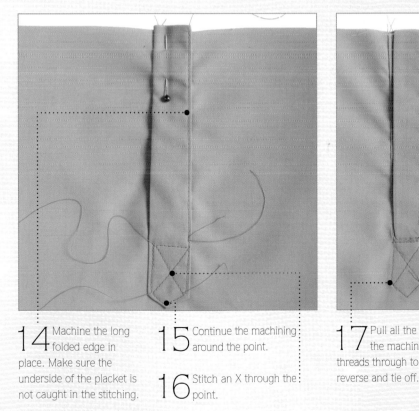

14 Machine the long folded edge in place. Make sure the underside of the placket is not caught in the stitching.

15 Continue the machining around the point.

16 Stitch an X through the point.

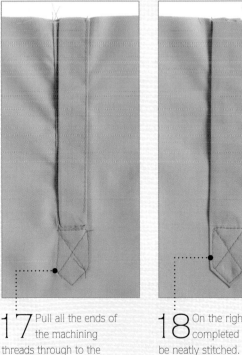

17 Pull all the ends of the machining threads through to the reverse and tie off.

18 On the right side, the completed placket will be neatly stitched.

Attaching a cuff

There are various types of cuff that can be attached to sleeve openings. The one-piece lapped cuff works well with a bound or faced opening. A two-piece shirt cuff is usually on a sleeve with a placket opening, but works equally well on a bound opening. The double cuff, or French cuff, is for men's dress shirts and tailored shirts for both ladies and men, and may be cut in one or two sections. It is usually found with a placket or bound opening.

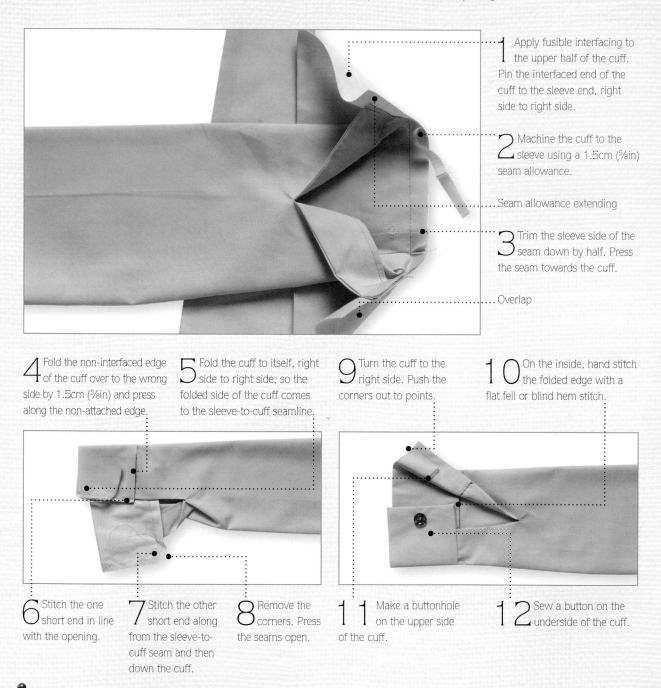

1 Apply fusible interfacing to the upper half of the cuff. Pin the interfaced end of the cuff to the sleeve end, right side to right side.

2 Machine the cuff to the sleeve using a 1.5cm (⅝in) seam allowance.

Seam allowance extending

3 Trim the sleeve side of the seam down by half. Press the seam towards the cuff.

Overlap

4 Fold the non-interfaced edge of the cuff over to the wrong side by 1.5cm (⅝in) and press along the non-attached edge.

5 Fold the cuff to itself, right side to right side, so the folded side of the cuff comes to the sleeve-to-cuff seamline.

9 Turn the cuff to the right side. Push the corners out to points.

10 On the inside, hand stitch the folded edge with a flat fell or blind hem stitch.

6 Stitch the one short end in line with the opening.

7 Stitch the other short end along from the sleeve-to-cuff seam and then down the cuff.

8 Remove the corners. Press the seams open.

11 Make a buttonhole on the upper side of the cuff.

12 Sew a button on the underside of the cuff.

SHIRT CUFF

1 Apply fusible interfacing to the upper cuff. Place it to the sleeve end, right side to right side, with a seam allowance extending at either end. Pin in place.

2 Machine using a 1.5cm (⅝in) seam allowance.

3 Place the right side of the under cuff to the right side of the upper cuff. Machine together around three sides, stitching in line with the sleeve opening.

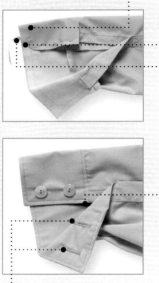

4 Trim down the under cuff side of the seam.

5 Remove bulk from the corners. Press.

6 Turn the cuff to the right side and press.

7 Turn under the raw edge of the under cuff and place to the end of the sleeve. With this type of cuff, the edge is machined in place.

8 Add buttonholes to the upper cuff and attach buttons to the under cuff.

DOUBLE CUFF

1 Apply interfacing to the whole of the cuff. Attach the cuff to the sleeve end, right side to right side, using a 1.5cm (⅝in) seam allowance.

2 Fold the cuff back on to itself, right side to right side.

3 Machine stitch the two sides in line with the sleeve opening.

4 Trim the bulk from the seams and corners.

5 Press, then turn the cuff through to the right side.

6 Fold the cuff up in half so that it is doubled.

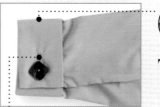

7 Hand stitch inside to finish the other edge of the cuff.

8 Insert a buttonhole through the top two layers of the cuff and sew a button on to the under cuff.

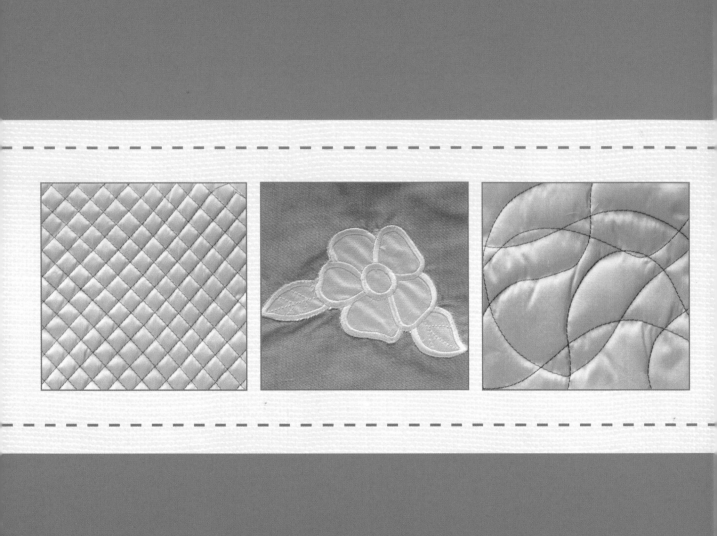

DECORATIVE TECHNIQUES

Finishing touches

Simple finishing touches can be used to good effect on many items. The term appliqué applies to one fabric being stitched to another in a decorative manner. The fabric to be appliquéd must be interfaced to support the fabric that is to be attached. Appliqué can be drawn by hand, then cut and stitched down, or it can be created by a computer pattern on the embroidery machine. The embroidery machine can also be used to create quilting, or this can be done by hand or with a sewing machine.

Hand-drawn appliqué

This technique involves drawing the chosen design on to a piece of double-sided fusible web, after which the design is fused in place on fabric prior to being stitched.

1 Draw a decorative shape, such as a flower, on to a piece of double-sided fusible web.

2 Using the iron, fuse the web on to your chosen fabric.

3 Cut out the shape from the fabric.

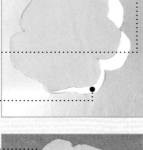

4 Place the shape, fusible web side down, where it is to be positioned on fabric and fuse in place.

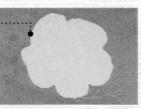

5 Using a wide, close zigzag stitch, stitch around the shape.

6 For a flower, stitch on top of the fabric appliqué to make petal shapes.

Machine appliqué

There are designs available for appliqué if you have an embroidery machine. You will need to use a special fusible embroidery backer on both the fabric for the appliqué and the base fabric.

1 Place the base fabric and appliqué fabric in the embroidery hoop and stitch out the first part of the design.

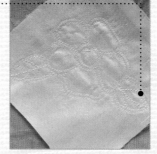

2 Trim the appliqué fabric back to the stitching lines.

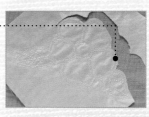

3 Complete the computerized embroidery.

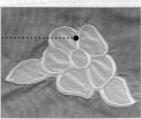

Quilting

This is a technique that involves stitching through two layers of fabric, one of which is a wadding. The stitching sinks into the wadding, creating a padded effect. Quilting can be done by hand, with a sewing machine, or using computerized embroidery.

COMPONENTS OF QUILTING

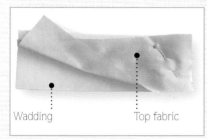

Wadding   Top fabric

HORIZONTAL QUILTING

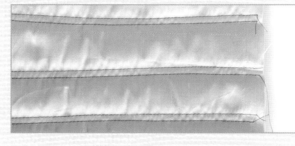

Tack the wadding and top fabric together. Stitch double lines with spaces between. Use a stitch length of 4.0 on your machine.

DIAMOND QUILTING

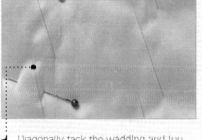

1 Diagonally tack the wadding and top fabric together.

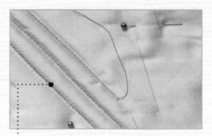

2 Set the machine to a stitch length of 4.0, with the needle on the one side of the foot. Stitch rows of machining diagonally across. Use the width of the machine foot as a guide to keep the rows parallel.

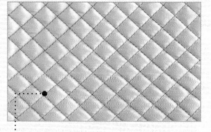

3 Stitch parallel rows in the opposite diagonal directions, to create diamond shapes.

← COMPUTERIZED QUILTING
Tack the wadding and top fabric together, then stitch on a quilted pattern with the embroidery machine.

FREEFORM QUILTING →
Tack the wadding and top fabric together. Stitch at random.

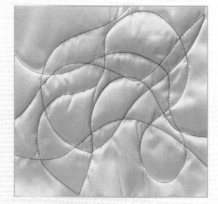

Roses and bows

On special-occasion wear a rose can add a superb finishing touch. When the raw edges of a rose are exposed, as in version 2 below, it also looks great made in tweed and suiting fabrics, to add a decorative finish to a tailored jacket. A bow that is permanently fixed in place is a beautiful embellishment on bridal wear.

ROSE VERSION 1

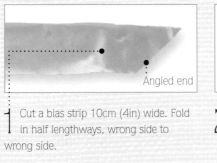

Angled end

1 Cut a bias strip 10cm (4in) wide. Fold in half lengthways, wrong side to wrong side.

2 Pin the raw edges together.

3 Insert two rows of gather stitches at the raw edge – one row at 1cm (⅜in) from the edge and the other row at 1.3cm (½in).

4 Pull up the gathers, grouping them together and leaving spaces between the groups. The groups and spaces will give the impression of petals.

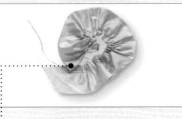

5 Hold the lower edge of one end in your left hand and loosely wrap the strip around.

6 When you have a rose shape, tuck any raw edges that show into the base.

7 Secure at the base edge with hand stitches.

ROSE VERSION 2

1 Cut a bias strip 10cm (4in) wide.

2 Insert two rows of gather stitches along the centre of the strip. Leave a gap of 3mm (⅛in) between the rows of stitching.

3 Pull up the gathers into groups and spaces (see step 4 above).

4 The groups and spaces will pull up to give a diagonal effect. Fold in half along the stitching lines.

5 Hold the end of the gathers in your left hand and wrap the strip around loosely.

6 Secure at the base with hand stitches. Although the edge is raw, fraying is minimal as the strip has been bias-cut.

BOW

1 To make the loops, cut a piece of silk or other fabric that is four times the length of the loop required and twice the width plus seam allowances.

2 Interline with dress net to the wrong side. Tack the net around the raw edge.

3 Fold in half, right side to right side. Stitch along the raw edge leaving a 1.5cm (⅝in) seam allowance.

4 Turn through to the right side. Fold so that the seamline is in the centre.

5 Bring the short end to the centre. Pin in place.

6 Tack through the centre, using double thread.

7 Pull along the tacking stitches to gather the centre.

8 Next make the two ends. Cut two pieces of fabric the required finished length and twice the required width plus seam allowances.

9 Tack dress net to the fabric.

10 Fold each piece of fabric in half, right side to right side, and stitch along the long raw edge and at an angle at one end.

11 Remove bulk from the corners.

12 Turn through to the right side. Press. Make sure there are sharp points.

13 To assemble the bow, wrap a piece of fabric around the gathered centre of the loops and stitch in place by hand.

14 Scrunch the raw ends of the ends together and hand stitch behind the loop.

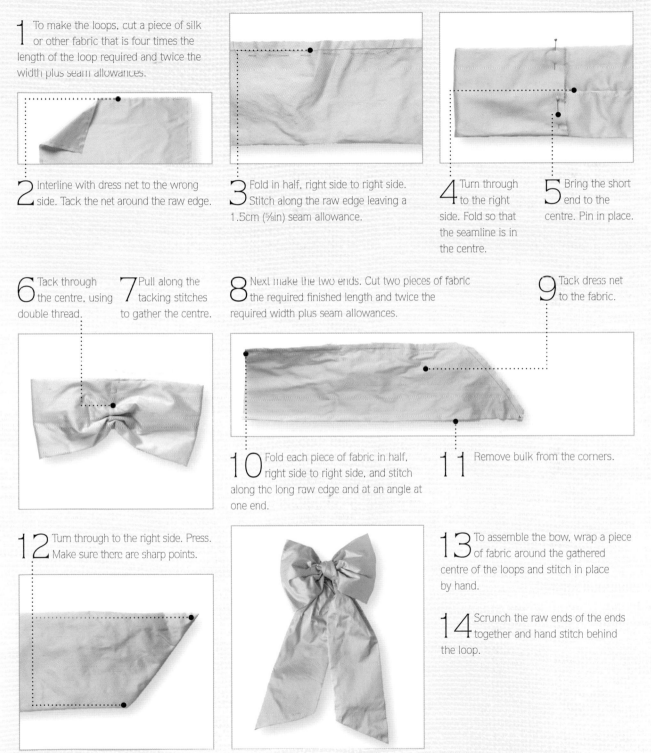

Glossary

Appliqué
One piece of fabric being stitched to another in a decorative manner.

Back stitch
A strong hand stitch with a double stitch on the wrong side, used for outlining and seaming.

Bias
45-degree line on fabric that falls between the lengthways and the crossways grain. Fabric cut on the bias drapes well. *See also* Grain.

Bias binding
Narrow strips of fabric cut on the bias. Used to give a neat finish to hems and seam allowances.

Binding
Method of finishing a raw edge by wrapping it in a strip of bias-cut fabric.

Blanket stitch
Hand stitch worked along the raw or finished edge of fabric to neaten, and for decorative purposes.

Blind hem stitch
Tiny hand stitch used to attach one piece of fabric to another, mainly to secure hems. Also a machine stitch consisting of two or three straight stitches and one wide zigzag stitch.

Blind tuck
A tuck that is stitched so that it touches the adjacent tuck without machine stitches showing. *See also* Tuck.

Bodice
Upper body section of a garment.

Boning
Narrow nylon, plastic, or metal strip, available in various widths, that is used for stiffening and shaping close-fitting garments, such as bodices.

Box pleat
Pleat formed on the wrong side of the fabric, and fuller than a knife pleat. *See also* Pleat.

Buttonhole
Opening through which a button is inserted to form a fastening. Buttonholes are usually machine stitched but may also be worked by hand or piped for reinforcement or decorative effect.

Buttonhole stitch
Hand stitch that wraps over the raw edges of a buttonhole to neaten and strengthen them. Machine-stitched buttonholes are worked with a close zigzag stitch.

Button shank
Stem of a button that allows room for the buttonhole to fit under the button when joined.

Casing
Tunnel of fabric created by parallel rows of stitching, through which elastic or a drawstring cord is threaded. Often used at a waist edge. Sometimes extra fabric is required to make a casing; this can be applied to the inside or outside of the garment.

Contour dart
Also known as double-pointed dart, this is used to give shape at the waist of a garment. It is like two darts joined together. *See also* Dart.

Crease
Line formed in fabric by pressing a fold.

Cross stitch
A temporary hand stitch used to hold pleats in place and to secure linings. It can also be used for decoration.

Cross tuck
Tuck that crosses over another by being stitched in opposite directions. *See also* Tuck.

Cutting line
Solid line on a pattern piece used as a guide for cutting out fabric.

Dart
Tapered stitched fold of fabric used on a garment to give it shape so that it can fit around the contours of the body. There are different types of dart, but all are used mainly on women's clothing.

Darted tuck
A tuck that can be used to give fullness of fabric at the bust or hip. *See also* Tuck.

Double-pointed dart
See Contour dart

Double ruffle
Decorative trim made from two plain ruffles where one side is longer than the other. Also a ruffle made from doubled fabric.

Drape
The way a fabric falls into graceful folds; drape varies with each fabric.

Drop
The length of fabric required to make a curtain, the "drop" being the measurement from top to bottom of the window.

Ease
Distributing fullness in fabric when joining two seams together of slightly different lengths, for example a sleeve to an armhole.

Ease stitch
Long machine stitch, used to ease in fullness where the distance between notches is greater on one seam edge than on the other.

Enclosed edge
Raw fabric edge that is concealed within a seam or binding.

Facing
Layer of fabric placed on the inside of a garment and used to finish off raw edges of an armhole or neck of a garment. Usually a separate piece of fabric, the facing can sometimes be an extension of the garment itself.

Felt
A natural wool fabric can felt when it is stimulated by friction and lubricated by moisture and the fibres bond together to form a cloth. Felting can also be done in a washing machine in a hot cycle.

Flat fell seam
See Run and fell seam.

Flat fell stitch
A strong, secure stitch used to hold two layers together permanently. Often used to secure linings and bias bindings.

French dart
Curved dart used on the front of a garment. See also Dart.

French seam
A seam traditionally used on sheer and silk fabrics. It is stitched twice, first on the right side of the work and then on the wrong side, enclosing the first seam.

Fusible tape
Straight grain tape used to stabilize edges and also replace stay stitching. The heat of the iron fuses it into position.

Galloon lace
Decorative lace trim shaped on both sides, used to edge a hem.

Gathers
Bunches of fabric created by sewing two parallel rows of loose stitching, then pulling the threads up so that the fabric gathers and reduces in size to fit the required space.

Goblet pleat
Decorative curtain heading in which the fabric is stitched into narrow tubes that are then stuffed with wadding. See also Pleat.

Grain
Lengthways and crossways direction of threads in a fabric. Fabric grain affects how a fabric hangs and drapes.

Gusset
Small piece of fabric shaped to fit into a slash or seam for added ease of movement.

Hem
The edge of a piece of fabric neatened and stitched to prevent unravelling. There are several methods of doing this, both by hand and by machine.

Hem allowance
Amount of fabric allowed for turning under to make the hem.

Hemline
Crease or foldline along which a hem is marked.

Hemming tape
Fusible tape with adhesive on both sides. Iron in place to fuse and secure hems that are difficult to hand stitch.

Herringbone stitch
Hand stitch used to secure hems and interlinings. This stitch is worked from left to right.

Herringbone weave
A zigzag weave where the weft yarn goes under and over warp yarns in a staggered pattern.

Hong Kong finish
A method of neatening raw edges particularly on wool and linen. Bias-cut strips are wrapped around the raw edge.

Interfacing

A fabric placed between garment and facing to give structure and support. Available in different thicknesses, interfacing can be fusible (bonds to the fabric by applying heat) or non-fusible (needs to be sewn to the fabric).

Interlining

Layer of fabric attached to the main fabric prior to construction, to cover the inside of an entire garment to provide extra warmth or bulk. The two layers are then treated as one. Often used in jackets and coats.

Keyhole buttonhole stitch

A machine buttonhole stitch characterized by having one square end while the other end is shaped like a loop to accommodate the button's shank without distorting the fabric. Often used on jackets.

Kick pleat

Inverted pleat extending upwards from the hemline of a narrow skirt to allow freedom when walking. *See also* Pleat.

Knife pleat

Pleat formed on the right side of the fabric where all the pleats face the same direction. *See also* Pleat.

Lapped seam

Used on fabrics that do not fray, such as suede and leather, the seam allowance of one edge is placed over the edge to be joined, then topstitched close to the overlapping edge. Also called an overlaid seam.

Lining

Underlying fabric layer used to give a neat finish to an item, as well as concealing the stitching and seams of a garment.

Locking stitch

A machine stitch where the upper and lower threads in the machine "lock" together at the start or end of a row of stitching.

Mitre

The diagonal line made where two edges of a piece of fabric meet at a corner, produced by folding.

Mock casing

Where there is an effect of a casing, but in fact elastic is attached to the waist, or is used only at the back in a partial casing.

Multi-size pattern

Paper pattern printed with cutting lines for a range of sizes on each pattern piece.

Nap

The raised pile on a fabric made during the weaving process, or a print pointing one way. When cutting out pattern pieces, ensure the nap runs in the same direction.

Notch

V-shaped marking on a pattern piece used for aligning one piece with another. Also V-shaped cut taken to reduce seam bulk.

Notion

An item of haberdashery, other than fabric, needed to complete a project, such as a button, zip, or elastic. Notions are normally listed on the pattern envelope.

Overedge stitch

Machine stitch worked over the edge of a seam allowance and used for neatening the edges of fabric.

Overlaid seam

See Lapped seam.

Pattern markings

Symbols printed on a paper pattern to indicate the fabric grain, foldline, and construction details, such as darts, notches, and tucks. These should be transferred to the fabric using tailor's chalk or tailor's tacks.

Pencil pleat

The most common curtain heading where the fabric forms a row of parallel vertical pleats. *See also* Pleat.

Pile

Raised loops on the surface of a fabric, for example velvet.

Pill

A small, fuzzy ball formed from tangled fibres which is formed on the surface of a fabric, making it look old and worn; it is often caused by friction. To remove fabric pills, stretch the fabric over a curved surface and carefully cut or shave off the pills.

Pinking

A method of neatening raw edges of fray-resistant fabric using pinking shears. This will leave a zigzag edge.

Pin tuck

Narrow, regularly spaced fold or gather. *See also* Tuck.

Piped tuck
See Corded tuck.

Piping
Trim made from bias-cut strips of fabric, usually containing a cord. Used to edge garments or soft furnishings.

Pivoting
Technique used to machine stitch a corner. The machine is stopped at the corner with the needle in the fabric, then the foot is raised, the fabric turned following the direction of the corner, and the foot lowered for stitching to continue.

Placket
An opening in a garment that provides support for fasteners, such as buttons, snaps, or zips.

Plain weave
The simplest of all the weaves; the weft yarn passes under one warp yarn, then over another one.

Pleat
An even fold or series of folds in fabric, often partially stitched down. Commonly found in skirts to shape the waistline, but also in soft furnishings for decoration.

Pocket flap
A piece of fabric that folds down to cover the opening of a pocket.

Raw edge
Cut edge of fabric that requires finishing, for example using zigzag stitch, to prevent fraying.

Rever
The turned-back front edge of a jacket or blouse to which the collar is attached.

Reverse stitch
Machine stitch that simply stitches back over a row of stitches to secure the threads.

Right side
The outer side of a fabric, or the visible part of a garment.

Rouleau loop
Button loop made from a strip of bias binding. It is used with a round ball-type button.

Round-end buttonhole stitch
Machine stitch characterized by one end of the buttonhole being square and the other being round, to allow for the button shank.

Ruching
Several lines of stitching worked to form a gathered area.

Ruffle
Decorative gathered trim made from one or two layers of fabric.

Run and fell seam
Also known as a flat fell seam, this seam is made on the right side of a garment and is very strong. It uses two lines of stitching and conceals all the raw edges, reducing fraying.

Running stitch
A simple, evenly spaced straight stitch separated by equal-sized spaces, used for seaming and gathering.

Seam
Stitched line where two edges of fabric are joined together.

Seam allowance
The amount of fabric allowed for on a pattern where sections are to be joined together by a seam; usually this is 1.5cm (⅝in).

Seam edge
The cut edge of a seam allowance.

Seamline
Line on paper pattern designated for stitching a seam; usually this is 1.5cm (⅝in) from the seam edge.

Selvedge
Finished edge on a woven fabric. This runs parallel to the warp (lengthways) threads.

Shell tuck
Decorative fold of fabric stitched in place with a scalloped edge. *See also* Tuck.

Shirring
Multiple rows of gathers sewn by machine. Often worked with shirring elastic in the bobbin to allow for stretch.

Slip hem stitch
Similar to herringbone stitch but is worked from right to left. It is used mainly for securing hems.

Straight stitch
Plain machine stitch, used for most applications. The length of the stitch can be altered to suit the fabric.

Stretch stitch
Machine stitch used for stretch knits and to help control difficult fabrics. It is worked with two stitches forwards and one backwards so that each stitch is worked three times.

Tacking stitch
A temporary running stitch used to hold pieces of fabric together or for transferring pattern markings to fabric.

Tailor's buttonhole
A buttonhole with one square end and one keyhole-shaped end, used on jackets and coats.

Tailor's tacks
Loose thread markings used to transfer symbols from a pattern to fabric.

Toile
A test or dry run of a paper pattern using calico. The toile helps you analyse the fit of the garment.

Top-stitch
Machine straight stitching worked on the right side of an item, close to the finished edge, for decorative effect. Sometimes stitched in a contrasting colour.

Top-stitched seam
A seam finished with a row of top-stitching for decorative effect. This seam is often used on crafts and soft furnishings as well as garments.

Trace tacking
A method of marking fold and placement lines on fabric. Loose stitches are sewn along the lines on the pattern to the fabric beneath, then the thread loops are cut and the pattern removed.

Tuck
Fold or pleat in fabric that is sewn in place, normally on the straight grain of the fabric. Often used to provide a decorative addition to a garment.

Underlay
Strip of fabric placed under the main fabric to strengthen it, for example under a pleat or buttonhole.

Understitch
Machine straight stitching through facing and seam allowances that is invisible from the right side; this helps the facing to lie flat.

Waistband
Band of fabric attached to the waist edge of a garment to provide a neat finish.

Warp
Lengthways threads or yarns of a woven fabric.

Warp knit
Made on a knitting machine, this knit is formed in a vertical and diagonal direction.

Weft
Threads or yarns that cross the warp of a woven fabric.

Weft knit
Made in the same way as hand knitting, this uses one yarn that runs horizontally.

Welt
Strip of fabric used to make the edges of a pocket.

Whip stitch
Diagonal hand stitch sewn along a raw edge to prevent fraying.

Wrong side
Reverse side of a fabric, the inside of a garment or other item.

Yoke
The top section of a dress or skirt from which the rest of the garment hangs.

Zigzag stitch
Machine stitch used to neaten and secure seam edges and for decorative purposes. The width and length of the zigzag can be altered.

Index

Acknowledgments

About the author
Alison Smith trained as an Art and Fashion Textile teacher, before becoming Head of Textiles at one of the largest schools in Birmingham, where she was able to pursue one of her key interests: the importance of teaching needlecrafts to boys, as well as girls. After successful spells as textiles tutor at the Liberty Sewing School, London, and the Janome Sewing School, Cheshire, Alison set up her own shop, Fabulous Fabric, and sewing school, Alison Victoria School of Sewing, in Ashby-de-la-Zouch, Leicestershire. Her school is the largest independent sewing school in England and offers courses and workshops on all aspects of dressmaking, tailoring, and corsetry.

Alison regularly lectures at specialist sewing shows, is a regular contributor to *Sewing World* magazine, and has appeared on ITV television series *Ladette to Lady* teaching dressmaking skills. She lives with her husband in Leicestershire, and has two grown-up children.

Author's acknowledgments
No book would ever be written without a little help. I would like to thank the following people for their help with the techniques and projects: Jackie Boddy, Nicola Corten, Ruth Cox, Helen Culver, Yvette Emmett, Averil Wing, and especially my husband, Nigel, for his continued encouragement and support, as well as my mother, Doreen Robbins, who is responsible for my learning to sew. The following companies have also provided invaluable help, by supplying the sewing machines, haberdashery, and fabrics: Janome UK Ltd, EQS, Linton, Adjustoform, Guttermann threads, the Button Company, YKK zips, Graham Smith Fabrics, Fabulous Fabric, Simplicity Patterns, and Freudenberg Nonwovens LP.

Dorling Kindersley would like to thank:
Heather Haynes and Katie Hardwicke for editorial assistance; Elaine Hewson and Victoria Charles for design assistance; Susan Van Ha for photographic assistance; Hilary Bird for indexing; Elma Aquino; Alice Chadwick-Jones; and Beki Lamb. Special thanks from all at DK to Norma MacMillan for her exceptional professionalism and patience.

Picture credits:
Additional photography: Laura Knox p70 tl, tr, 72 t, 74 tr, br, 76 b
Illustrator: Debajyoti Datta
Patterns: John Hutchinson, pp66–67, 76
Additional artwork: Karen Cochrane p67 r